Annotated Teacher's Edition

WRITERS
INC
SKILLSBOOK
Editing and Proofreading Practice

a resource of student activities
to accompany
Writers INC
Level 10

WRITE SOURCE®

GREAT SOURCE EDUCATION GROUP
a Houghton Mifflin Company
Wilmington, Massachusetts

A Few Words About the
Writers INC SkillsBook: Level 10

Before you begin . . .

The *SkillsBook* provides you with opportunities to practice the editing and proofreading skills presented in the *Writers INC* handbook. The handbook contains guidelines, examples, and models to help you complete your work in the *SkillsBook*.

Each *SkillsBook* activity includes a brief introduction to the topic and refers you to the pages in the handbook that offer additional information and examples. The "Proofreading Activities" focus on punctuation and the mechanics of writing. The "Language Activities" highlight each of the eight parts of speech. The "Sentence Activities" provide practice in sentence combining and in correcting common sentence problems.

The **Extend**

Many activities include an **Extend** at the end of the exercise. Its purpose is to provide ideas for follow-up work that will help you apply what you have learned to your own writing.

Authors: Pat Sebranek and Dave Kemper

Project Manager: Mary Anne Hoff

Writers and Editors: Laura Bachman, Diane Barnhart, Mark Bazata, Andria Hayday, Scott Hazeu, Stuart Hoffman, Seth Johnson, Karen Park-Koenig, Lois Krenzke, Jon Leitheusser, Barb Lund, Larry Powers, Randy Rehberg, Connie Stephens, Ken Taylor, Maureen Winkler, and Claire Ziffer

Printed in the United States of America

International Standard Book Number: 0-669-47190-9 (student edition)

1 2 3 4 5 6 7 8 9 10 - DBH - 04 03 02 01 00

International Standard Book Number: 0-669-47192-5 (teacher's edition)

1 2 3 4 5 6 7 8 9 10 - DBH - 04 03 02 01 00

TABLE OF CONTENTS

Proofreading Activities

Language Activities

Sentence Activities

Sentence Basics

PROOFREADING ACTIVITIES

The activities in this section of your *SkillsBook* include sentences that need to be checked for punctuation, mechanics, or correct word choices. Most of the activities also include helpful handbook references. In addition, the **Extend** activities provide follow-up practice of certain skills.

Pretest: Punctuation

Place periods, commas, and apostrophes where they are needed in the following paragraphs.

1   If you're a tourist heading to southern California, you're probably on

2   your way to an amusement or theme park. But don't overlook a third

3   possibility: Mission San Juan Capistrano. It is part of a chain of historic

4   missions—21 in all—that stretches from San Diego to San Francisco.

5   For some people, the missions represent the high point of Spanish   *(optional)*

6   civilization in North America. For others, they serve as a painful reminder

7   of the days when Spaniards forced thousands of Native Americans to build

8   these missions, work in the fields, and change their religious beliefs. Today,

9   the missions have become one of California's main tourist attractions, and

10   they are an important link to California's multicultural past.

Place commas, quotation marks, and underlining (for italic) in the following paragraph.

1   Kevin Starr, the state librarian of California, talked about the Spanish

2   missions in an interview with the <u>New York Times</u>. He said, "The missions

3   do have a spell—a hold—over California. And today, as we become

4   increasingly a Latin or a Spanish nation again—Hispanics will soon be the

5   country's largest minority—we begin to appreciate Spanish history as part

6   of United States history." Starr went on to say that California, like the

7   rest of the Southwest, would not be the same without the historic

8   missions.

> **Place colons, hyphens, and dashes where they are needed in the following paragraph.**

1 California's most famous mission, San Juan Capistrano, is crumbling.

2 Six-inch cracks weaken a sagging dome, and swallows have constructed

3 nests in crevices. Recently the Great Stone Church, which was erected in

4 1806, had a budget for renovation that would have set its builders' heads

5 spinning (or)— $10 million! With that kind of money, you might imagine that

6 the 200-year-old church could be fully restored to its original glory. The

7 goal, however, is much simpler (or)— keep the mission's walls and roofs from

8 falling down on someone's head. (That actually happened once. Just six

9 years after the Great Stone Church was finished, an earthquake collapsed

10 the roof, killing all 40 worshippers inside.)

> **Add colons, periods, and commas where they are needed in the following paragraph.**

1 Mission San Juan Capistrano is open to the public from 8:30 a.m. to

2 5:00 p.m. daily. For more information, write to the following address: P. O.

3 Box 697, San Juan Capistrano, CA 92693.

> **Put a _Q_ in the blank if the title should be punctuated with quotation marks; put an _I_ in the blank if the title should be italicized (underlined).**

_I_ **1.** Time (magazine)

_I_ **2.** New York Times (newspaper)

_Q_ **3.** The Star-Spangled Banner (song)

_Q_ **4.** The Road Not Taken (poem)

_I_ **5.** World Book (encyclopedia)

_I_ **6.** Queen Elizabeth II (ship)

_Q_ **7.** ESPNNET SportsZone (electronic file)

_I_ **8.** 60 Minutes (TV program)

_Q_ **9.** From Trash to Treasures (magazine article)

End Punctuation

Turn to sections 455.1 and 467.1-467.5 in *Writers INC* for information and examples of end punctuation.

> **Place** periods, question marks, and exclamation points where they are needed in the following narrative. Also put in the necessary capital letters.

1   ~~a~~ **A** small Japanese restaurant recently opened in our town**.** "~~l~~**L**et's go**!**"

2   exclaimed my friend John**.** ~~h~~**H**e and I both like trying new things, so this

3   was the perfect place for our next meal out**.** John wondered what kind of

4   tables would be used**.** ~~w~~**W**ould they be those low, low tables**?** ~~w~~**W**ould we be

5   expected to sit on the floor**?**

6   "I think people kneel and sit on the backs of their legs," I said**.**

7   "~~t~~**T**hat could get very tiring," John replied, "but let's go anyway**.**"

8   ~~w~~**W**e ordered sushi (it was later that I found out sushi is cold rice

9   garnished with raw fish), Hakusai soup, tempura, and, for dessert, some

10   Okinawan sweet fritters**.**

11   "~~d~~**D**o you know how to use these**?**" John asked, holding up a pair of

12   chopsticks**.** "~~h~~**H**ow are we going to eat soup without a spoon**?**"

13   "I'll show you," I offered**.** I demonstrated by picking up my bowl and

14   slurping the soup**.**

15   "~~n~~**N**o way," John said. "~~y~~**Y**ou can't make that much noise**!**"

16   I replied, "~~i~~**I**t is one of the few noises that you are allowed to make

17   at a Japanese dining table**.**"

18   ~~w~~**W**e followed the Japanese customs reasonably well**.** ~~t~~**T**he food was

19   beautifully served**.** I declared it "a fine culinary adventure**.**"

Extend: Write three to five sentences, each one making a statement about a different type of food. Then rewrite each of these sentences twice. First, turn each statement into a question; then turn each statement into an exclamation.

Review: End Punctuation

> **Add** end punctuation and capital letters where they are needed below.

1   My friend Tri was explaining to me that origami is the Oriental art

2   of folding paper to make shapes. "What kinds of things can you make with

3   origami?" I asked.

4   "The most popular shapes represent birds, fish, and insects," he

5   answered. "More than 1,000 designs are known to exist. The possibilities

6   are endless. (or !) Some origami designs have movable parts that imitate the

7   action of the creature or object. For example, you can make a crane whose

8   wings flap when you pull the tail."

9   "What materials does origami require?" I questioned.

10   Tri responded, "All you need are paper and your imagination. You can

11   find special origami paper in hobby stores and specialty shops, but almost

12   any paper will work. Some people even use aluminum foil or tissue paper."

13   "Can you cut the paper?" I asked.

14   "That's actually a topic of debate," he acknowledged. "Some modern

15   designs do require scissors. In contrast, traditional origami forbids the

16   artist to cut, paste, or decorate the paper; only folding is allowed."

17   I then asked him, "Who created origami?"

18   "The Chinese invented it," he said, "though the Japanese perfected the

19   art, and it has now spread throughout the world. Origami was originally

20   used in religious ceremonies. The Moors introduced origami to Spain, where

21   paper-folding artists made decorative playthings. Today, origami is popular

22   throughout the world among artists, teachers, and students."

Commas Between Independent Clauses

To form a compound sentence, insert a comma followed by a coordinating conjunction (*and, but, or, nor, for, yet, so*) between the two independent clauses. Turn to 457.1 in *Writers INC*. Also turn to 522.2 for information about compound sentences.

> **Create** five new compound sentences by combining information from the sentences listed below. Use a comma and a coordinating conjunction between the independent clauses. Use *and, but,* and *so* at least once. You may edit the original sentences as needed.

Answers will vary.

Medieval knights were trained to fight on horseback.
They could also fight hand to hand.
Overlords gave knights land for their services.
Some knights retired as wealthy men.
Knights were famous for using swords and shields.
They also wielded maces, lances, and battle-axes.
Some knights were crusaders.
They devoted their lives to religious quests.
Medieval knights did not carry guns.
Knighthood continues today.
Knighthood no longer represents just a military role.

1. _Medieval knights were trained to fight on horseback, but they could also fight hand to hand._

2. _Overlords gave knights land for their services, so some knights retired as wealthy men._

3. _Medieval knights were famous for using swords and shields, but they did not carry guns._

4. _Some knights were crusaders, and they devoted their lives to religious quests._

5. _Knighthood continues today, but it no longer represents just a military role._

6. _Medieval knights could fight hand to hand, but they also wielded maces, lances, and battle-axes._

Commas in a Series & to Separate Equal Adjectives

The following examples show how to use commas to separate words and phrases in a series and how to use commas to separate equal adjectives. Turn to 458.3 and 457.2 in *Writers INC*.

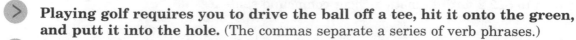 **Playing golf requires you to drive the ball off a tee, hit it onto the green, and putt it into the hole.** (The commas separate a series of verb phrases.)

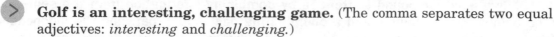 **Golf is an interesting, challenging game.** (The comma separates two equal adjectives: *interesting* and *challenging*.)

> **Insert commas where they are needed.**

1. Golf courses have many different hazards, including trees, roughs, water, and sand traps.

2. The world's most famous and most difficult courses are Saint Andrews in Scotland, Augusta National in Georgia, and Pebble Beach in California.

3. Prestigious tournaments take place at these beautiful, challenging courses.

4. The top four tournaments in men's golf are the PGA, the Masters, the U.S. Open, and the British Open.

5. The top four women's events are the duMaurier Classic in Canada, the U.S. Women's Open, the LPGA, and the Dinah Shore Tournament.

6. Talented, experienced golfers can drive a ball more than 200 yards, reach the green in two strokes, and finish the hole with a single putt.

7. Five of the most notable male golfers of the past century are Bobby Jones, Ben Hogan, Arnold Palmer, Jack Nicklaus, and Tiger Woods.

8. "Babe" Didrikson-Zaharias, Nancy Lopez, Pat Bradley, and Amy Alcott are some of the most gifted, successful female golfers of the past century.

9. To be a champion golfer, you need to spend years perfecting your drives, your chip shots, your putting, and your patience.

Extend: Write four sentences about a sport or game. In two sentences, use words or phrases in a series. In the other two, include equal adjectives. Use commas correctly.

Commas After Introductory Phrases & Clauses

A comma is used to separate an introductory phrase or clause from the rest of the sentence; it is also used to set off items in a date. Turn to 458.4, 459.1, and 460.1 in *Writers INC* for examples. Then read the examples below carefully. Most readers can tell when the introductory material ends and the main clause begins, but it's still a good idea to learn to distinguish phrases and clauses. (The information about phrases and clauses is on pages 520-521 in *Writers INC*.)

> *Perhaps best known for his theory describing pressure within a fluid,* **the great mathematician Blaise Pascal was born on June 19, 1623, in France.** (The first comma sets off the introductory phrase, which is a participial phrase modifying "Pascal." Also note how commas set off the date.)

> *Before he was 12 years old,* **Blaise Pascal had mastered the works of earlier mathematicians.** (The comma sets off the introductory adverb clause.)

Insert commas where they are needed in the sentences below.

1. When he was only 24 years old, Pascal developed serious health problems and moved to Paris.

2. While living in Paris, he became interested in probability theory.

3. After experimenting with probability in many different ways, he developed Pascal's triangle.

4. In Pascal's triangle, the rows of numbers are designed so that each number is the sum of the two numbers above it.

5. Continuing his work in the field of physics, Pascal produced the principle called Pascal's Law.

6. Often used to help design and develop new devices, Pascal's Law led to the invention of hydraulic jacks and air brakes.

7. Although many of his peers doubted that a vacuum could exist, Pascal helped prove that air has weight and its absence can produce a vacuum.

8. Following a severe bout with depression, Pascal had a religious experience on November 23, 1654, that changed his life.

9. After Pascal entered a monastery in January 1655, he became a monk.

10. From 1658 until his death▲Pascal lived at the monastery and worked on many projects.

11. By writing a defense of the Christian faith▲Pascal became famous in yet another way.

12. After he died▲fragments of his uncompleted manuscript were found and published in a work titled *Pensées*.

13. Writing about his theory that there is a limit to what a human can understand▲Pascal established himself as a philosopher and theologian.

14. Still considered one of the greatest mathematicians and philosophers of all time▲Pascal died on August 19▲1662▲at the age of 39.

Fill in the following blanks. Turn to 458.4 and 459.1 in *Writers INC.*

1. Introductory phrases are often prepositional phrases or ___*participial*___ phrases.

2. When a prepositional phrase follows the independent clause, the ___*comma*___ is often omitted.

3. You may also omit the ___*comma*___ if the introductory phrase is ___*short*___ .

4. When an adverb clause ___*follows*___ the main clause and begins with *although, even though, while,* or another conjunction expressing a ___*contrast*___ , a comma is used.

5. A comma is not used if the adverb clause following the main clause is needed to ___*complete the meaning of the sentence*___ .

Extend: Write five sentences about someone you know. Begin each of your sentences with an introductory phrase or clause. Include dates using commas in at least two of your sentences.

Review: Commas 1

> **Insert commas where they are needed.**

1. When it was launched in 1958, the *Edmund Fitzgerald* was the largest, strongest ore ship on the Great Lakes.

2. Neither its strength, its size, nor its experienced captain could prevent the *Edmund Fitzgerald* from sinking on November 10, 1975, in Lake Superior.

3. Loaded with 26,000 tons of iron ore pellets, the *Edmund Fitzgerald* sailed from Superior, Wisconsin, on November 10, 1975.

4. The sunny November day looked calm, but a storm with strong, blustery winds and waves in excess of 15 feet lay ahead.

5. As the storm gained strength, Captain Ernest McSorley bore north across Lake Superior.

6. Seeking the shelter of the Canadian shore and Whitefish Bay, the capable, quick-thinking captain continued to bear north.

7. But luck was not with the captain, the crew, or the ship, for both the radar system and its backup failed.

8. Not only did the ship's radar system fail, but the storm also took out the electrical power to Whitefish Point's light and radio beacon.

9. The light came back on, but the radio beacon did not.

10. Captain McSorley's final, brief message at 7:10 p.m. was "We're holding our own."

11. Gordon Lightfoot's song "The Wreck of the *Edmund Fitzgerald*" tells the tale of the ship, the storm, and the tragedy.

Commas to Set Off Contrasted Elements & Appositives

Commas are used to set off appositives, explanatory words, and items in an address. Turn to 458.1, 458.2, and 460.2 in *Writers INC* for additional information.

Insert commas where they are needed below.

---

1. Our teacher, Mr. Goodman, assigned a project on volcanoes.

2. My cousin, a freshman in college, has seen a volcano.

3. I sent a letter to him at 889 West Dayton Street, Madison, Wisconsin 54421, to ask for some information about volcanoes.

4. I knew that my cousin, a very observant person, would have good facts.

5. My cousin sent a letter back to me at 39924 Raven Drive, Lake Villa, Illinois 60046.

6. He wrote me that he had seen Mauna Loa, a volcano in Hawaii.

7. A volcano can spew magma, hot molten rock, hundreds of feet into the air.

8. The least violent type of eruption, a Hawaiian eruption, is characterized by very fluid lava and an occasional lava fountain.

9. The most violent eruption, a Peleean eruption, includes a violent ejection of volcanic ash.

10. Stromboli, an active volcano off the coast of Italy, erupts constantly.

11. My cousin, an avid photographer, sent me some photographs of volcanoes.

12. He also gave me the name of a volcanologist he knows who lives at 32454 Oak Drive, Los Angeles, California 90025.

Extend: Write three to five sentences about a tourist attraction you'd like to visit. Include an appositive or explanatory words in each sentence, using commas to set them off correctly.

Other Uses of Commas

Use commas to set off dialogue, nouns of direct address, and interjections. Turn to 460.3-460.5 in *Writers INC* for examples.

> **Insert** commas where they are needed below.

1. "Today," our science teacher said, "we are going to learn about thunderclouds."

2. "Mrs. Stellflag, what is a thundercloud?" Henry asked.

3. "Good grief, you don't know what a thundercloud is?" Sally said in an amazed voice.

4. "Thunderclouds are formed when warm, moist air rises toward cooler air," Mrs. Stellflag replied.

5. "Mrs. Stellflag, is that when the water condenses?" Kristy wondered.

6. "That's right. When the warm, moist air hits the cold air, Kristy, the water and dust particles create raindrops," answered Mrs. Stellflag.

7. "The clouds that are formed," Mrs. Stellflag continued, "are called cumulonimbus clouds."

8. "So, Mrs. Stellflag, are those the huge, towerlike clouds?" Jaleel asked.

9. "My goodness, you students really know a lot about this," she said.

10. "These clouds commonly produce large gusts of wind," Mrs. Stellflag continued, "and can also produce tornadoes."

11. "Yeah, I remember the thunderstorm on July 4, 1999, because it took out three of our huge oak trees," Laura added.

12. "Don't forget that thunderstorms are always accompanied by lightning," Mrs. Stellflag warned, "which adds to their destructive power."

Extend: Write a conversation between two people discussing recent weather. Use commas to set off dialogue, nouns of direct address, and interjections. (See page 170 in *Writers INC* for a sample dialogue.)

Commas with Nonrestrictive Phrases & Clauses 1

Nonrestrictive phrases and clauses *are not* essential to the meaning of the sentence. Restrictive phrases and clauses *are* essential. Study the examples below. Turn to 459.2 in *Writers INC* for further information.

> Ferdinand Magellan, *whose Spanish name is Fernão de Magalhães,* was the leader of the first expedition around the world. (nonrestrictive clause)

> The sailor *who actually completed the expedition* was Juan Sebastián del Cano. (restrictive clause)

Label each sentence below. Write *R* if it contains a restrictive phrase or clause, or *N* if it contains a nonrestrictive phrase or clause. Insert commas to set off the nonrestrictive phrases and clauses.

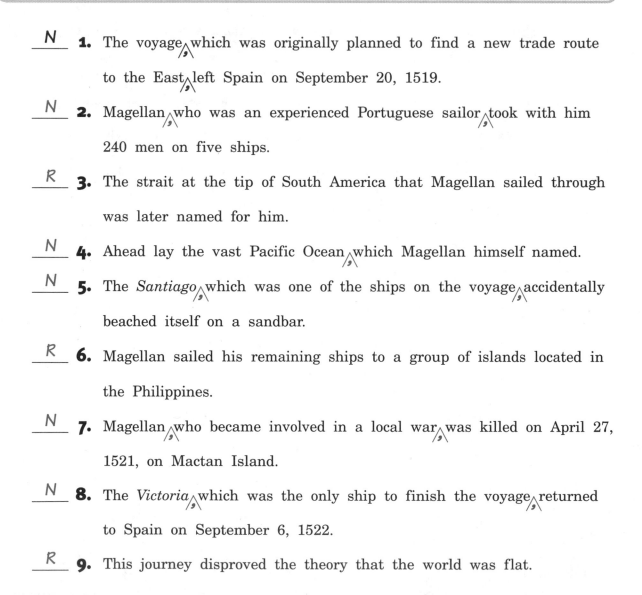

N 1. The voyage‸which was originally planned to find a new trade route to the East‸left Spain on September 20, 1519.

N 2. Magellan‸who was an experienced Portuguese sailor‸took with him 240 men on five ships.

R 3. The strait at the tip of South America that Magellan sailed through was later named for him.

N 4. Ahead lay the vast Pacific Ocean‸which Magellan himself named.

N 5. The *Santiago*‸which was one of the ships on the voyage‸accidentally beached itself on a sandbar.

R 6. Magellan sailed his remaining ships to a group of islands located in the Philippines.

N 7. Magellan‸who became involved in a local war‸was killed on April 27, 1521, on Mactan Island.

N 8. The *Victoria*‸which was the only ship to finish the voyage‸returned to Spain on September 6, 1522.

R 9. This journey disproved the theory that the world was flat.

Commas with Nonrestrictive Phrases & Clauses 2

Nonrestrictive phrases and clauses (sometimes called nonessential word groups) can be removed from a sentence without changing its basic meaning. Always use commas to set off nonrestrictive phrases and clauses. Turn to 459.2 in *Writers INC* and study the examples.

> **Insert** commas in the sentences below to set off nonrestrictive phrases and clauses. (Not all sentences need commas.)

1. Programs of the American Red Cross, which are funded by contributions, aim to prevent suffering among all people in time of war or peace.

2. In 1864, Jean Henri Dunant founded an organization of volunteers to aid any person, regardless of nationality, wounded in war.

3. The Red Cross, which grew from Dunant's organization, now has societies in more than 135 countries.

4. Aid to disaster victims, which is provided free of charge, includes food, clothing, medical service, and shelter.

5. Families separated by war, disasters, or other emergencies are often reunited by Red Cross societies throughout the world.

6. Its national transplant service, begun in 1984, provides bone, skin, and organs to doctors and their patients.

7. The Red Cross volunteers who serve in military medical facilities provide assistance to members of the armed forces.

8. Many safety programs, including the familiar first aid, swimming, and baby-sitting courses, are offered by local Red Cross chapters.

9. Red Cross youth activities, which are designed to develop leadership skills, range from volunteer hospital service to international friendship projects.

Extend: Write four sentences about a natural disaster (earthquake, tornado, hurricane, etc.). Two of the sentences should contain a nonrestrictive clause; the other two should include a restrictive clause. Use commas where necessary.

Review: Commas 2

> **Insert commas where they are needed in the sentences below.**

1   The concept of "breaching the peace," known today as "disorderly

2   conduct," has its roots in England. It dates back to a time when the

3   monarch, who was believed to be the supreme ruler, proclaimed a royal

4   right to peace. Whenever someone committed a crime against the royal

5   laws, the offender was arrested for disturbing "the king's peace."

6   Today the term "breach of peace" is seldom used. However, on October

7   30, 1994, at about 1:00 a.m., my father and I came to understand the

8   meaning of this phrase when the doorbell woke us.

9   A voice outside said, "Mr. Hurley, I need to speak to you and your son

10   Reginald." My father opened the door to find two plainclothes police officers.

11   "What's the problem?" my father asked.

12   "According to our reports, you and your son were disturbing the peace

13   up until about 30 minutes ago," one police officer said.

14   "Well," Father began, "what did we supposedly do?"

15   The police officer replied, "We understand that you and your son have

16   a plastic clown's head, which you obtained from the St. Bartholomew's

17   fund-raiser, and that you put the clown's head on the end of a pole. You

18   then took it to the home of Nelson Giles on 143 Surf Street, held it up to

19   his window, and made loud laughing noises until you woke him."

20   About this time, Mr. Giles appeared from behind a tree laughing

21   uncontrollably. "I'd like you to meet my cousins John and Karl. We really

22   had you, didn't we?"

Semicolons to Join Independent Clauses

Semicolons may be used to connect closely related sentences or independent clauses, sometimes with conjunctive adverbs. For examples and a list of conjunctive adverbs, turn to 461.4-461.5 in *Writers INC*.

> **Join** the following pairs of sentences using either a semicolon alone or a semicolon with a conjunctive adverb.

Answers will vary.

1. Brazil is a vast country; It is almost as big as the United States.

2. Spanish is spoken throughout much of South America; *however,* The official language of Brazil is Portuguese.

3. Brazil is the largest country in South America; It occupies almost half the continent.

4. Brazil is a populous country; *in fact,* It has more inhabitants than all the other South American countries combined.

5. The Amazon, one of the earth's largest rivers, flows through Brazil; It carries more water than any other river.

6. One of Brazil's greatest resources is the rain forest; *however,* It is quickly disappearing.

7. Regional clothing styles are distinctive; For example, women in the state of Bahia wear colorful skirts, bright blouses, and many bracelets.

8. Brazil has more than 6,000 miles of coastline; Thousands of people go to the beaches to swim, fish, and boat.

9. Soccer is the favorite sport; *in fact,* One Brazilian soccer star, Pele, became known as the world's greatest soccer player.

10. There is an average of one car for every 15 people; *therefore,* Most Brazilians travel by bus.

Extend: Write six to eight very short sentences about the city or state in which you live. Exchange papers with a classmate. Combine one another's sentences using semicolons.

Semicolons to Separate Word Groups Containing Commas

Semicolons separate groups of words (within a sentence) that already contain commas. The items in each group must be related. Turn to 462.2 in *Writers INC* for an example.

> **Write** sentences that include lists of the items below. Use semicolons to punctuate each sentence.

Answers will vary.

1. *Things found in the woods: animals, plants, rocks*

   While in the woods, I saw chipmunks, deer, and rabbits; ferns, mushrooms, and ivy; quartz, granite, and sandstone rocks.

2. *Favorite foods: desserts, fruits, vegetables*

   My favorite foods are ice cream, apple pie, and brownies; seedless grapes, cherries, and strawberries; carrots, green beans, and asparagus.

3. *Things in your room: snacks, books, clothes*

   I feel comfortable in my room among the potato chips, pizza crusts, and licorice; dictionaries, textbooks, and paperbacks; jeans, socks, and shoes.

4. *Places you've been (or want to visit): states, national parks, other countries*

   Someday I will visit California, Wyoming, and Montana; Yosemite, Yellowstone, and Glacier National Parks; England, India, and China.

5. *Things to pack for a trip: clothes, personal items, books*

   I will pack shorts, T-shirts, and jeans; my toothbrush, comb, and deodorant; my journal, a dictionary, and a novel.

Colons 1

The examples below illustrate how colons are used in the salutation of a business letter, between numbers indicating time, and to emphasize a word or a group of words. Turn to 462.3-462.5 in *Writers INC*.

> **Dear Mr. Baker:**
> (The colon follows a salutation in a business letter.)

> **My curfew is 9:30 p.m. on weekdays.**
> (The colon separates the numbers *9* and *30* to indicate time.)

> **We had to find the puzzle's missing piece: the mysterious black one.**
> (The colon is used to emphasize the phrase *the mysterious black one*.)

Insert colons where they are needed in the letter below.

---

1   Dear Mrs. Klein

2   We are happy to inform you that we have found something of yours a

3   small purse. We know that you left it in our restaurant sometime between

4   8 00 p.m. and 9 30 p.m. last Friday.

5   You may come and pick up your purse anytime we are open. Our

6   hours are from 8 00 a.m. to 9 45 p.m. on weekdays and from 10 00 a.m.

7   to 10 00 p.m. on weekends.

8   We will be able to verify your identity by using the picture

9   identification we found in the purse your driver's license.

10   There is just one last issue we need to address the reward. We

11 appreciate a reward being offered, but we won't be able to accept it.

12 Rather, we recommend you do this visit us again in the future.

13   Sincerely,

14   The Red River Inn Staff

Extend: Write three to five sentences about a time you lost something. Use at least one colon in each sentence to indicate time or to emphasize a word or group of words.

Colons 2

Colons are used to introduce a list; to distinguish between title and subtitle, volume and page, and chapter and verse in literature; and to introduce a sentence, a question, or a quotation. Turn to 463.1-463.3 in *Writers INC*.

> **Insert** colons where they are needed in the sentences below.

1. Booker T. Washington focused on three things during his lifetime: education, freedom, and civil rights.

2. He tells his story in his book *Up from Slavery: An Autobiography by Booker T. Washington.*

3. Booker T. Washington once made this observation: "My experience is that there is something in human nature which always makes an individual recognize and reward merit."

4. Washington held many different jobs: salt-furnace laborer, coal miner, house servant, night janitor, and, ultimately, teacher.

5. As a teacher, Washington taught African Americans the subjects that he believed were most important for success: writing, reading, and agriculture.

6. He remembers thinking as a child that reading was very important: "I recall that I had an intense longing to learn to read. I determined . . . that, if I accomplished nothing else in life, I would in some way get enough education to enable me to read."

7. Washington summed up his belief in the future with these words: "In the long run, the world is going to have the best, and any difference in race, religion, or previous history will not long keep the world from what it wants."

Extend: Compose three to five sentences about a book you've read. Use a colon in each sentence to introduce a list or to introduce a sentence, question, or quotation.

Review: Semicolons & Colons

> **Insert** colons and semicolons correctly in the sentences below.

1. I decided to call my grandmother yesterday ⌄; I hadn't talked to her in a long time.

2. The doctor will not be in until 10:00 a.m. tomorrow ⌄; however, you can go to the clinic if you need immediate care.

3. Ms. Krebopple asked one question before class started ⌄: "Did everyone remember to bring his or her book?"

4. With the party coming up, Christoph made a list of things to do ⌄: water the lawn, order the cake, and hire a clown.

5. Darcy read aloud the inscription from John 8 ⌄: 32—"The truth will set you free."

6. There is one thing you must remember when hiking that trail ⌄: stay away from poison ivy.

7. The storm became impossible to ignore ⌄: thunderclouds darkened the sky, lightning flashed, and thunder rumbled.

8. At our supermarket you will find detergent, scrub brushes, and toilet-bowl cleaners in aisle 6 ⌄; bread, peanut butter, and jelly in aisle 11 ⌄; and soup, crackers, and seasonings in aisle 15.

9. Our heroine was stuck in the abandoned warehouse ⌄; meanwhile, her trusty sidekick was stuck in traffic.

10. In class we talked about two things ⌄: the rights of the homeless and the problems with the Social Security Administration.

Hyphens 1

A hyphen is used to make compound words (*son-in-law, president-elect*), to join the words in compound numbers (*twenty-one, ninety-nine*), to form new words beginning with certain prefixes (*self-made, ex-mayor*), to indicate a span of time (*1902-1982*), and to join two or more words that serve as a single adjective (*up-to-date, cream-filled*). Turn to 463.4, 464.1, 464.3, 464.5, and 465.2 in *Writers INC* for more information.

> **Insert** hyphens where they are needed in the sentences below.

1. My great-grandmother has been eighty-one for three minutes and twenty-two seconds.

2. A water-repellent tent is a must on any camping trip.

3. Grandpa always admired self-made men and women, the pull-yourself-up-by-the-bootstraps type.

4. During her first term as senator (1993-1999), Ms. Millicent supported campaign-finance reform.

5. Is that what is called ready-to-wear clothing?

6. On Friday, we will have a half-hour lunch.

7. Great-grandfather likes Stanley's chocolate-chip cookies.

8. The coach has a change-your-attitude look on his face.

9. He was a make-my-day type of teacher.

10. A worm crawled out of the half-eaten apple.

11. I think the dates for the Civil War were 1860-1865.

12. Did Liam say his mother-in-law was a delight?

13. I must remember to use a hyphen in numbers twenty-one to ninety-nine.

14. The soon-to-be father fainted.

15. Small-minded people will dislike the change.

Hyphens 2

A hyphen is used to join a letter to a word, to join the elements of a written-out fraction, and to join the numbers in a vote or a score. A hyphen is also used when two or more words share a common element that appears only with the last term. Turn to 463.5, 464.1-464.2, and 464.5 in *Writers INC*.

Insert hyphens where they are needed in the following sentences.

---

1. It was a hot day, and my T-shirt was sticking to my back.

2. Work on the deck was about two-thirds done.

3. Our radio was tuned to a ball game; the Sox were up 2-0.

4. The house we were working on was an A-frame from the late '70s.

5. It belonged to Jack's mother, who was always taking pre- and post-repair photographs.

6. We were using three- and four-inch nails.

7. The screws we used were three-fourths of an inch long.

8. I asked the guys if they wanted to change to the Cubs game, and the vote was 4-1 in favor.

9. As I was getting up to change the station, Jerry asked me to get him the five-, seven-, and nine-sixteenths wrenches.

10. That is when I discovered that one-third of the tools were missing.

11. Before long, we watched as the police car made a U-turn and pulled up.

12. Then Jack's four-year-old son appeared.

13. "I'm building a T-house," he said proudly. (He meant "tree house.")

14. We laughed and then voted 5-0 not to have him arrested for taking our tools.

Extend: Write four sentences about building something. In two of the sentences, use a hyphen to join two or more words that serve as a single adjective. In the other two sentences, use a hyphen to join words sharing a common element that appears only with the last term.

Dashes

Dashes are used to indicate a sudden break or change in a sentence, to set off an introductory series, to set off parenthetical material, to show interrupted speech, and to emphasize a word or word group at the end of a sentence. Turn to 466.1-466.5 in *Writers INC*.

Write the number of the rule in *Writers INC* that explains why a dash is used in each example below.

466.1 (or) 466.3
1. It used to be a nice room—bright, clean, and cheerful—until my brother moved in with me.

466.2
2. Discipline, honesty, love—these are what the world needs.

466.4
3. I—must reach—the control box—before it is too late.

466.3
4. It was 1945—the year World War II ended—when Jimmy finally came home.

466.5
5. The unique chime made the clock a piece of furniture that people would have loved—to throw out a window.

466.2
6. A cup of flour, a teaspoon of baking soda, a pinch of salt—all I needed to make the paste was right here.

466.3
7. It was Mr. Peabody—the elderly man who lives on Lilac Road—who donated the rare book to the library.

466.4
8. I—can't—breathe—because—the aliens are turning off the oxygen mixer.

466.1 (or) 466.3
9. We heard the noise—clank, ding, bong—and I knew that it would be a long time before the car would be zip-zap-zooming anywhere.

466.5
10. With two whole dollars in my pocket, I was really rolling—right down Poorman's Alley.

Write two sentences of your own that use dashes to set off an introductory series in a sentence.

Answers will vary.

Eating pizza, going to a movie, hanging with friends—these are my

favorite weekend activities.

Strong winds, changing temperatures, rain mixed with snow—March is

here.

Review: Hyphens & Dashes

> **Insert** hyphens or dashes where they are needed in the sentences below.

1. My brother-in-law is very friendly.

2. I don't think a U-turn would be wise here.

3. Four-, six-, and eight-foot boards—those are the only oak boards we have in stock.

4. This half-eaten pear is the worst thing I've ever seen in your sock drawer.

5. Two-thirds of the people in the audience think that the score should have been 4-3.

6. Sometimes I can be a scaredy-cat person.

7. Some things in the room—the lamp, the desk, the couch—simply do not match anything.

8. The bug-eyed young man—alone and terrified—screamed at the bear.

9. My great-great-grandmother made banana bread—truly scrumptious banana bread.

10. The senate vote yesterday was 54-46 for the new tax bill.

11. I'm not sure that mid-January is the best time for a swimming party.

12. My sister is a pro at what she does best—annoying me to death.

13. Grease, mud, dust, and dirt—what would a garage be without them?

14. Only one-fourth of the votes supported our ex-mayor.

15. Her self-centered attitude is not appealing to most people.

16. The bell-like shape of the house made it an oddity.

17. Yes—well, no—well, maybe—well, I don't know.

18. My sixteen-year-old sister likes to drive—drive me crazy, that is.

Quotation Marks with Dialogue

Quotation marks are used to set off dialogue from the rest of a sentence. Turn to 468.3 and 469.1 in *Writers INC* for more information and examples. Commas are used to set off a speaker's exact words. Turn to 460.3 in *Writers INC*.

> **Add** quotation marks and commas where they are needed.

1   As he listens to the physics teacher, Bill whispers to Sarah, "Wake me

2   up if I fall asleep."

3   Ms. Quing says, "Quasars are the most luminous objects in the universe.

4   The brightest known quasar has a luminosity 30,000 times that of the

5   Milky Way." She continues, "Cosmological quasar distances are calculated

6   from recessional velocities by the equation $v = H(0)d$."

7   Bill mutters, "Quasars, phasers, equations. It all sounds like science

8   fiction to me."

9   Ms. Quing continues, "H(0) is a constant of proportionality estimated to

10   be . . ." Bill begins to doze.

11   "Captain Quasar, sir, something is showing up on my monitor. It

12   appears that a mental shutdown is being reported at Agazzi High School,"

13   Corporal Cosmo announces.

14   Quasar barks, "Mr. Phaser, increase warp speed to factor eight."

15   "Aye, aye, sir," Phaser replies.

16   An intercom voice says, "We're having problems with the warp drive,

17   Captain. It'll take two hours to wake up."

18   "Wake up! Wake up!" Sarah whispers loudly as Ms. Quing heads in

19   their direction.

Extend: Write a short conversation between two or more friends about a favorite television show. Punctuate the dialogue correctly. (See page 175 in *Writers INC* for tips about writing dialogue.)

Quotation Marks with Direct Quotations

Quotation marks are placed before and after direct quotations. They also set off words that are being used in a special way. Turn to 468.2 and page 469 in *Writers INC*.

> **Put quotation marks around direct quotations and words used in special ways.**

1   Mr. Oquendo, my social studies teacher, said, "Presidents and other

2   politicians are good sources of quotations." He told us that Calvin Coolidge,

3   who was given the nickname Silent Cal, was his favorite politician.

4   I asked, "How can a person known as Silent Cal be quotable?"

5   "Why don't you find out?" Mr. Oquendo asked in return.

6   So I did. Silent Cal's slogan was "Keep Cool with Coolidge." Ironically,

7   the word "uncool" came to mind when I considered Coolidge, who was a

8   sour-faced man. A reporter once wrote, "It looks like he is always sucking

9   on lemons."

10   Coolidge thought that government should leave business alone and not

11   spend money helping people. "The chief business of the American people is

12   business," he stated. Describing America in the 1920s, he said, "Civilization

13   and profits go hand in hand." When he left office, he commented, "Perhaps

14   one of the most important accomplishments of my administration has been

15   minding my own business." Although some people benefited from this

16   so-called Coolidge Prosperity, many others would not have called it

17   "prosperity." Some of Coolidge's policies led to the Great Depression.

18   I guess Mr. Oquendo was right; the nickname Silent Cal was ironic.

19   One history book concluded, "Cal really wasn't silent: He gave more

20   speeches than any of the 29 presidents before him!"

Extend: Does a friend of yours have a favorite saying? ("That's the way it goes," "Later, dude," etc.) Write a short dialogue between you and your friend containing one of these sayings.

Double & Single Quotation Marks

Single quotation marks are used to punctuate a quotation within another quotation. Turn to 469.1-469.3 in *Writers INC* for an explanation and example.

> **Add** single and double quotation marks where they are needed.

1   My English teacher, Mr. Gobel, said, "The first time that the term

2   'football player' appeared in print was in Shakespeare's *King Lear,* when

3   Kent insults Oswald, saying, 'you base [lowlife] foot-ball player.'"

4   Mr. Gobel explained, "It's important to understand that in England,

5   'football' is the term for soccer, so Kent is actually calling Oswald a lowlife

6   soccer player.

7   "But football, even back then, was considered a rough game," Mr. Gobel

8   continued. "From 1314 to 1603, it was banned by 10 different kings,

9   including Henry VIII. Imagine Henry VIII saying, 'No more football or off

10 with your heads!' Everyone laughed.

11 Mr. Gobel was just warming up to his subject. He stated, "In 1823,

12 William Ellis of Rugby School in England picked up the football [soccer

13 ball] and ran with it. The game of rugby football was invented. With it,

14 rules changed, and a new term came into being: 'tackle.'"

15 After a dramatic pause, Mr. Gobel said, "Finally, American football

16 developed from rugby." He paused again, smiled, and said, "Enough terms.

17 Your assignment for the weekend is to watch the Super Bowl. Class

18 dismissed!"

Extend: Write three sentences your teacher might use to explain literary terms to your class. In addition to using his or her own words, imagine that your teacher is quoting directly from *Writers INC* pages 233-241. This means you will have to use double *and* single quotation marks to punctuate your sentences correctly.

Italics (Underlining) & Quotation Marks 1

Quotation marks or italics (shown by underlining) identify the titles of books, movies, songs, lectures, videos, and other works, as well as the names of ships and aircraft. Turn to 468.1 and 470.1-470.2 in *Writers INC* for information and examples.

> **Add** quotation marks or underlining to correctly set off titles and special names in the sentences below.

1. Many people are interested in disasters such as the sinking of the <u>Titanic</u> or the crashing of the <u>Hindenburg</u>.

2. Films about the ill-fated <u>Titanic</u> include <u>Titanica</u>, an IMAX movie; <u>A Night to Remember</u>, a British production; and <u>Titanic</u>, a recent Hollywood extravaganza.

3. <u>A Night to Remember</u> was based on a book written in 1955 by Walter Lord. In 1985 Lord wrote a sequel, <u>The Night Lives On</u>. The short story "Lifeboat," by James W. Herndon, also describes this famous disaster.

4. As the <u>Titanic</u> sank, the band supposedly played "Nearer My God to Thee."

5. The <u>American Heritage</u> magazine article "Titanic: Not-So-True Romance" reports that survivors remember the band's last song being "Dream of Autumn."

6. <u>Titanic: A New Musical</u> opened on Broadway in 1997. The play included the song "Dressed in Your Pajamas" in the Grand Salon.

7. The <u>Discovery of the Titanic</u>, a book written by Robert D. Ballard, provides detailed information about the ship's remains on the seafloor.

8. Explorers have dived the 12,468 feet to the wreck in the manned submersibles the <u>Nautile</u> and the <u>Alvin</u> A robotic ship, <u>Jason, Jr.</u>, has explored inside the wreck.

9. A recent lecture at the Maritime Museum, entitled "Let It Be," strongly recommended an end to all future explorations of the <u>Titanic</u>.

Extend: Write four or five sentences about your favorite films, stories, books, TV shows, or CD's. Use quotation marks or underlining to correctly identify the titles.

Italics (Underlining) & Quotation Marks 2

Quotation marks or italics (shown by underlining) identify the titles of lectures, plays, magazines, CD's, TV shows, and other works. Turn to 468.1 and 470.1-470.2 in *Writers INC*.

> **Add** quotation marks or underlining to correctly set off titles.

1. Our history teacher gave a lecture titled "The '60s and '70s: Been There, Done That."

2. In 1966, Star Trek began its run on television. The pilot episode, "The Cage," starred only two members of the original cast. NBC wanted a second pilot, so "Where No Man Has Gone Before" was produced.

3. The top single at the end of 1971 was the theme from the movie Shaft.

4. In one of his book's chapters, titled "The Schizophrenic Sixties," pop-culture author Charles Panati wrote, "Hippies in San Francisco . . . began to tie-dye every garment that would absorb color."

5. Go-go boots were also a '60s fashion hit. In an interview with Spin magazine, Madonna said, "Nancy Sinatra was my first pop idol . . . with go-go boots, miniskirt, and fake eyelashes." Sinatra sang "These Boots Are Made for Walkin'."

6. Roger McGuinn of the Byrds wore tinted granny glasses on TV's Ed Sullivan Show and on the album cover of Turn! Turn! Turn! Soon after, everyone was wearing granny glasses.

7. In that era, Harper Lee's novel To Kill a Mockingbird won the Pulitzer prize, and the musical A Chorus Line won a prize for drama.

8. The Godfather was the most popular novel of the '70s.

Extend: Write three to five sentences describing popular fads, books, TV shows, and films. Use quotation marks and underlining correctly to identify the titles.

Review: Quotation Marks & Italics (Underlining)

> **Put** single quotation marks, double quotation marks, and underlining where needed.

1   The documentary film <u>The Civil War</u> uses diaries and journals to

2   describe this important event in United States history. For instance, after

3   four years of fighting, food was scarce in the Confederacy. All kinds of

4   stories were later told about just how desperate things actually became.

5   In his journal, one soldier wrote, "We found no one who will exchange

6   eatables for Confederate money. So we are devouring our clothes."

7   Generals Grant and Lee had been fighting each other in Petersburg,

8   Virginia, for nine months. Lee asked the Confederate Congress for more

9   men and supplies: "I have been up to see Congress, and they do not seem

10   able to do anything except eat peanuts and chew tobacco." Lee even asked

11   that slaves be used in the army, and the Confederate Congress agreed.

12   The <u>Richmond Examiner</u> reported: "The country will not deny General Lee

13   anything he may ask for."

14   But it was not enough. Soon Federal troops entered Richmond, the

15   Confederacy's capital. One Confederate officer described the chaos in the

16   city as follows: "Every now and then, as a magazine [shell] exploded, a

17   column of white smoke rose . . . followed by a deafening sound. The

18   ground seemed to rock and tremble. . . . Hundreds of shells would explode

19   in the air. . . . Then all was still, for the moment, except for the dull

20   roar and crackle of the fast-spreading fires."

21   The Confederates left Richmond, some singing "Dixie." Their White

22   House soon became Union headquarters. Walking through the ruined city

23 afterward, a reporter for the <u>New York World</u> wrote, "There is no sound of

24 life, but the stillness of a catacomb. . . ."

25   Lee's army headed west in search of food. General John B. Gordon

26 said about Lee's retreat, "The lines were alternately forming, fighting, and

27 retreating, making one continuous battle. A boy soldier came running by.

28 When asked why he was running, he shouted back, "I'm running 'cause I

29 can't fly!"

30   Lee stopped at Appomattox Court House where he soon surrendered to

31 Grant with these words: "I suppose, General Grant, that the object of our

32 present meeting is fully understood. The terms I propose are those stated

33 . . . in my letter of yesterday."

Complete each statement below using the term "inside" or "outside."

1. Periods and commas are always placed _____*inside*_____ quotation marks.

2. An exclamation point or a question mark is placed _____*inside*_____ quotation marks when it punctuates the quotation or title.

3. An exclamation point or a question mark is placed _____*outside*_____ quotation marks when it punctuates the main sentence.

4. Semicolons and colons are always placed _____*outside*_____ quotation marks.

Apostrophes to Form Possessives 1

The possessive form of a noun shows ownership. Ownership can be singular (*Joe's book*) or plural (*teachers' cars*). Turn to 472.3-472.4 in *Writers INC* for more information.

> **Add** an apostrophe and, when needed, an *s* to any noun that should be possessive.

1. One of Cleveland's biggest attractions is the Rock and Roll Hall of Fame, a fantastic showcase for musicians and their achievements.

2. The Hall of Fame's founders were leaders in the music business. They created the museum to recognize the industry's most important contributors.

3. Elvis Presley, Buddy Holly, Chuck Berry, and Ray Charles were four of the Hall's first inductees.

4. One exhibit features Elvis Presley. It includes Elvis' *(or)* 's report card, his army uniform, and one of his guitars.

5. Presley's epithet, "The King of Rock and Roll," fits Mississippi's best-known rocker. Many of the King's songs topped the charts; in fact, he recorded more Top 40 hits (107) and more Top 10 hits (38) than any other artist.

6. Each year, the Rock and Roll Hall of Fame Foundation's nominating committee reviews hundreds of performers' careers.

7. Many nominees' music could be considered gospel, blues, or country as well as rock and roll.

8. Each year's ballots go to about 1,000 of the world's experts on rock and roll.

9. The experts' votes determine who gets into the Hall of Fame.

10. An inductee's fame must stand the test of time, because an artist's eligibility doesn't begin until 25 years after his or her first record is released.

Extend: Write three to five sentences about someone you think should be in the Rock and Roll Hall of Fame. Use at least three nouns that show possession. Check your sentences for the correct use of apostrophes.

Apostrophes to Form Possessives 2

To show possession correctly, remember that the word immediately before the apostrophe is the owner. Turn to 472.3-473.4 in *Writers INC*.

> **Add** an apostrophe and, when it is needed, an *s* to any noun that should be possessive.

1. Artists who predate the rock era can be elected to the Rock and Roll Hall of Fame, if they inspired rock's major performers.

2. Jazz's best-known trumpeter, Louis Armstrong, is in the Hall of Fame. In 1964, Armstrong's version of "Hello, Dolly" knocked a string of Beatles' singles off the top of the charts.

3. Most rock bands break up after a few years together, but not the Rolling Stones. Formed in 1962, the Stones are the world's oldest rock band.

4. The band's origin dates back to the boyhood friendship of Mick Jagger and Keith Richards. Richards' family moved out of Jagger's neighborhood, but the friends later reunited in London.

5. Set up in 1989, the Rolling Stones' *(optional)* exhibit features the groups' costumes, instruments, and concert videos.

6. Another popular exhibit—glass panels covered with rock stars' signatures—was moved into the Hall of Fame in 1998.

7. In the Hall, you can listen to the inductees' music at four computerized kiosks, which contain a musical database of 25,000 songs.

8. Sarah says she won't get a moment's peace until she helps fulfill her mother-in-law's wish: a trip to Cleveland's Rock and Roll Hall of Fame.

9. Sarah's and her mother-in-law's tickets have already been purchased.

Extend: Write three to five sentences about a place that you would like to visit. Include plural and singular nouns that show possession. Check your writing for the correct use of apostrophes.

Apostrophes to Form Possessives 3

Possession can be shared by more than one noun. Turn to 473.4 in *Writers INC*.

> **Add** an apostrophe, or an apostrophe and **s**, where needed.

1. The Marx Brothers were one of the funniest groups to act in vaudeville's palaces, Hollywood's films, and Broadway's theaters.

2. Groucho's, Harpo's, and Chico's real names were Julius, Arthur, and Leonard.

3. Two other brothers, Milton and Herbert, appeared in the act from time to time. Milton's and Herbert's stage names were Gummo and Zeppo.

4. The Marx Brothers made 12 films, but producers and directors didn't fully know how to use Harpo's, Groucho's, and Chico's talents.

5. Often the brothers' zaniness was bogged down by bad songs and boring subplots. Only *Animal Crackers, Duck Soup,* and *Horsefeathers* gave the brothers full freedom to go wild.

6. Music played a part in the brothers' films. In *Animal Crackers,* Groucho, Chico, and Harpo's opening musical number showed their combined talents. Groucho sang while Chico played the piano and Harpo played the harp.

7. Hungerdunger, Hungerdunger, Hungerdunger, and McCormack's law office is one of the settings in *Animal Crackers.*

8. Some comedy teams are famous for one special routine. Examples include Abbott and Costello's "Who's on First," Martin and Lewis' (or) Lewis's "Crazy Conductor," and Rowan and Martin's "I Didn't Know That."

9. But every one of the Marx Brothers' films is filled with Groucho's, Harpo's, and Chico's own unique gags.

Extend: Think of objects or activities that you and several of your friends share. Write sentences describing these objects or activities. Use the correct possessive forms of your names.

Apostrophes to Form Possessives 4

To show the possessive form of a compound noun, place the possessive ending after the last word. Turn to 473.1 in *Writers INC* for information and examples.

> **Underline** the correct choice in each italicized pair below.

1. My *(sister-in-law's, sister's-in-laws)* dream was really weird.

2. In it, she was the president of the United States, and I was the *(speaker of the House of Representatives', speaker's of the House of Representatives)* dog walker.

3. Our new president, my sister-in-law, began changing the government according to Article II, Section 3 of the Constitution. The *(commander in chief's, commander's in chiefs)* plan started with adjourning Congress.

4. She told the senators and representatives not to come back until they agreed on a budget. Her *(plan of attack's, plan's of attack)* direction then switched to international matters.

5. My sister-in-law appointed my *(brother's-in-laws, brother-in-law's)* uncle as secretary of state. The new *(secretary of state's, secretary's of states)* first duty was to issue free passports to every United States citizen.

6. Then the three of us gave a party for the secretary-general of the United Nations and the *(secretary-general's, secretary-generals')* family.

7. The fun really started when the soup was served. The *(aide-de-camp's, aide's-de-camp)* hands were shaking so badly that he spilled a bowl of soup in his lap.

8. Finally my *(sister's-in-laws, sister-in-law's)* alarm clock rang, and she escaped from this political nightmare.

Extend: Write three to five sentences about a dream or daydream. Use correct possessive endings on at least three compound nouns.

Other Uses for Apostrophes

Apostrophes show where letters or numbers have been left out. They are also used to form plurals and contractions. Turn to 472.1-472.2 in *Writers INC*.

> **Add** apostrophes where they are needed.

1. Some clocks don't have 1's, 2's, or 3's on their faces; only lines indicate where those numbers would be.

2. I've even seen watches that don't have anything but the hands on their faces.

3. "Bye, Mom! We're goin' swimmin'!" Alf shouted as he and Ralph ran out the door.

4. I can't believe it's been 20 years since I graduated in '81.

5. Ramundo's four C's and two D's on his report card won't make his father very happy.

6. The instructions for the bread machine list a bunch of *do's* and *don't's*.

7. They're recycling many of the fashions from the '60s and '70s.

8. Kids are even movin' and groovin' to songs from that era.

9. Make 'n' Bake cookie mix is my favorite.

10. My curfew used to be ten o'clock, but now it's later.

11. It isn't unusual to hear public speakers use a lot of *uh's* and *um's*.

12. Doreen mistakenly used %'s in her paper when she should have spelled out "percent."

13. Angie pecked him on the cheek and said, "G'night!"

14. The forty-niners enjoyed ridin' and ropin' when they weren't prospectin' for gold.

Extend: Write three to five sentences analyzing your latest report card. Use apostrophes in your writing to form contractions and the plural forms of letters or numbers.

Review: Apostrophes

> **Add** an apostrophe and, when it is needed, an *s* to each noun or pronoun that should be possessive. Also insert apostrophes in other places where needed.

1   In 1848, James Marshall discovered gold at John Sutter's sawmill. The

2   next year, 50,000 people headed to California's goldfields. The luckiest

3   prospectors' dreams came true: they found gold. Other people became rich by

4   selling supplies to the area's many miners.

5   In a few months, 75 percent of San Francisco's men had left their homes,

6   giving in to the goldfields' allure. When the news of gold reached the East

7   Coast in '49, many easterners also headed west. But it was at least three

8   months' journey to California. Ships had to sail around South America or stop

9   at Panama, where men trekked across Panama's isthmus to catch a second ship

10 on the other side. Other forty-niners traveled by land, crossing Nebraska's

11 plains and Colorado's mountains. Everyone's wagons started rolling before six

12 o'clock and didn't stop until dark.

13 Gold fever spread to Colorado's, Nevada's, and Montana's rivers and

14 mountains. In 1859 in Nevada, Henry Comstock and his partners put their X's

15 on the claim that produced the Comstock Lode, one of the United States' richest

16 silver mines. At first, the Comstock Lode's miners threw away the black rock

17 mixed in with the gold, not knowing that they'd found pure silver. Soon, a

18 silver fever overtook miners, and they flocked to the Comstock Lode. Virginia

19 City, Nevada, one of Nevada's most colorful mining towns, sprang up.

20 Today, Virginia City's opera house, saloons, steam locomotive, old houses,

21 and boardwalks keep its history alive. Tourists enjoy the city's old-time

22 atmosphere.

Pretest: Capitalization

> **Add** the necessary capitalization to the following dialogue.

1 **O**ur history teacher, **m**s. **r**adu, asked us if we could name the **s**even **w**onders

2 of the **a**ncient **w**orld without looking in our book, ***w**orld **h**istory for **e**veryone.*

3 **J**ust about everyone in **w**orld **h**istory 101 knew that the **e**gyptian pyramids

4 at **g**iza, **e**gypt, had to be on the list. We had just read the chapter called

5 "**E**gypt's **m**ummies **y**ield **t**heir **s**ecrets." **D**harma **g**rant, the class brain, waved

6 her hand: "**T**he **h**anging **g**ardens of **b**abylon are one of the ancient wonders," she

7 said. "**T**hey were built by **k**ing **n**ebuchadnezzar II around 600 **b**.**c**.**e**. for his wife."

8 **A**fter thinking of only two answers, we were stumped; so **m**s. **r**adu said

9 she'd give us a hint: "**A**ll of the wonders are found in the **m**iddle **e**ast, in

10 countries surrounding the **m**editerranean **s**ea."

11 **W**hen she got no response, she asked, "**D**on't any of you remember learning

12 **g**reek and **r**oman mythology in junior high? **W**ho was the father of the **g**reek

13 gods? **S**urely, someone knows that answer."

14 **F**rom the back of my brain, I dredged up the one name that had lodged

15 there during my days at **g**rover **c**leveland **j**unior **h**igh **s**chool. "**Z**eus!" I

16 exclaimed. "**H**e was the king, or something."

17 "**E**xactly," said Ms. **r**adu. (**S**he was trying to keep from smiling.) "The

18 statue of **z**eus, at **o**lympia, **g**reece, is the third ancient wonder." Instead of

19 extending the misery, she told us the other four places: a lighthouse at

20 **a**lexandria, **e**gypt; a temple at **e**phesus, **t**urkey; a statue on the island of **r**hodes;

21 and a mausoleum (that's a large tomb) in **t**urkey.

22 "**W**hy isn't the **g**reat **w**all of **c**hina on the list?" someone asked. "**M**y father

23 said it's one of the only things on ~~e~~arth that you can see from outer space." [E]

24 "~~g~~reat question," ~~m~~s. ~~r~~adu replied. "~~H~~ow about someone from the ~~s~~mithville [G] [M R] [H] [S]

25 ~~s~~cience ~~c~~lub answering that one." [S] [C]

26 "~~m~~aybe they didn't know about it," ~~b~~riana ~~j~~ones said. "~~c~~hina is much [M] [B J C]

27 farther east than the ~~m~~iddle ~~e~~ast, and ~~at&t~~ wasn't around back then." [M E] [AT T]

28 "~~b~~rilliant," ~~m~~s. ~~r~~adu said. "~~b~~ut now let's do a ~~u~~-turn and think about today's [B] [M R] [B] [U]

29 world. What are the most amazing structures in the modern world? And don't

30 give me any lame answers like the ~~s~~mithville ~~b~~aptist ~~c~~hurch or the [S] [B] [C]

31 headquarters for the ~~s~~mithville ~~d~~emocratic ~~c~~lub." [S] [D] [C]

32 ~~w~~e came up with the highest buildings in the world, the ~~p~~etronas ~~t~~owers in [W] [P] [T]

33 ~~k~~uala ~~l~~umpur, ~~m~~alaysia, and famous places where people worship, such as ~~s~~t. [K] [L] [M] [S]

34 ~~p~~eter's ~~b~~asilica in ~~r~~ome. [P] [B] [R]

35 ~~o~~ther students said they thought that natural wonders were greater than [O]

36 those made by human hands and named the ~~h~~imalayan ~~m~~ountains in ~~t~~ibet and [H] [M] [T]

37 the ~~g~~rand ~~c~~anyon in the ~~u~~nited ~~s~~tates to make their point. [G] [C] [U] [S]

38 ~~h~~oward ~~m~~eyerhoff said that a simple ~~a~~-frame home could be as beautiful as [H] [M] [A]

39 some ancient temple or modern skyscraper, but that's the kind of weird answer

40 you can expect from ~~h~~oward—summer, winter, spring, or fall. [H]

Capitalization 1

Proper names are always capitalized, as are the following:

> races (Hispanic), nationalities (French), languages (Swahili), and religions (Hinduism)

> organizations (Lions Club), associations (World Soccer Federation), and teams (Milwaukee Mustangs)

> titles (Mrs.) and acronyms (NAACP)

> letters used to indicate shape and form (T-shirt).

Turn to 475.1-477.5 in *Writers INC* for more information and examples.

Place capital letters wherever they are needed.

1.   *S* senator *S* susan *R* ricketts, my father's classmate and neighbor, was a *R* republican first, but then made a *U* u-turn and became a *D* democrat.

2. At *G* greenfield *H* high *S* school, she had the lead role in *M* my *F* fair *L* lady.

3. *S* she began her ascent as a star center fielder for the *G* greenfield *S* super *S* slugs.

4. *I* in college, she met a lot of future campaign volunteers through the *Y* young *R* republicans, *A* amnesty *I* international, and the *T* toastmasters *C* club.

5. *W* while still in college, she wrote two books: *H* how to *S* speak *K* knowledgeably *A* about *G* gravy and *A* a *C* college *S* student's *E* economic *R* reform *E* efforts.

6. Her father encouraged her to study for her *P* ph.*D* d., which she did—specializing in international affairs.

7. She took the *R* ricketts name when she married her husband.

8. *W* when *I* i see her, *I* i teasingly call her "*S* senator *D* dr. *M* mrs. *R* ricketts."

9. *S* she replies, "*I* i have more titles than the *G* greenfield *P* public *L* library."

10. *S* she speaks *S* spanish, *F* french, and *E* english and can make an audience laugh in all three languages.

Extend: Try writing a few sentences about what you plan to do in the next 5 to 10 years. Be serious or silly, but use many examples of proper capitalization.

Capitalization 2

The following words are capitalized:

> names for the Supreme Being (God, Allah, Jehovah); the names for holy books, such as the Bible, the Koran, and the Talmud

> days of the week, the months, holidays and holy days (Christmas, Hanukkah, Kwanza)

> trade names (Irish Spring soap, Ford trucks)

> periods and events in history (the Renaissance, Battle of Normandy); political parties (Democratic Party, Libertarian Party)

Turn to 475.1-477.5 in *Writers INC* to review capitalization rules.

Place capital letters wherever they are needed.

1. $\overset{T}{\cancel{t}}$he $\overset{M}{\cancel{m}}$esozoic $\overset{P}{\cancel{p}}$eriod came after the $\overset{P}{\cancel{p}}$ermian $\overset{E}{\cancel{e}}$ra according to our science teacher, $\overset{D}{\cancel{d}}$r. $\overset{S}{\cancel{s}}$amuelson.

2. $\overset{I}{\cancel{i}}$t didn't matter what people were—$\overset{D}{\cancel{d}}$emocrat, $\overset{R}{\cancel{r}}$epublican, $\overset{I}{\cancel{i}}$ndependent— everyone was shocked when $\overset{P}{\cancel{p}}$resident $\overset{K}{\cancel{k}}$ennedy was assassinated.

3. $\overset{G}{\cancel{g}}$randma $\overset{E}{\cancel{e}}$dith believes in $\overset{G}{\cancel{g}}$od, $\overset{G}{\cancel{g}}$randma $\overset{K}{\cancel{k}}$atherine believes in $\overset{A}{\cancel{a}}$llah, and $\overset{G}{\cancel{g}}$reat-$\overset{A}{\cancel{a}}$unt $\overset{T}{\cancel{t}}$illy believes in $\overset{B}{\cancel{b}}$uddha.

4. $\overset{K}{\cancel{k}}$elty's birthday is $\overset{O}{\cancel{o}}$ctober 13, which sometimes falls on a $\overset{F}{\cancel{f}}$riday.

5. $\overset{I}{\cancel{i}}$'m afraid $\overset{J}{\cancel{j}}$oel will miss the $\overset{R}{\cancel{r}}$epublican $\overset{R}{\cancel{r}}$eform $\overset{P}{\cancel{p}}$arty's rally on $\overset{S}{\cancel{s}}$aturday since he'll be honoring $\overset{R}{\cancel{r}}$osh $\overset{H}{\cancel{h}}$ashanah.

6. $\overset{D}{\cancel{d}}$id any of the men who signed the $\overset{D}{\cancel{d}}$eclaration of $\overset{I}{\cancel{i}}$ndependence suffer consequences?

7. $\overset{M}{\cancel{m}}$y neighbor $\overset{R}{\cancel{r}}$aquel $\overset{Z}{\cancel{z}}$eneh ran for a seat in the $\overset{H}{\cancel{h}}$ouse of $\overset{R}{\cancel{r}}$epresentatives on the $\overset{L}{\cancel{l}}$ibertarian $\overset{P}{\cancel{p}}$arty platform.

8. The $\overset{N}{\cancel{n}}$ational $\overset{A}{\cancel{a}}$eronautics and $\overset{S}{\cancel{s}}$pace $\overset{A}{\cancel{a}}$dministration ($\overset{NASA}{\cancel{nasa}}$) maintains the $\overset{D}{\cancel{d}}$ryden $\overset{F}{\cancel{f}}$light $\overset{R}{\cancel{r}}$esearch $\overset{C}{\cancel{c}}$enter at $\overset{E}{\cancel{e}}$dwards $\overset{A}{\cancel{a}}$ir $\overset{F}{\cancel{f}}$orce $\overset{B}{\cancel{b}}$ase in $\overset{C}{\cancel{c}}$alifornia.

Extend: For each capitalization error you made in this activity, write two sentences containing correct examples of that rule.

Capitalization 3

Turn to 475.1-477.5 in *Writers INC.*

Place capital letters wherever they are needed.

1. The ~~a~~uburn ~~u~~niversity ~~t~~igers play the ~~u~~niversity of ~~w~~ashington ~~h~~uskies ~~m~~onday.
   A *U* *T* *U* *W* *H* *M*

2. President ~~r~~eagan probably never considered joining the ~~l~~ibertarian ~~p~~arty.
   R *L* *P*

3. I wonder if the ~~m~~agna ~~c~~arta was signed on a ~~t~~uesday or a ~~w~~ednesday.
   M *C* *T* *W*

4. The ~~n~~ew ~~e~~ngland ~~p~~atriots' home stadium is located in a suburb of ~~b~~oston.
   N *E* *P* *B*

5. Christians celebrate ~~j~~esus ~~c~~hrist's birth in ~~d~~ecember.
   J *C* *D*

6. This year, the ~~c~~hinese ~~n~~ew ~~y~~ear will be celebrated in early ~~f~~ebruary.
   C *N* *Y* *F*

7. Sam will take ~~u~~ncle ~~c~~harlie to an ~~a~~frican storytelling performance next ~~s~~unday.
   U *C* *A* *S*

8. Joey says it's un-~~a~~merican to eat apple pie without cinnamon ice cream.
   A

9. The chief engineer does not know why we lost communication with ~~a~~pollo 13.
   A

10. It happened when they shot the satellite into orbit around ~~m~~ars.
    M

11. How well can you see the ~~m~~ilky ~~w~~ay from ~~a~~laska?
    M *W* *A*

12. About 165,000 native ~~h~~awaiians live in ~~h~~awaii, the ~~a~~loha ~~s~~tate.
    W *H* *A* *S*

13. Turn north at ~~f~~irst ~~a~~merican ~~b~~ank.
    F *A* *B*

14. Have you read the book *~~a~~ngela's ~~a~~shes* by ~~f~~rank ~~m~~cCourt?
    A *A* *F* *M*

15. Many ~~e~~gyptians are ~~m~~uslims; they practice the ~~i~~slamic religion.
    E *M* *I*

16. My grandparents, who go to ~~f~~lorida for the winter, are called "snowbirds" by the
    F
    people who live in the ~~s~~outh.
    S

17. Professor ~~g~~irell, who lives next door, teaches religious subjects, and he has
    G
    studied the ~~b~~ible, the ~~k~~oran, and the ~~t~~almud.
    B *K* *T*

18. His home is located on ~~s~~ugarloaf ~~r~~oad, not ~~p~~ark ~~l~~ane.
    S *R* *P* *L*

Extend: For each capitalization error you made in this activity, write two sentences containing correct examples of that rule.

Review: Capitalization

> Correct the capitalization in the following student writing.

1   when i was a little boy, bunde, minnesota, was the cultural center of my
     (W) (I) (B) (M)

2   life. bunde was a tiny village planted beside minnesota highway 7, about 100
     (B) (M) (H)

3   miles straight west of minneapolis. in fact, the village wasn't even a village;
     (M) (I)

4   the place consisted of eight houses, egbert foken's farm, a church, the
     (E) (F)

5   parsonage, and bunde cemetery.
     (B) (C)

6   my great-aunt, minnie (*aunt minkya* we called her), lived in a bulky
     (M) (M) (A) (M)

7   two-story house at the west end of bunde. aunt minnie's apple orchard stood
     (B) (A) (M)

8   between her house and the little square home where grandma ulferts lived with
     (G) (U)

9   uncle harry, her 35-year-old son. just north of my grandma lived old mrs.
     (U) (H) (J) (M)

10   gruising; and north of her lived mrs. bode with her 40-year-old son, clarence.
     (G) (M) (B) (C)

11   before he died, clarence's father, dr. bode, had been the minister at the
     (B) (C) (D) (B)

12   bunde christian reformed church, which was built next to his home and was
     (B) (C) (R) (C)

13   well-known for its christmas service. just east of the church, the bodies of
     (C) (J)

14   about 200 norwegian and german settlers rested beside dr. bode under the tall
     (N) (G) (D) (B)

15   trees and thick sod in the church cemetery. south of the cemetery, old
     (S)

16   mrs. alberts lived behind a screen of long-haired willow trees and thick
     (M) (A)

17   honeysuckle—all of which hid her tiny chicken coop and the old, steep-roofed,

18   pale green house that looked like a cuckoo clock.

19   each day, in cars and trucks on minnesota highway 7, hundreds of
     (E) (M) (H)

20   strangers shot through that little gathering of trees and buildings and

21   gravestones. i suspect that few of them realized that the blur they saw was
     (I)

22   really the cultural oasis for our farm community.

Pretest: Plurals & Spelling

Write the correct spelling above each underlined word that is misspelled. Write **C** above each underlined word that is spelled correctly.

1   *sandwiches*   *C*
     Peanut butter and jelly <u>sandwichs</u> are almost an American <u>institution</u>.

2   *C*
     Maybe you're one of the <u>unfortunates</u> who steers away from peanut butter

3   *fattening*   *Studies*
     because you think it's too <u>fatening</u>. Take note: <u>Studys</u> at Harvard University

4   *successful*
     show that peanut butter can be part of a <u>suceful</u> weight-loss program because

5   *C*   *happiness*
     peanut butter satisfies the <u>appetite</u>. It's the <u>happyness</u> factor. You eat less

6   because you feel full.

7   *geniuses (or) genii*   *C*
     Who were the <u>geniusses</u> who "invented" PB&J sandwiches? We'll <u>probably</u>

8   never know, but if they could have patented their invention, they could be

9   *lives*
     enjoying <u>lifes</u> of luxury now.

10   *approximately*
     There are <u>approximatly</u> 850 peanuts in every 18-ounce jar of peanut butter.

11   *through*
     I'd say our family goes <u>thru</u> at least one jar a week, so in a year—let me see—

12   *jarfuls*
     that would be 52 <u>jarsful</u> of peanut butter and 44,200 peanuts! Where do they

13   all come from?

14   *glorious*   *C*
     Peanuts have a <u>gloryous</u>, multicultural past. They <u>originated</u> in the

15   *likely*   *ancient*
     Western Hemisphere, most <u>likly</u> in Brazil, and were domesticated in <u>anceint</u>

16   times by Native Americans in both North and South America. Of course, all

17   *schoolchildren*   *C*
     <u>schoolchildrens</u> learn about the <u>contributions</u> of George Washington Carver,

18   *scientist*
     the African American <u>sceintist</u> who developed hundreds of uses for peanuts

19   *potatoes*   *countries*
     and sweet <u>potatos</u>. But today, the two largest peanut-producing <u>countrys</u> in

20   the world are not even in the Western Hemisphere. China and India are the

21   *C*   *incidentally*
     <u>front-runners</u> in peanut production. (The United States, <u>incidentaly</u>, ranks

22   fifth.)

23   By high school graduation, the *average* avrage American has eaten 1,500 peanut

24   butter sandwiches—many in their school *lunches* lunchs. What are the criteria *C* for a

25   great PB&J? If you limit yourself to peanut butter and grape jelly, you're being

26   too much of a *purist* pureist. Besides, what do you do when you discover that some

27   *really* realy inconsiderate member of your family has used the last two *spoonfuls* spoonsful of

28   jelly in the jar and then set it back in the refrigerator *C* without telling anyone?

29   *Necessity* Necesity, as they say, is the mother of invention. Honey or that "marshmallow

30   in a jar" will do in a pinch, but the former is sticky and the *latter* later is gooey.

31   Applesauce, sliced bananas, *pitted* pited dates, chutney, *candies* candys, and even dill pickles

32   are favored by those with adventurous *C* (some would say weird) *C* taste buds.

33   Restaurants that specialize in PB&J's are *cropping* croping up across the country.

34   Most feature *loaves* loafs of gourmet breads and peanut butter ground to your

35   specifications, *C* like gourmet coffee. They should try adding cinnamon *C* or raisins,

36   don't you think?

37   Let's face it—when you get down to everyday life, it's our *stomachs* stomaches that

38   do most of the talking. Right now, mine is reminding me of all those happy

39   *memories* memorys I have of eating *delicious* delishous PB&J sandwiches. In my family, we

40   discovered what we *believe* beleive is an *improvement* improvment on this great American staple.

41   Toast your PB&J as you would a *grilled* griled-cheese sandwich. At our house, we

42   absolutely love them!

Plurals 1

The plurals of many nouns are formed by adding *s* to the singular, but there are some exceptions. *Remember:* A dictionary generally lists only irregular plural forms. If the plural form isn't listed, follow rules 478.1-479.5 in *Writers INC*.

> **Write** the plural of each word below. **Consult a dictionary if necessary.**

1. cupful ___cupfuls___
2. disc ___discs___
3. alley ___alleys___
4. buoy ___buoys___
5. radio ___radios___
6. self ___selves___
7. lunch ___lunches___
8. jeep ___jeeps___
9. melody ___melodies___
10. soprano ___sopranos___
11. leaf ___leaves (or) leafs___
12. reef ___reefs___
13. beach ___beaches___
14. typist ___typists___
15. injury ___injuries___
16. potato ___potatoes___
17. puff ___puffs___
18. wharf ___wharves (or) wharfs___
19. child ___children___
20. gentleman ___gentlemen___

21. fistful ___fistfuls___
22. ox ___oxen (or) ox___
23. tankful ___tankfuls___
24. louse [the insect] ___lice___
25. grandchild ___grandchildren___
26. antenna ___antennae (or) antennas___
27. mouthful ___mouthfuls___
28. fungus ___fungi (or) funguses___
29. phenomenon ___phenomena (or) phenomenons___
30. brother-in-law ___brothers-in-law___
31. chief of protocol ___chiefs of protocol___
32. agency ___agencies___
33. wolf ___wolves___
34. hairdo ___hairdos___
35. trolley ___trolleys___
36. tomato ___tomatoes___
37. maid of honor ___maids of honor___
38. editor in chief ___editors in chief___
39. mosquito ___mosquitoes (or) mosquitos___
40. echo ___echoes (or) echos___

Extend: Write five sentences using the plurals that give you the most difficulty.

Plurals 2

The plurals of many nouns are formed by adding *s* to the singular, but there are some exceptions. Turn to 478.1-479.5 in *Writers INC*.

> **Write** the correct plural above each underlined noun.

1. Logging *camps* camp in northern Minnesota, Wisconsin, and Michigan contained colorful *people* person who lived colorful *lives* life.

2. The camps were exciting *places* place to live, but *jobs* job were demanding, and *days* day were long.

3. The *loggers* logger often used *rivers* river to transport the cut *logs* log from the *forests* forest to the *sawmills* sawmill.

4. Sometimes the limbless tree *trunks* trunk would get jammed up in a river bend, resulting in *logjams* logjam that explosives *experts* expert had to clear with dynamite.

5. It took many people to run a logging camp; for instance, *feeders* feeder or barn *bosses* boss would feed the *horses* horse and clean the *barns* barn.

6. *Blacksmiths* Blacksmith made and fitted *horseshoes* horseshoe; they also made or repaired iron *parts* part for *sleighs* sleigh, *wagons* wagon, and other equipment.

7. Bull *cooks* cook (also called barroom *men* man or chore *boys* boy) filled the wood *boxes* box, swept the *bunkhouses* bunkhouse, and fed the *pigs* pig.

8. *Clerks* Clerk worked in the *stores* store or managed the *wanigans* wanigan (supply chests or storage *shacks* shack on wheels).

9. They ordered *supplies* supply; the *5's* 5, *18's* 18, or *28's* 28 in their *records* record were often impossible to decipher.

10. "Cruiser" (also called *estimators* estimator, *land lookers* land looker, or *valuers* valuer) estimated the value of the standing timber.
Cruisers

Extend: Make a list of plural words that are correct examples of the one rule (478.1 to 479.5) that causes you the most difficulty.

Spelling 1: *i* before *e*

Write *i* before *e* except after *c*, or when sounded like $\bar{a}$ as in *neighbor* and *weigh*. Eight exceptions to this rule are included in the following sentence: Neither sheik dared leisurely seize either weird species of financiers. Additional exceptions are *their, height, counterfeit, heir,* and *foreign*. Turn to 484.1 in *Writers INC.*

Fill in the blanks below with the correct spelling of each word.

Write *i* before *e* . . .

1. f—ld *field*

3. br—f *brief*

2. rel—f *relief*

4. p—ce *piece*

except after *c*,

1. conc—ve *conceive*

2. dec—ve *deceive*

or when sounded like $\bar{a}$ as in *neighbor* and *weigh*.

1. fr—ght *freight*

3. w—ght *weight*

2. v—n *vein*

4. r—gn *reign*

Fill in the blanks, writing the correct spelling of each word using *ie* or *ei*.

1. If you want to *(rec—ve)* _____ *receive* _____ a passing grade in English, you must work hard on your spelling.

2. If you *(bel—ve)* _____ *believe* _____ that good spelling is unnecessary these days, you are only *(dec—ving)* _____ *deceiving* _____ yourself.

3. You would probably also trust in the little red-suited elf who rides in a *(sl—gh)* _____ *sleigh* _____ pulled by *(—ght)* _____ *eight* _____ tiny *(r—ndeer)* _____ *reindeer* _____ .

4. Learning how to *(ach—ve)* _____ *achieve* _____ in spelling is not easy.

5. There are several important steps you must learn to follow if you are to become a heavy *(w—ght)* _____ *heavyweight* _____ in the sport of spelling.

6. First of all, you must learn to be *(pat—nt)* _____patient_____ ; good spelling takes time.

7. Second, you must check the correct pronunciation of each word you are attempting to learn. A dictionary is the best *(fr—nd)* _____friend_____ to consult for word pronunciation.

8. As you are checking your dictionary, take a *(br—f)* _____brief_____ look at the meaning and history of each word. This information will help you recall the spelling of the word because you can now *(perc—ve)* _____perceive_____ where and how this word might be used.

9. Before you close the dictionary, look away from the page and try to *(v—w)* _____view_____ , or see, each word in your mind. Write the word on your paper using only your mind's eye for *(conc—ving)* _____conceiving_____ the proper spelling.

10. Learn some spelling rules. You should begin by *(s—zing)* _____seizing_____ the opportunity to learn the four rules presented in *Writers INC*.

11. Use memory techniques to *(retr—ve)* _____retrieve_____ the correct spelling for words you use often.

12. Make a list of the words you misspell and *(rev—w)* _____review_____ them as often as you can. Use the tips we just covered. Your spelling will begin to *(y—ld)* _____yield_____ better grades and pride in yourself.

Extend: Memorize the sentence containing exceptions to the "*i* before *e*" rule. (Neither sheik dared leisurely seize either weird species of financiers.) Write it without looking at the original. Then check your spelling.

Spelling 2: Consonant Endings

If the last syllable of a word is accented when spoken aloud, the spelling rule for doubling consonants may apply. Study rule 484.2 in *Writers INC*, but always check your dictionary for exceptions.

Write an accent mark above the stressed syllable in each word below. If you are unsure, say the word aloud or check a dictionary.

1. omit´
2. lín ger
3. díf fer
4. for get´
5. re gret´

6. re fer´
7. con cur´
8. hón or
9. be gin´
10. con fer´

11. cóv er
12. com mit´
13. con trol´
14. e quip´
15. pre fer´

16. gál lop
17. oc cur´
18. múr mur
19. ad mit´
20. hú mor

Add the suffix *able*, *ing*, or *ed* to each word below. Use each suffix at least four times.

Answers may vary.

1. omit *omitted*
2. linger *lingering*
3. differ *differed*
4. forget *forgettable*
5. regret *regrettable*
6. refer *referring*
7. concur *concurred*

8. honor *honoring*
9. begin *beginning*
10. confer *conferred*
11. cover *covered*
12. commit *committed*
13. control *controllable*
14. equip *equipped*

15. prefer *preferable*
16. gallop *galloped*
17. occur *occurring*
18. murmur *murmuring*
19. admit *admitted*
20. humor *humored*
21. color *coloring*

Add one of the following suffixes to each word below: *ence/ance*, *ont/ant*, or *er*.

1. concur *concurrent*
2. wrap *wrapper*
3. occur *occurrence*
4. admit *admittance*

5. refer *reference*
6. bat *batter*
7. differ *different*
8. flip *flippant*

9. color *colorant*
10. quit *quitter*
11. stop *stopper*
12. control *controller*

Spelling 3: Silent e

If a word ends with a silent *e*, drop the *e* before adding an ending that begins with a vowel. Do not drop the *e* when adding a suffix that begins with a consonant. Exceptions to the silent *e* rule occur when the final *e* is preceded by either *c* or *g*, and these exceptions are true only when adding *able* or *ous*. (*Truly, awful,* and *argument* are additional exceptions. Turn to 484.3 in *Writers INC*.)

 state—stating—statement   like—liking—likeness

> **Combine** the following words with the suffixes listed. Remember both the silent *e* rule and the exceptions.

1. nature + al *natural*

2. nine + ty *ninety*

3. store + age *storage*

4. true + ly *truly*

5. guide + ance *guidance*

6. peace + able *peaceable*

7. lone + ly *lonely*

8. advise + able *advisable*

9. sense + less *senseless*

10. desire + able *desirable*

11. state + ment *statement*

12. fame + ous *famous*

13. excite + ment *excitement*

14. hope + less *hopeless*

15. lone + some *lonesome*

16. care + less *careless*

17. safe + ty *safety*

18. nerve + ous *nervous*

19. live + able *livable*

20. arrive + al *arrival*

> **Add** the suffix *ing* to each of the following words. Again, remember the rule.

1. come + ing *coming*

2. hope + ing *hoping*

3. use + ing *using*

4. argue + ing *arguing*

5. ache + ing *aching*

6. believe + ing *believing*

7. love + ing *loving*

8. divide + ing *dividing*

9. feature + ing *featuring*

10. lose + ing *losing*

Spelling 4: Final *y*

When *y* is the last letter in a word and it is preceded by a consonant, change the *y* to *i* before adding a suffix (unless the suffix itself begins with an *i*). Turn to 484.4 and 478.2 in *Writers INC*.

 carry—carrier—carrying

 reply—replied—replying

Combine the following words and suffixes. Remember: Do not change *y* to *i* if *y* is preceded by a vowel.

1. beauty + ful _beautiful_

2. easy + ly _easily_

3. marry + age _marriage_

4. journey + s _journeys_

5. chimney + s _chimneys_

6. monkey + ed _monkeyed_

7. hungry + er _hungrier_

8. turkey + s _turkeys_

9. employ + er _employer_

10. hurry + ed _hurried_

11. try + ing _trying_

12. lady + es _ladies_

Combine the words and suffixes below.

1. busy + ly _busily_

2. destroy + ed _destroyed_

3. library + es _libraries_

4. territory + al _territorial_

5. ready + ness _readiness_

6. diary + es _diaries_

7. lovely + est _loveliest_

8. ninety + es _nineties_

9. twenty + eth _twentieth_

10. attorney + s _attorneys_

11. bury + ed _buried_

12. safety + es _safeties_

13. annoy + s _annoys_

14. sully + es _sullies_

15. necessary + ly _necessarily_

16. likely + hood _likelihood_

17. secretary + al _secretarial_

18. vary + able _variable_

19. defy + ance _defiance_

20. scrappy + ness _scrappiness_

Add the missing letter: either *y* or *i*.

1. hill_*i*_ness

2. var_*i*_ous

3. dela_*y*_ed

4. merc_*i*_ful

5. funn_*i*_est

6. bab_*y*_ish

7. fur_*i*_ous

8. bur_*i*_al

9. carr_*y*_ing

Combine each word below with the suffix listed beside it.

1. The dictionary defines a *contest* as "a struggle for superiority or victory." *Vary* + *ous* _____*Various*_____ words describe such struggles more precisely.

2. A boxing contest, for example, is called a *bout*. So is a struggle with an illness. Neither situation is very *enjoy + able* _____*enjoyable*_____ , and *bout convey + s* _____*conveys*_____ this better than the word *contest*.

3. When two political candidates "struggle for victory," the contest is called a *campaign*. Campaigns are also *employ + ed* _____*employed*_____ in warfare. Either way, the struggle is usually *fury + ous* _____*furious*_____ and *weary + some* _____*wearisome*_____ .

4. Politicians combat their *adversary + es* _____*adversaries*_____ with words. When words fail, soldiers *battle* their *enemy + es* _____*enemies*_____ with deadlier weapons. The political struggle is called a *debate;* the military struggle is called a *skirmish*, a *confrontation*, a *battle*, a *campaign*, or a *war*.

Extend: If a word has only one syllable, the final *y* is not changed when adding either *ly* or *ness*. Combine the words and suffixes below.

1. shy + ness _____*shyness*_____

2. pretty + ly _____*prettily*_____

3. sly + ly _____*slyly*_____

4. dry + ness _____*dryness*_____

Review: Plurals & Spelling

Complete each word below by adding either *ei* or *ie*.

1. w_*ei*_ght
2. ch_*ie*_f
3. v_*ie*_w
4. dec_*ei*_ve
5. r_*ei*_gn
6. n_*ei*_ghbor
7. y_*ie*_ld
8. fr_*ie*_nd
9. for_*ei*_gn

Place accent marks in the underlined word below. Then add the suffix listed.

1. prefer′ + ed _preferred_
2. omit′ + ed _omitted_
3. admit′ + ance _admittance_
4. forget′ + ful _forgetful_
5. equip′ + ed _equipped_
6. control′ + ing _controlling_
7. regret′ + able _regrettable_
8. ′counsel + ed _counseled (or) counselled_
9. begin′ + ing _beginning_
10. ′differ + ing _differing_

Combine the following words with the suffixes listed.

1. lone + ly _lonely_
2. desire + able _desirable_
3. care + less _careless_
4. store + age _storage_
5. safe + ty _safety_
6. true + ly _truly_
7. fame + ous _famous_
8. guide + ance _guidance_
9. argue + ing _arguing_
10. lose + ing _losing_
11. lone + some _lonesome_
12. nine + ty _ninety_
13. use + ing _using_
14. live + able _livable_
15. state + ment _statement_
16. peace + able _peaceable_

Combine the words and suffixes below.

1. easy + ly _easily_
2. journey + s _journeys_
3. bury + ed _buried_
4. library + es _libraries_

5. mercy + ful _merciful_
6. lucky + ly _luckily_
7. turkey + s _turkeys_
8. chimney + s _chimneys_

Make the following words plural. Some have irregular spellings.

1. wife _wives_
2. belief _beliefs_
3. knife _knives_
4. roof _roofs_
5. wolf _wolves_
6. chief _chiefs_
7. cliff _cliffs_
8. child _children_
9. ox _oxen (or) ox_
10. mouse _mice_
11. goose _geese_
12. tooth _teeth_
13. woman _women_
14. syllabus _syllabi (or) syllabuses_

15. thief _thieves_
16. fife _fifes_
17. life _lives_
18. loaf _loaves_
19. strife _strifes_
20. puff _puffs_
21. elf _elves_
22. editor in chief _editors in chief_
23. son-in-law _sons-in-law_
24. runner-up _runners-up_
25. drive-in _drive-ins_
26. lean-to _lean-tos_
27. two-year-old _two-year-olds_
28. vertebra _vertebrae (or) vetebras_

Numbers 1

Depending on the situation, numbers are represented by words or numerals. Business, scientific, legal, and technical writings tend to use numerals. In other areas, numbers are often written out. Become familiar with the basic guidelines in *Writers INC*, covering the most common ways to use numbers. Turn to 480.1-480.4 in *Writers INC*.

Underline each misused number and write the correction above it.

1. Halley's comet is named after the English astronomer Edmund Halley, who
   observed it in sixteen eighty-two. *(1682)*

2. It takes Halley's comet about seventy-five years to complete its orbit and return *(or) 75*
   to our skies.

3. For the last two thousand years, it has followed this schedule. *2,000 (optional)*

4. The most recent passing of Halley's comet took place February ninth, *9*
   nineteen eighty-six. *1986*

5. The European Space Agency's *Giotto*, a satellite, once came within
   six hundred and five kilometers of the comet. *605*

6. Halley's comet appears to rotate on its axis once every two point two days. *2.2*

Use numbers to demonstrate each rule that is listed below.

Answers will vary.

1. You may use a combination of numerals and words for very large numbers.

   The world's population recently passed 6 billion.

2. Numbers being compared or contrasted should be kept in the same style.

   The art class was limited to children aged six to ten.

3. If time is expressed in words, spell out the number.

   Schoolchildren are dismissed at half past three.

Extend: Write sentences for the following: (1) Start a sentence with your age. (2) Include the date and year of your birth in another sentence. (3) In one more sentence, include the time you eat dinner and how much time you usually spend eating.

Numbers 2

Regardless of size, numbers are always spelled out at the beginning of a sentence and on the center line of a personal check. Numbers used in the same way should be treated the same way—all should be either written as words or written as numbers. (The three cats, two dogs, and fifty mice ate 20 cans of food. *Notice that* cans *represents a new category, so the numeral* 20 *is used.*) Turn to 480.1-480.4 in *Writers INC.*

> **Underline** each misused number and write the correction above it.

1. The Colosseum in Rome is an immense superstructure that stands forty-nine *[49]*
   meters high and covers an area one hundred eighty-nine *[189]* meters long and
   one hundred fifty-six *[156]* meters wide.

2. Construction of the Colosseum began in C.E. sixty-nine *[69]* and was completed in
   eighty *[80]* C.E.

3. 76 *[Seventy-six]* of the Colosseum's 80 *[eighty]* bays served as entryways.

4. The outer wall had 4 *[four]* stories and could accommodate fifty thousand *[50,000 (optional)]* spectators.

5. The arena measured eighty-six *[86]* meters by fifty-four *[54]* meters.

> **Use** the following numbers in sentences that demonstrate the rule that is listed.

Answers will vary.

1. (2, 9) Numbers from one to nine are usually written as words.

   There are two dogs and nine cats at the animal shelter.

2. (99) Use words to express numbers that begin a sentence.

   Ninety-nine students are on a field trip.

3. (15) If numbers are used infrequently in a piece of writing, you may spell out those that can be written in one or two words.

   I've skipped breakfast fewer than fifteen times this year.

Extend: Write sentences that correctly demonstrate the use of numbers for the three exceptions listed at 480.1 in *Writers INC.*

Abbreviations

Abbreviations are used to shorten a word or phrase. Too many abbreviations (or abbreviations that are not clearly explained) can confuse a reader. Turn to pages 481-483 in *Writers INC.*

Spell out the following abbreviations.

1. NE _northeast_
2. COD _collect on delivery (or) cash on delivery_
3. dept. _department_
4. CDT _central daylight time_
5. qt _quart_

6. Ore. _Oregon_
7. etc. _and so forth (Latin et cetera)_
8. ed. _edition (or) editor_
9. MS _manuscript, Mississippi, (or) multiple sclerosis_
10. g _gravity (or) gram_

Abbreviate the following words and phrases.

1. Colorado _CO_
2. cup _c._
3. incorporated _inc._
4. that is _i.e. (Latin id est)_
5. Internal Revenue Service _IRS_

6. please reply _R.S.V.P. (or) r.s.v.p._
7. kilogram _kg_
8. Illinois _IL_
9. population _pop._
10. percent _pct._

List three acronyms and three initialisms that you want to learn. Include the phrases they represent. Turn to page 483.

Answers will vary.

Acronyms	Initialisms
1. _____	1. _____
2. _____	2. _____
3. _____	3. _____

Extend: Look through one or two of your textbooks from another class, searching for abbreviations, acronyms, and initialisms. Write them down. Exchange lists with a classmate to see how many each of you can identify.

Review: Numbers & Abbreviations

> **Underline** any number or abbreviation used incorrectly and write the correction above. **Finally, answer the questions.**

June 9, 1942

1. The top secret Manhattan Project was begun 6/9/42.

World War   United States

2. Adolf Hitler and the Nazis were winning WW II. The U.S. and its allies needed

a powerful weapon to stop them.

3. Albert Einstein and other scientists worked with the Corps of Engineering to

as soon as possible

help develop a nuclear bomb ASAP.

Three thousand   *Tennessee*

4. 3,000 people living in the Oak Ridge, TN, area were relocated to make way for

three

3 supersecret military factories.

5. Speed was necessary, so contractors had to build prefabricated homes for the

hour

workers, sometimes in less than an hr.

(or) twelve

6. Anyone over the age of 12 did not enter or leave the city without his or her

security badge and personal identification number (PIN).

7. Today, Oak Ridge manufacturers produce heat-resistant ceramics that protect

23,000

space shuttles up to twenty-three thousand °F.

34,000

8. Some thirty-four thousand ceramic tiles are used as heat shields on the shuttle.

9. Superconductor ceramics are also helping to create "floating" trains that will

200-300   *miles per hour (optional)*

travel two hundred to three hundred mph.

10. How do you present numbers that begin a sentence?

Numbers at the beginning of a sentence must be expressed as words.

11. How do you express time with either A.M. or P.M.?

When A.M. or P.M. is used, use numerals.

12. How do you express the numbers 10 and above?

These numbers are usually written as numerals.

Pretest: Using the Right Word

> **Write** the correct word above each underlined word that is used incorrectly.

1   Every August, our neighborhood holds _it's_ [*its*] annual dessert-lovers potluck.

2   (It may not be _real_ [*very (or) really*] healthful, but it sure is fun.) Melvin Brown always brings

3   his dog Bono. That's fine with everyone because Bono, a cocker spaniel, is _real_ [*really (or) very*]

4   well-behaved, and he doesn't try to _steel_ [*steal*] treats from anyone's plate.

5   We had this year's potluck last week. Everything was going along _good_ [*well*]

6   until we _herd_ [*heard*] the awful screech of car _breaks_ [*brakes*] and _than_ [*then*] a sickening thump.

7   _Pore_ [*Poor*] Bono had wandered away from the party and had been hit by a passing

8   car; he was _laying_ [*lying*] in a quiet heap by the side of the road.

9   A hush _past_ [*passed*] over the crowd as Melvin and I ran to Bono's side and tried to

10   determine _weather_ [*whether*] he had been badly hurt. We didn't _no_ [*know*] if Bono would be

11   _alright_ [*all right*], but we did know that he needed emergency medical help, and _their_ [*there*] was

12   no time to _loose_ [*lose*].

13   When we reached the emergency room, Bono, with Melvin _besides_ [*beside*] him, was

14   not the only animal there. We had to _set_ [*sit*] and wait while the vet attended _too_ [*to*]

15   two other animals. A cat called Patches was brought in suffering from the

16   _affects_ [*effects*] of smoke inhalation. _It's_ [*Its*] owner, _who's_ [*whose*] name was Juan, was covered in

17   soot from the fire. An older dog was carried in by a tearful woman who

18   exclaimed, "My _dear_ [*dear*] Conchetta has _feinted_ [*fainted*], and she won't wake up!"

19   The personnel on the _seen_ [*scene*] at the clinic were _all together_ [*altogether*] calm and

20   reassuring. They reminded me of the cast of a TV show about a vet who

21   handles pet emergencies. Unlike medical shows, which probably won't _learn_ [*teach*]

22   you _alot_ [*a lot*] about real medicine, this show features actual vets, pets, and pet

23   owners. One thing I've learned by watching the show is that pet owners often

      accept   *their*

24   ~~except~~ complete responsibility when something happens to ~~there~~ pets.

      Poor   *letting*   *sight*

25   ~~Pour~~ Melvin kept kicking himself for ~~leaving~~ Bono out of his ~~site~~. But,

26   of course, accidents just happen, and there's no point in making yourself

                       already   *Anyway*

27   feel worse than you ~~all ready~~ do. ~~Anyways~~, Bono was finally x-rayed. His

                             break   *set*

28   left rear leg had a pretty bad ~~brake~~, so the vet decided to ~~sit~~ it in a

                 wear   *for*   *weeks*

29   splint. Bono will have to ~~ware~~ the splint ~~fore~~ about six ~~weaks~~.

                                  among

30   The neighbors took up a collection ~~between~~ themselves to help Melvin

      through   *heal*

31   ~~threw~~ the financial part of this emergency. Money can't ~~heel~~ Bono, but it

                       meet   *really (or) very*

32   can certainly help Melvin ~~meat~~ this unexpected expense. I'm ~~real~~ proud of

      way   *One*

33   the ~~weigh~~ my neighbors acted like . . . well, like real neighbors. ~~Won~~ of

34   them even bought Melvin a little present: a leash for Bono.

Using the Right Word 1

The following exercise uses some words that sound or look like other words and are often used incorrectly. Turn to pages 491-500 in *Writers INC* for more information.

> **Check** each underlined word. If it is wrong, write the correct word above it.

1   For my oral history report, I <u>choose</u> <u>too</u> speak with my great-grandmother *chose to*

2   about the Great Depression. She was born in 1910 and <u>emigrated</u> <u>to</u> the *immigrated*

3   United States with her family in 1920. The '20s were <u>an</u> prosperous and *a*

4   exciting time. It <u>seamed</u> like the prosperity might last forever. <u>Than</u> of <u>coarse</u>, *seemed* *Then* *course*

5   the stock market crashed in October of 1929.

6   My great-grandmother said she had never <u>scene</u> so much hardship <u>between</u> *seen* *among*

7   the people as that caused by the Great Depression. Hundreds of banks

8   foreclosed on homes and businesses in <u>a</u> unsuccessful attempt to keep *an*

9   themselves afloat. Companies went out of business because the banks wouldn't

10 <u>borrow</u> them any money, forcing <u>they're</u> employees onto the streets. *lend* *their*

11 People did whatever they could <u>too</u> make money, from selling pencils, *to*

12 apples, and other <u>wears</u> on street corners to collecting bits of <u>medal</u> and other *wares* *metal*

13 waste that they might be able to sell <u>fore</u> a few <u>scents</u>. It was a difficult <u>weigh</u> *for* *cents* *way*

14 to support a family and put <u>meet</u> on the table. *meat*

15 Everyone <u>new</u> the Great Depression couldn't go on forever, but everyone *knew*

16 also <u>new</u> <u>there</u> wasn't going to be a quick fix. Being <u>pour</u> wasn't something *knew* *poor*

17 that happened <u>too</u> other people; instead, it was something that happened to *you*. *to*

18 Eventually the government put programs into <u>affect</u> that helped <u>two</u> end *effect* *to*

19 the Great Depression, but <u>its</u> still regarded as one of the most trying times in *it's*

20 American history.

Extend: Write sentences using these words: *they're, their, there* and *effect, affect*. Ask a classmate to check your sentences.

Using the Right Word 2

Many words look or sound alike but have different meanings. They are often misused in conversation and in writing. Other words are somewhat similar in meaning, but are often used incorrectly. Turn to pages 491-500 in *Writers INC* for help.

> **Check** each underlined word. If it is wrong, write the correct word above it.

1 Last week I ~~excepted~~ *accepted* an invitation ~~two~~ *to* go with some friends to the

2 traveling circus and carnival. I hadn't gone <u>to</u> a circus since I was a little kid,

3 and it sounded like <u>a lot</u> of fun.

4 We wanted to see a great ~~amount~~ *number* of things, and we ~~new~~ *knew* we'd have a hard

5 time choosing ~~who~~ *which* to see first. I suggested that we split up and ~~meat~~ *meet* later. We

6 ~~choose~~ *chose* ~~too~~ *to* go together ~~too~~ *to* the magician's tent—which was fine with me because

7 I wanted to go ~~their~~ *there* ~~anyways~~ *anyway*.

8 After the magician was ~~threw~~ *through* with his show, I took a ~~brake~~ *break* and had

9 something to eat. Food at the circus is ~~real~~ *very (or) really* expensive. I bought a corn dog and

10 ~~an~~ *a* soda. As I enjoyed my food, I watched a monkey showing off ~~it's~~ *its* tricks. It

11 ~~laid~~ *lay* down on the ground and pretended it had <u>fainted</u>. Then it got up, walked

12 right ~~passed~~ *past* me, and jumped into its owner's arms.

13 ~~Latter~~ *Later* in the day, one of my friends asked me to ~~borrow~~ *lend* him some money.

14 He'd ~~all ready~~ *already* spent his on games, and he didn't have enough to get something

15 ~~too~~ *to* eat. I grumbled a bit, but I ~~new~~ *knew* he'd pay me back.

16 I didn't want ~~two~~ *to* ~~waist~~ *waste* any more time, so I said I'd see him later. ~~Than~~ *Then* I

17 headed to the midway. I won ~~a~~ *an* eagle-shaped eraser from the woman ~~whom~~ *who* was

18 guessing people's ~~waits~~ *weights*.

19 Before I ~~new~~ *knew* it, it was time to go home. Even though we'd all eaten far ~~to~~ *too*

20 much junk food and spent way ~~to~~ *too* much money, we'd had ~~alot~~ *a lot* of fun.

Using the Right Word 3

Some words that sound or look alike are often used incorrectly. Turn to pages 491-500 in *Writers INC.*

> **Circle** the correct choice in each set of words in parentheses.

1. I would (die, dye) if someone (died, dyed) my hair!

2. You (choose, chose) which (desert, dessert) you want; I already (choose, chose) mine.

3. Of (coarse, course) I knew the sandpaper would be (coarse, course).

4. My grandfather said he'd never (scene, seen) a (scene, seen) as horrific as the aftermath of the Battle of Normandy.

5. I wanted to (accept, except) the invitation to the party; everyone (accept, except) Jaron was going.

6. It was (plain, plane) that the (plain, plane) wasn't going anywhere soon.

7. How can a (be, bee) (be, bee) so small and yet (be, bee) so frightening?

8. George Washington thought (a, an) turkey would make (a, an) better national emblem than (a, an) eagle.

9. For some reason, Joel (blew, blue) up only the (blew, blue) balloons.

10. There is (to, too, two) much (to, too, two) do for just the (to, too, two) of you.

11. I (knew, new) the team was getting (knew, new) equipment, but I didn't (know, no) that (know, no) one else (knew, new).

12. It's never a (waist, waste) of time to clean up all the (waist, waste) at a campsite.

13. (Their, There, They're) not allowed to go (their, there, they're) without all (their, there, they're) shots and medications.

14. (Who, Whom) else knows the person to (who, whom) you were speaking?

Extend: Write sentences using these words: *accept, except; real, very.* Exchange papers with a classmate and check each other's work.

Using the Right Word 4

The English language has many words that sound and look similar or are close enough in meaning to make it difficult to know which word should be used when. Turn to pages 491-500 in *Writers INC* for help.

Check each underlined word. If it is wrong, write the correct word above it.

---

1. When I was younger, I had a *whole* hole bunch of ideas about what I wanted to *be* bee

   when I grew up.

2. I think I *knew* new even *then* than what I wanted most: to be a veterinarian.

3. I love all kinds of critters, from pets like cats and dogs *too* *to herd* heard animals like

   cows and sheep.

4. This *past* passed summer I volunteered at an animal rescue center, and now I *know* no

   that a career as a vet takes more than just love.

5. My team was *led* lead by a student in her *sixth* year *here* hear at the university.

6. She taught us that *there* they're is *a lot* alot more to being a good "animal doctor" *than* then

   knowing how to *heal* heel the sick and injured.

7. Sometimes *it's* its necessary *to* too euthanize (put to sleep) an animal if it's in *too* to much

   pain or if it poses a danger to others.

8. When you *lose* loose an animal this way, *its* it's death is hard to *accept* except.

9. The most uplifting *sight* site all summer was a mountain lion giving *birth* berth.

10. *Some* Sum of the animals *seemed* seamed perfectly happy to let us take care of them, while

    others absolutely seemed to hate us.

11. I didn't always have fun at the rescue center, but I was never *bored* board—and I

    learned that animal medicine certainly isn't *for* fore the *fainthearted* feinthearted.

Extend: Make a list of the words you had trouble with in the exercise above. Write a sentence using each of these words correctly. Check your work using pages 491-500 in *Writers INC*.

Review: Using the Right Word

> **Circle** the correct choice in each set of words in parentheses.

1. *(Their,* **There,** *They're)*! That's what I'm talking about! They always think *(their, there,* **they're***)* going to get everything *(***their,** *there, they're)* way!

2. *(Wood,* **Would***)* you rather chop the *(***wood,** *would)*, or *(wood,* **would***)* you rather stack the *(***wood,** *would)*?

3. My father says you should never *(borrow,* **lend***)* money to family or friends, which is weird, because I *(***borrow,** *lend)* money from him all the time.

4. *(***Poor,** *Pore, Pour)* Paul. Why did his teammates *(poor, pore,* **pour***)* a pitcher of lemonade over his head? Now his *(poors,* **pores,** *pours)* are all clogged.

5. Back *(than,* **then***)* there were more laborers *(***than,** *then)* managers.

6. Kadeem made some *(***allusion,** *illusion)* to the fact that everything we were about to see would be an *(allusion,* **illusion***)*.

7. Ravi became *(board,* **bored***)* very quickly as he watched the Kung Fu master breaking one *(***board,** *bored)* after another.

8. Jody *(***threw,** *through)* the ball as hard as she could. It arced cleanly *(threw,* **through***)* the air and sailed right *(threw,* **through***)* Mrs. Jackson's attic window.

9. The *(***amount,** *number)* of trash left behind at the campground is directly related to the *(amount,* **number***)* of people who stayed there.

10. The conductor told many anecdotes, but the one about the woman who gave *(***birth,** *berth)* in a train *(birth,* **berth***)* was the most memorable.

11. We had done *(good,* **well***)*. In fact, we had done such a *(***good,** *well)* job that our supervisor told us that if we did the next job just as *(good,* **well***)*, she'd give us a day off!

12. *(Its,* It's*)* not beyond repair; all *(its,* it's*)* pieces are right here.

13. There were *(to,* too, *two)* many of us *(to,* too, two*)* fit into one car.

14. The doctor said Jason should *(wait,* weight*)* a week before he checked his *(wait, weight)* again.

15. I have *(know,* no*)* idea how Patrice *(knew,* new*)* the *(knew,* new*)* schedule. As far as I *(know,* no*)*, *(know,* no*)* one but you and I *(knew,* new*)*.

16. When a family *(adapts,* adopts*)* a child, they need time to *(adapt,* adopt*)* to the changes a new child brings.

17. You need to *(accept,* except*)* the fact that no one *(accept,* except*)* the supervisor is permitted to use this phone.

18. Just as Sam decided to *(lay,* lie*)* on the couch for a nap, his younger sister decided to *(lay,* lie*)* her big stuffed animal there.

19. *(Set,* Sit*)* that heavy box down on the floor. Then *(set,* sit*)* in this chair and catch your breath.

20. *(Who,* Whom*)* said, "Ask not for *(who,* whom*)* the bell tolls; it tolls for thee"?

21. Although all *(personal,* personnel*)* at the Big Company have their own cubicles, they are not allowed to post any *(personal,* personnel*)* materials in them.

22. The weather definitely *(affects,* effects*)* a person's mood; seeing the sun after a week of rain can *(affect,* effect*)* a feeling of exhilaration.

23. Malcolm couldn't think of a *(complement,* compliment*)* for his friend's shaved head, so he said, "Wow, the shape of your head sure *(complements,* compliments*)* your face."

24. Upon *(farther,* further*)* examination, it appears the rat went *(farther,* further*)* into the maze than we originally thought.

25. Mom *(continually,* continuously*)* tells me not to watch TV *(continually, continuously).*

Review: Proofreading Activities

> **Write out** the full word or phrase for these common abbreviations.

1. a.m. _before noon (ante meridiem)_
2. vs. _versus_
3. oz. _ounce_
4. ex. _example_
5. mdse. _merchandise_

6. misc. _miscellaneous_
7. tbsp _tablespoon_
8. r.s.v.p. _please reply (répondez s'il vous plaît)_
9. etc. _and so forth (et cetera)_
10. pg. _page_

> **Correct** errors in punctuation, capitalization, spelling, plurals, numbers, and abbreviations in the sentences below. Write the corrections, when necessary, above the errors.

1. The Mount ~~r~~Rushmore ~~nat. mem.~~ National Memorial is located on ~~Hwy.~~ Highway 16, 25 ~~mi. s.w.~~ miles southwest of Rapid City, ~~SD~~ South Dakota.

2. The heads of 4 four ~~U.S. Pres.~~ United States presidents are carved into the side of the mountain: George Washington, Thomas Jefferson, Abraham Lincoln, and Theodore Roosevelt.

3. These ~~carveings~~ carvings are protected by the ~~Nat.~~ National ~~p~~Park Service and the ~~Dept.~~ Department of the ~~i~~Interior.

4. The memorial can be ~~veiwed~~ viewed 24 ~~hrs.~~ hours a day, 365 days a ~~yr.~~ year.

5. ~~l~~Located in the ~~b~~Black ~~h~~Hills, this mountain was chosen for its finely textured granite and the lack of ~~viens~~ veins showing ~~throughout~~ throughout the stone.

6. It also had the unusual feature of a smooth, ~~three-hundred~~ 300-foot ~~perpendiculer~~ perpendicular face of granite on the ~~e.~~ east side, perfect for carving.

7. On ~~Aug.~~ August 10, 1927, thousands watched as the artist and sculptor, Gutzon Borglum, made his ~~decleration~~ declaration to begin construction.

8. ~~a~~A blacksmith shop, tool buildings, and artist ~~studioes~~ studios were built first.

Elaborate
9. ~~Elaberate~~ winches ,devices used for hauling or pulling ,were also constructed.

enormous
10. These held the workers in midair as they chiseled the ~~enormus~~ faces.

length *feet* *height* *six*
11. The ~~lenth~~ of Washington's nose is 20 ft; His head is the ~~hieght~~ of a 6-story building.

meters
12. If he were carved from head to toe, he would be 140 ~~m~~ tall.

accurate measurements *first*
13. In order to get ~~acurate mesurements~~, Borglum ~~1st~~ carved a model.

metal
14. A ~~medal~~ shaft was placed on the upper center of the model's head.

attached
15. A protractor was ~~atached~~ to the base of the shaft.

angles
16. The ~~angels~~ were kept equal on both the model and the mountain, while
lengths *measured* *12*
the ~~lenths~~ were ~~measurred~~ in a ratio of 1 to ~~twelve~~ inches.

injuries *hazardous*
17. There were ~~injurys~~ during the ~~hazzardous~~ construction, but no deaths.

suffered
18. The most significant "injury" on the project was ~~sufferred~~ by Thomas
assistant
Jefferson when an ~~assistent~~ used too much dynamite to create his outline.

19. As with a haircut, the artist can chisel granite here and there to "fix" the sculpture ,but unlike a haircut, granite does not grow back.

20. Jefferson's head was moved from Washington's right to his left. The last
completed without incident
two presidents were ~~compleeted w/o incedent~~.

stopped *October* *World War*
21. Carving ~~stoped~~ in ~~Oct.~~ 1941, the eve of America's involvement in ~~WW~~ II.

monument occurred years
22. The final dedication of the ~~monnument occured~~ 50 ~~yrs.~~ later, even though
completely
it was never ~~completly~~ finished.

(or) one million dollars
23. The total construction cost was nearly $1,000,000, considerably more
than Congress wanted to spend during the great depression.

considered *unique*
24. Now, however, it is ~~considerred~~ a small price to pay for a ~~unque~~ memorial
history
to those who shaped our ~~histery~~.

LANGUAGE ACTIVITIES

The activities in this section provide a review of the different parts of speech. Most of the activities also include helpful handbook references. In addition, the **Extend** activities encourage follow-up practice of certain skills.

Pretest: Nouns

Underline the words used as nouns in the following sentences.

1. Two <u>students</u>, <u>Shannel Lumpkin</u> and <u>Monique Anderson</u>, got a firsthand <u>chance</u> to learn about another <u>culture</u>.

2. Recently, they won all-expenses-paid <u>trips</u> to <u>East Africa</u>.

3. On their three-week <u>journey</u>, the two <u>students</u> from <u>De LaSalle Education Center</u> and their <u>principal</u>, <u>Gayle Lee</u>, visited the <u>Masai Tribe</u> and saw a snake <u>farm</u>.

4. They also spent <u>time</u> as <u>guests</u> of a <u>family</u> in <u>Arusha</u>.

Indicate the function of each of the underlined nouns in the following sentences. Use **S** for subject, **PN** for predicate noun, **IO** for indirect object, **DO** for direct object, and **OP** for object of the preposition. Use **POS** for nouns showing ownership.

1. Both <u>students</u> *(S)* are thankful for their <u>journey</u> *(OP)*.

2. They both felt that many things in <u>East Africa</u> *(OP)* were impressive.

3. For example, <u>East Africa's</u> *(POS)* young people show <u>elders</u> *(IO)* great <u>respect</u> *(DO)*.

4. Lumpkin and Anderson also noticed the <u>lack</u> *(DO)* of <u>materialism</u> *(OP)* and the safe <u>streets</u> *(DO)*.

5. The <u>experience</u> *(S)* changed both <u>Lumpkin's</u> *(POS)* and <u>Anderson's</u> *(POS)* lives.

6. They say they gained <u>appreciation</u> *(DO)* for both <u>cultures</u> *(OP)*.

7. As this and other exchanges take place between <u>communities</u> *(OP)*, the <u>world</u> *(S)* becomes a little smaller.

8. Such programs help people become a little more appreciative of their <u>differences</u> *(OP)* and <u>similarities</u> *(OP)*; the <u>world</u> *(S)* becomes a <u>community</u> *(PN)*.

Identifying Nouns

A common noun names a person, a place, a thing, or an idea. A proper noun names a *particular* person, place, thing, or idea. Proper nouns are capitalized. A collective noun refers to a group or a unit. For more information, turn to page 501 in *Writers INC*.

> **Underline** the common nouns, capitalize the proper nouns, and write **COL** above the collective nouns in the following narrative.

1   For some <u>reason</u>, <u>maps</u> and I don't get along. Even folding the foolish

2   <u>things</u> correctly is an <u>exercise</u> in <u>futility</u>.

3   When it comes to <u>directions</u>, my <u>family</u> [COL] thinks I'm somewhere south of

4   ~~u~~selessville as a <u>navigator</u>. My <u>father</u> says I cannot find my <u>way</u> out of a paper

5   <u>bag</u>, and sometimes I'm inclined to agree. My <u>mother</u> says, "Be kind. At least

6   he doesn't get lost in the <u>neighborhood</u>." I have a <u>pair</u> [COL] of <u>brothers</u> who are less

7   kind.

8   I think it's safe to say that I am not a <u>descendant</u> of ~~m~~agellan [M]. Whether

9   I'm looking for a small <u>shop</u> or the ~~m~~ain [M] ~~s~~treet [S] ~~c~~inema [C], you can be sure I will

10   find the most "scenic" <u>route</u> possible. Once while driving my <u>friends</u> to a <u>movie</u>,

11   I made a wrong <u>turn</u>. It took me an <u>hour</u> to find the right <u>street</u> again. What

12   an <u>embarrassment</u>!

13   To improve my cloudy <u>sense</u> of <u>direction</u>, I once enrolled in an orienteering

14   <u>class</u> in northwest ~~m~~ontana [M]. It didn't help. Luckily, I have no <u>problem</u> asking

15   <u>people</u> for <u>directions</u>. And upon my <u>arrival</u>—anywhere—I can always begin

16   with "A funny <u>thing</u> happened on my <u>way</u>. . ."

Extend: Think of a place you once visited. Describe that place to a friend in the form of a postcard. Exchange postcards with a classmate and underline all the nouns in each other's message.

Singular & Plural Nouns

Number indicates whether a noun is singular or plural. (You need to know the number of the noun you use as a subject, because the verb you choose must agree with that noun.) Turn to 502.1 in *Writers INC*.

> **Write** an **S** above the underlined nouns that are singular and a **P** above the underlined nouns that are plural in the following sentences.

1. $\overset{P}{\underline{People}}$ who live in an American $\overset{S}{\underline{city}}$ may live side by side with many $\overset{P}{\underline{animals}}$.

2. Birds and $\overset{P}{\underline{squirrels}}$ are common, and you might even be able to find $\overset{P}{\underline{deer}}$ or coyotes.

3. But in other $\overset{P}{\underline{parts}}$ of the $\overset{S}{\underline{world}}$, different animals are found on city $\overset{P}{\underline{streets}}$.

4. In $\overset{S}{\underline{Thailand}}$, thousands of wild monkeys live in $\overset{P}{\underline{parks}}$ and on rooftops.

5. Monkeys are sacred in the Buddhist $\overset{S}{\underline{religion}}$, and for $\overset{P}{\underline{hundreds}}$ of years $\overset{P}{\underline{monkeys}}$ have been welcome in Thailand's Buddhist $\overset{P}{\underline{temples}}$.

6. Once $\overset{P}{\underline{cities}}$ grew up around the $\overset{P}{\underline{temples}}$, monkeys could no longer retreat to the $\overset{S}{\underline{forest}}$ and began to live alongside the city $\overset{P}{\underline{dwellers}}$.

7. Most of the $\overset{P}{\underline{monkeys}}$ live quiet, peaceful $\overset{P}{\underline{lives}}$, and some are even adopted as $\overset{P}{\underline{pets}}$.

8. But some are very aggressive and will steal $\overset{P}{\underline{ice\ cones}}$ right out of people's $\overset{P}{\underline{hands}}$ as they exit convenience $\overset{P}{\underline{stores}}$.

9. Luckily, only a few $\overset{P}{\underline{people}}$ are injured by monkeys each year—the monkeys are more $\overset{P}{\underline{rascals}}$ than $\overset{P}{\underline{bullies}}$.

10. Each year, a hotel in one Thai $\overset{S}{\underline{city}}$ sets out a $\overset{S}{\underline{feast}}$ of fruit, rice, nuts, and candy for its primate $\overset{P}{\underline{friends}}$.

11. For more information, see the January 1999 $\overset{S}{\underline{issue}}$ of $\overset{S}{\underline{\textit{Smithsonian Magazine}}}$.

Extend: For more practice distinguishing the number of a noun, turn to page 55 in the handbook. Ask a classmate to read the paragraph at the bottom of the page and pause after each noun, at which time you identify its number as singular or plural.

Functions of Nouns

Nouns can be used six different ways. Study the chart below and turn to *Writers INC* for more information.

Writers INC	Function	Symbol	Example
519.1	*subject*	**S**	*Burglars* steal.
502.3, 507.3	*predicate noun*	**PN**	Burglars are *thieves*.
508.1	*direct object*	**DO**	Burglars steal your *possessions*.
508.1	*indirect object*	**IO**	Burglars gave *Grandpa* a scare.
515	*object of preposition*	**OP**	Burglars pried the jewels out of his *hands*.
502.3	*possessive noun*	**POS**	Burglars stole *Grandma's* jewelry.

> **Label** the function of each underlined noun in the following statements, using the symbols from the chart above.

          S   PN

1. Jade Snow Wong is a potter.

        OP   POS

2. A potter is someone who shapes pottery by hand on a potter's wheel.

    OP   OP

3. She was born in 1922 and grew up in Chinatown in San Francisco.

  POS   S   DO

4. Jade Snow Wong's ability to make pottery made her father happy and her

  DO

mother sad.

      S   PN   PN

5. Jade has said, "Creativity is 90 percent hard work and 10 percent inspiration."

    IO   DO

6. Wong gave her ordinary bowls beautiful glazes.

    DO

7. She wanted the dishes to be used every day.

    S   POS   S

8. When Jade Snow Wong and her glazed pots became famous, people's attitudes

toward her changed.

  OP   DO

9. In 1989, Jade Snow Wong wrote *Fifth Chinese Daughter,* her popular

autobiography.

                 PN   PN

10. Later she became a highly regarded writer and an outstanding educator.

Extend: Write about a skill or talent you have. Use nouns and pronouns in all of the six ways. Ask a classmate to identify each of the nouns and pronouns you use.

Nominative, Possessive, & Objective Cases of Nouns

In the *nominative case,* a noun is used as the subject or the predicate nominative. In the *possessive case,* the noun shows ownership or possession. In the *objective case,* the noun is used as the direct object, the indirect object, or the object of a preposition. Turn to 502.3

Writers INC	Case	Function	Symbol	Example
519.1	Nominative	*subject*	**S**	The *car* wouldn't start.
502.3		*predicate noun*	**PN**	The car is a *lemon.*
508.1	Objective	*direct object*	**DO**	Jake's driving gives me the *creeps.*
508.1		*indirect object*	**IO**	Jake's driving gives *me* the creeps.
515		*object of preposition*	**OP**	He drives with one *hand.*
502.3	Possessive	*possessive noun*	**POS**	*Hannah's* driving skills are much better.

> **Label** the function of the underlined nouns in the following statements using the symbols from the chart above. Indicate the case of each underlined noun (**N** for nominative, **O** for objective, and **POS** for possessive) on the blanks.

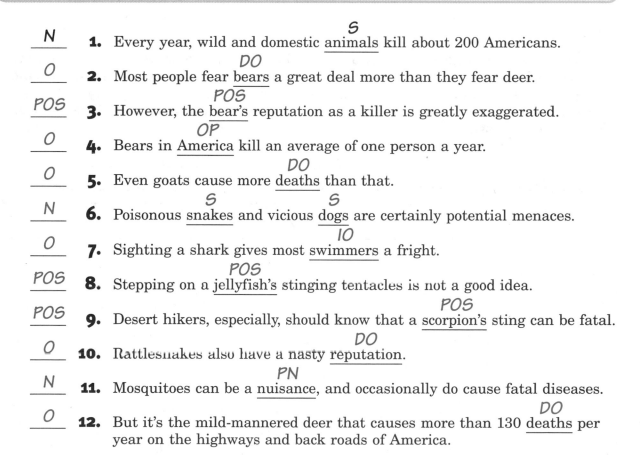

__N__ **1.** Every year, wild and domestic <u>animals</u> kill about 200 Americans. *S*

__O__ **2.** Most people fear <u>bears</u> a great deal more than they fear deer. *DO*

__POS__ **3.** However, the <u>bear's</u> reputation as a killer is greatly exaggerated. *POS*

__O__ **4.** Bears in <u>America</u> kill an average of one person a year. *OP*

__O__ **5.** Even goats cause more <u>deaths</u> than that. *DO*

__N__ **6.** Poisonous <u>snakes</u> and vicious <u>dogs</u> are certainly potential menaces. *S   S*

__O__ **7.** Sighting a shark gives most <u>swimmers</u> a fright. *IO*

__POS__ **8.** Stepping on a <u>jellyfish's</u> stinging tentacles is not a good idea. *POS*

__POS__ **9.** Desert hikers, especially, should know that a <u>scorpion's</u> sting can be fatal. *POS*

__O__ **10.** Rattlesnakes also have a nasty <u>reputation</u>. *DO*

__N__ **11.** Mosquitoes can be a <u>nuisance</u>, and occasionally do cause fatal diseases. *PN*

__O__ **12.** But it's the mild-mannered deer that causes more than 130 <u>deaths</u> per year on the highways and back roads of America. *DO*

Extend: Write a short paragraph describing an unusual animal. Exchange papers with a classmate and identify the case of each noun. Discuss your answers and check your handbook to determine if your answers are correct.

Using Nouns

Choose specific nouns when writing sentences. (Turn to page 130 in *Writers INC.*)

Fill in the chart below. The nouns in each row should be more and more specific as you move from left to right.

General Noun	Specific Noun	More Specific	Most Specific
person	writer	novelist	William Faulkner
color	primary color	red	scarlet
food	legume	bean	pinto bean
plant	bush	flowering bush	lilac
animal	pet	cat	Siamese
woman	doctor	heart specialist	Dr. Rosa Perkins

Select your own general nouns or nouns from your own writings. List them in the column on the far left. As you fill in the chart, make your nouns progressively more specific as you did in the exercise above. (If you absolutely cannot carry a noun out to the fourth column, don't worry. It may mean that you have already made it as specific as possible.)

General Noun	Specific Noun	More Specific	Most Specific

Extend: Write five sentences using your most specific nouns from the charts above. Include a few strong, vivid verbs to make your sentences as effective as possible.

Review: Nouns

Function				Case		Number
subject	**S**	direct object	**DO**	nominative **N**		singular
predicate noun	**PN**	indirect object	**IO**	objective **O**		plural
object of preposition	**OP**	possessive	**POS**	possessive **POS**		

Underline the nouns in the sentences below. Next, list them on the numbered lines in the same order that they appear in the sentences. Fill in the information required for each noun, using the symbols from the chart and words for *singular* and *plural*.

- Jack went to the concert with Maria's brothers.
- Our teachers gave my class many lectures about tardiness.
- Rosa is a renowned photographer.
- My cats' names are Hobesters and Maddie.

	NOUN	FUNCTION	CASE	NUMBER
1.	Jack	S	N	singular
2.	concert	OP	O	singular
3.	Maria's	POS	POS	singular
4.	brothers	OP	O	plural
5.	teachers	S	N	plural
6.	class	IO	O	singular
7.	lectures	DO	O	plural
8.	tardiness	OP	O	singular
9.	Rosa	S	N	singular
10.	photographer	PN	N	singular
11.	cats'	POS	POS	plural
12.	names	S	N	plural
13.	Hobesters	PN	N	singular
14.	Maddie	PN	N	singular

Pretest: Pronouns

Circle the correct pronoun from the set in parentheses.

1. No astronauts have ever received more publicity than Neil Armstrong and Edwin "Buzz" Aldrin, for it was (**they,** them) who first walked on the surface of the moon.

2. Most of America watched (they, **them**) take the first moon walk on July 20, 1969.

3. How long will it be before some enterprising entrepreneur offers trips to the moon for people like you and (I, **me**)?

4. It was (**I,** me) who gave my brother, Aaron, a copy of Frommer's *The Moon: A Guide for First-Time Visitors.*

5. Now (**he,** him) and his friend Ahmed are planning their trip to the moon in their spare time.

6. I accidentally learned about their plans when I overheard (he, **him**) and Ahmed talking about it.

7. I believe my brother's personal conversation should be between (he, **him**) and his friend, but when it involves a trip to the moon, (**who,** whom) can resist listening?

8. Even though Aaron realized that the Frommer book is not completely serious, it obviously gave Ahmed and (he, **him**) their harebrained scheme.

9. I think Aaron (**himself,** hisself) would go tomorrow except for one thing: there are no flights available to civilians.

10. Between you and (**me,** I), I think one of the big attractions of going to the moon for (**them,** they) is the possibility of doing spectacular flips and effortless slam dunks in low gravity.

Number & Person of Personal Pronouns

The *number* of a pronoun can be either singular or plural. The *person* of a pronoun indicates whether that pronoun is speaking *(I, we)*, is spoken to *(you)*, or is spoken about *(he, she, it)*. Turn to 505.1-505.2 in *Writers INC* for more information and examples.

Write sentences using personal pronouns as subjects. Use the number and person listed in the parentheses.

Answers will vary.

1. (first person, singular)

I love to read books aloud to small children.

2. (third person, plural)

They plunged down the steep embankment.

3. (second person, singular)

You are a funny person.

4. (first person, plural)

We removed our shoes and socks and played tag on the beach.

5. (third person, singular)

He doesn't seem guilty.

6. (second person, plural)

You are the winners who deserve the trophy.

7. (first person, singular)

I will look in the rafters for the cat.

8. (third person, plural)

They are going to bring lunch.

Extend: Without looking at your handbook, write out your own explanation of *number* and *person* of a pronoun. Use these words in your explanation: *singular, plural, first person, second person,* and *third person.*

Functions of Pronouns

Pronouns function the same way that nouns do. Study the chart below and turn to 506.1 in *Writers INC*.

Writers INC	Function	Symbol	Example
519.1	*subject*	**S**	*You* need to change your clothes.
506.1	*predicate nominative*	**PN**	"That is *you*," she remarked about my shirt.
508.1	*direct object*	**DO**	The river's current pulled *him* under.
508.1	*indirect object*	**IO**	Frank gave *me* some paperback books.
515	*object of preposition*	**OP**	This isn't about *me*.
506.1	*possessive pronoun*	**POS**	*His* shoes were ruined by the rain.

Label how the underlined pronouns function in the following statements, using the symbols from the chart above.

        POS
1. Deciduous trees lose their leaves every autumn.

  S
2. They are unlike coniferous trees in that respect.

  S   *OP*
3. He said the boy wouldn't go without him.

      POS   *PN*
4. "I know my own weaknesses, and chocolate cake is one," explained the man.

         DO
5. Maggie will drive us to the swim meet.

  S   *POS*   *POS*
6. "You have to use your fingertips, not your palms," the volleyball coach advised.

      IO
7. Corinne did me a favor by making breakfast today.

         OP   *POS*
8. The dog jumped on her, wagging its tail.

POS   *S*
9. My lunch was missing, and I was mad.

    S   *DO*   *OP*
10. Did you see them give the flowers to her?

  S   *POS*
11. They like to serve hominy to their guests.

POS   *IO*
12. Your mother gave me a sandwich.

     S *DO*
13. "Did they find it?" asked Inez.

POS   *POS*
14. Our families take their vacations together.

Extend: Write your own sentences using pronouns in each of the six ways shown above.

Nominative, Possessive, & Objective Cases of Pronouns

The *case* of a personal pronoun is determined by how that pronoun is used in a sentence—as a subject, an object, or a possessive. Turn to 506.1 in *Writers INC* for more information and examples.

> **Underline** the personal pronouns in the sentences below. **Label** the case of each pronoun. Use **N** for nominative case, **POS** for possessive case, or **O** for objective case.

1.   **N**   **POS**   **O**
He sold his bike to me last week

2. **N**   **POS**   **N**
You should play in our chess tournament because you're such a good competitor.

3. **N**   **O**   **POS**
They need to give her a ride to her workplace.

4. **POS**   **N**
Kendra and Leona came to our store so they could buy pet food.

5. **O**
The teacher expects a lot of you, Lisa.

6. **N**   **POS**
When do you think Sara and Duncan will arrive at your home?

7. **N**   **O** **POS**
She will help you with your job search.

8. **N**   **N**
How did they find a song we both liked?

10. **O**   **POS**
Maria, please let us know your arrival time.

11. **POS**
Why did Jerry take his soccer ball home?

12. **O**
Jennifer gave me a copy of the CD.

13. **POS**   **N**
Yang went out to move his car, but it was gone.

14. **N**   **O**
Is it time for us to eat dinner?

15. **N**   **O**
Have you ever heard him sing?

16. **N**   **O**
I saw the cat and brought it home.

17. **POS**
Make her sandwich first.

18. **N**   **O** **POS**
They thanked me for my help.

19. **POS**   **POS**
Its climate was too damp for my health.

20. **N**   **N**   **O**
He and she will plan the schedule for us.

Extend: Choose six pronouns from the chart on page 506 in *Writers INC*. Correctly use each one in a sentence.

Review: Pronouns 1

> **Underline** the personal pronoun in each sentence below. In the first blank, indicate the number of the pronoun with **S** for singular or **P** for plural. In the second blank, identify the person with a **1, 2,** or **3** for first, second, or third person.

P 1 **1.** Last night <u>our</u> cat caught a mole in the backyard.

P 1 **2.** Grandpa is taking <u>us</u> to see a movie at the new cinema.

S 2 **3.** Justin, ask Grandpa if <u>you</u> can go along.

P 3 **4.** <u>They</u> decided to buy a new car, after all.

P 2 **5.** Did Dan invite all of <u>you</u> to join the office softball team?

S 3 **6.** <u>He</u> plans to get shirts with the company logo.

> **Label** the function of each underlined pronoun by writing the appropriate symbol above it. Use **S** for subject, **PN** for predicate nominative, **DO** for direct object, **IO** for indirect object, **OP** for object of a preposition, and **POS** for possessive. In the blanks below, indicate the case for each underlined pronoun by writing **N** for nominative, **O** for objective, and **P** for possessive.

N **1.** *S* <u>It</u> is going to be a long day.

O **2.** This magazine belongs to *OP* <u>me</u>.

N O **3.** Would *S* <u>you</u> like to borrow *DO* <u>it</u>?

O N **4.** Sheila brought *IO* <u>them</u> a cake that *S* <u>she</u> had baked.

N P **5.** *S* <u>She</u> wants to use *POS* <u>my</u> colored pencils.

N O **6.** *S* <u>He</u> forgot *DO* <u>them</u>.

N O **7.** When *S* <u>you</u> finish cleaning the bathroom, help *DO* <u>me</u> vacuum.

P O **8.** *POS* <u>My</u> mother planted fifteen oak trees, but six of *OP* <u>them</u> died.

P P **9.** *POS* <u>Our</u> teacher is *POS* <u>your</u> Grandma!

N P **10.** *S* <u>I</u> didn't know *POS* <u>their</u> house was robbed.

Relative Pronouns

A relative pronoun (*that, which, whose, who, whom*) relates an adjective clause to the noun or pronoun it modifies (as in "the team *who wins . . .* "). Turn to 503.4 and the chart on page 504 in *Writers INC* for more information.

> **Underline** the relative pronouns in the sentences below. Circle the noun or pronoun that each relative pronoun modifies.

1. (Snakes,) which are limbless reptiles, have been feared by humans for centuries.

2. (Those) who do not take precautions around certain snakes could find themselves in real danger.

3. (Snakes,) which include about 2,400 different species, live almost everywhere on the planet.

4. The world's longest recorded snake was an Asiatic reticulated (python) that was more than 33 feet long.

5. Some snakes kill their prey by (constriction,) which does not crush the animal but suffocates it.

6. (People) who study snakes are called herpetologists.

7. (Snakes) whose venom is fatal to humans number fewer than 300 species.

8. The (venom) that snakes carry either destroys nerve cells or attacks blood tissue.

9. Most (cobras,) which live mainly in India, have (poison) that attacks the nervous system.

10. (Humans,) whom snakes avoid whenever possible, are among the most dangerous predators of snakes.

Extend: Write five sentences about reptiles. Use each of the five relative pronouns (listed at the top of this page) in adjective clauses. Turn to 459.2 in *Writers INC* for helpful information about punctuating your clauses.

Indefinite, Interrogative, & Demonstrative Pronouns

Indefinite pronouns represent someone (or something) not specifically named or known (*everybody, anyone, each*). Interrogative pronouns ask questions (*who? which? what?*). Demonstrative pronouns point out people or things without naming them (*this can't be, these are fine*). Turn to 504.1-504.3 in *Writers INC* for more information.

> **Label** the underlined pronouns below. Use *I* for an indefinite pronoun, *D* for a demonstrative pronoun, and *IT* for an interrogative pronoun.

1 Almost <u>everyone</u> *[I]* knows Ben Franklin was an inventor, a printer, a public

2 servant, and a writer. <u>Many</u> *[I]* know that he proved lightning was caused by

3 electricity. <u>Some</u> *[I]* know that he said, "Little strokes fell great oaks." But <u>who</u> *[IT]*

4 knows that he loved to read—especially books by John Bunyan, Plutarch,

5 Daniel Defoe, and Cotton Mather? <u>Those</u> *[D]* were Franklin's favorites because he

6 said he learned so much from them.

7 <u>What</u> *[IT]* caused Franklin's formal schooling to end when he was 10 years old?

8 <u>That</u> *[D]* happened largely because he was the 15th child in a family of 17, and his

9 father needed his help. <u>This</u> *[D]* would seem to be a tragedy, and for <u>many</u> *[I]* of us it

10 would be. But not for Franklin. <u>Nothing</u> *[I]* would stop his education. He said,

11 "The doors of wisdom are never shut." Because of his positive attitude, Franklin

12 became <u>one</u> *[I]* of the best-educated and most successful people of his time. <u>Which</u> *[IT]*

13 of his many successes was Franklin's greatest? <u>That</u> *[D]* is hard to say.

14 <u>No one</u> *[I]* would leave Franklin's name off a list of most famous Americans.

15 <u>Few</u> *[I]* would leave his name off a list of the 10 most famous Americans. <u>Most</u> *[I]* of

16 us recognize Franklin's face on coins, paper money, and postage stamps. <u>These</u> *[D]*

17 are only a few ways that our country still honors this great man.

Extend: Write five sentences about some of Franklin's other accomplishments (developed a volunteer fire department, invented the Franklin stove and bifocals, and discovered that poorly ventilated rooms promote disease). Use an indefinite pronoun, an interrogative pronoun, and a demonstrative pronoun at least once.

Reflexive & Intensive Pronouns

Reflexive and intensive pronouns are formed by adding *-self* or *-selves* to personal pronouns (*myself, yourselves*). Turn to 503.3 in *Writers INC* for definitions and examples.

> **Write** a sentence, changing the pronoun in parentheses to either a reflexive or an intensive pronoun.

Answers will vary.

1. (them) reflexive

The paratroops called themselves Charlie Brown's Army.

2. (our) reflexive

We went to see the tornado damage for ourselves.

3. (him) intensive

David himself will make sure all the pledges are collected.

4. (it) intensive

The anger itself was understandable, but the way he expressed it

wasn't.

5. (her) intensive

After Maggie was robbed, she herself called the authorities to

report the theft.

6. (your) reflexive

You are responsible for yourself.

7. (my) reflexive

I couldn't help but think to myself, what an incredibly courageous

thing that was to do.

Extend: Choose two reflexive and two intensive pronouns. Use each in a sentence.

Review: Pronouns 2

> **Underline** the pronouns in the sentences below. On the lines write *relative*, *indefinite*, *interrogative*, *demonstrative*, *reflexive*, or *intensive* to identify each pronoun.)

   intensive   **1.** Joey can lift the boxes <u>himself</u>.

   demonstrative   **2.** <u>This</u> is not the meal <u>that</u> we ordered.

   relative

   interrogative   **3.** <u>Who</u> left a skateboard on the stairs?

   reflexive   **4.** Mr. White said, "Give <u>yourself</u> a pat on the back."

   relative   **5.** Jim's dog, Daisy, <u>who</u> saved our neighbor's cat, has been given an award.

   reflexive   **6.** Jerry dragged <u>himself</u> to Grandma's house to mow the lawn.

   indefinite   **7.** <u>Everything</u> is out of place in Leon's room.

   relative   **8.** Lori visited the capitol, <u>which</u> has a bronze dome.

   interrogative   **9.** <u>What</u> is Keiko doing with a 10-pound bag of potatoes?

   demonstrative   **10.** Is <u>that</u> the correct way to hold a hammer?

   indefinite   **11.** <u>Few</u> understand the feeling of seasickness.

   relative   **12.** Elena thinks the watch <u>that</u> was found crushed in the parking lot is Dan's.

   interrogative   **13.** <u>Which</u> one do you want?

   indefinite   **14.** <u>Nobody</u> in class could name every U.S. president.

   intensive   **15.** Derrick and Ron <u>themselves</u> cleaned the apartment before moving in.

Pretest: Verbs

Do the following three things for each sentence below: (1) underline all the main verbs once, (2) underline all the auxiliary (or helping) verbs twice, and (3) write the tense of each verb on the blank (*present, past, future, present perfect, past perfect,* or *future perfect*).

_____past_____ **1.** On August 17, 1999, a powerful earthquake <u>hit</u> western Turkey.

_____past_____ **2.** Before the sun <u>came</u> up that day, tens of thousands of
past perfect sleeping people <u>had been</u> <u>killed</u> by the giant quake—a 7.4 on the Richter scale.

_____present_____ **3.** <u>Is</u> the North Anatolian Fault in Turkey similar to the San Andreas Fault in California?

present perfect **4.** Scientists <u>have</u> <u>found</u> them to be similar in size and <u>have</u>
present perfect <u>found</u> movements in the tectonic plates to be similar.

_____present_____ **5.** So-called "tectonic earthquakes" <u>occur</u> when the major and
_____present_____ minor plates in the earth's crust <u>move</u>.

_____future_____ **6.** <u>Will</u> scientists and engineers <u>predict</u> future earthquakes
_____future_____ and <u>prevent</u> loss of life and property?

_____past_____ **7.** In 1975, the Chinese accurately <u>predicted</u> a major
_____past_____ earthquake at Haicheng and <u>gave</u> the city's residents evacuation orders.

_____past_____ **8.** The warning <u>saved</u> thousands of lives.

_____present_____ **9.** Scientists now <u>investigate</u> bulges in land surfaces, changes in the magnetic field, and even the behavior of animals.

_____present_____ **10.** <u>Is</u> it possible that in the next 15 years earthquake
future perfect prediction <u>will</u> <u>have</u> become more precise and reliable?

Identifying Main Verbs

Verbs express action (*waved, wink, says*) or state of being (*is, are, be*) and serve as predicates in sentences. Both action verbs and linking verbs can serve as the main verb (without helping verbs) in a sentence. Turn to page 507 in *Writers INC* for more information.

> **Underline** the main verbs in the following paragraphs.

1   Most Egyptians <u>live</u> near the Nile River or the Suez Canal, the country's

2   two major waterways. On the east bank of the Nile <u>lies</u> Cairo, Egypt's capital

3   and largest city. It <u>overflows</u> with people. About 7 million people <u>reside</u> in the

4   city of Cairo, but almost 13 million people <u>live</u> in the Cairo metropolitan area.

5   The people of Cairo <u>cope</u> with typical urban problems. Housing shortages

6   <u>cause</u> hardships. Many people <u>crowd</u> into small apartments or <u>build</u> makeshift

7   huts on roofs of apartment buildings or on land belonging to someone else.

8   Many <u>live</u> in poverty. Others <u>enjoy</u> modern conveniences and government

9   services. Extremes of wealth and poverty can be <u>seen</u> in Cairo and other

10   Egyptian cities. Attractive residential areas <u>exist</u> beside vast slums. Some of

11   the poorest people in Cairo <u>take</u> refuge in historic tombs on the city's outskirts

12   in an area known as the City of the Dead.

13   Cairo's Al-Azhar University was <u>founded</u> in A.D. 970 and <u>is</u> one of the

14   world's oldest universities. It <u>serves</u> as the world's leading center of Islamic

15   teaching. About 90 percent of the Egyptians <u>practice</u> Islam, the Muslim

16   religion. Islam <u>influences</u> family life, social relationships, business activities,

17   and government affairs. Muslims <u>pray</u> five times daily, <u>give</u> money or products

18   to the poor, <u>fast</u>, and, if possible, <u>make</u> a pilgrimage to Mecca, Saudi Arabia, the

19   sacred city of Islam.

Extend: Label the verbs you underlined in the last paragraph as *action* or *linking*.

Auxiliary Verbs

Auxiliary (helping) verbs include all the forms of *have, do, be, can, may, shall,* and *will.* (The verbs *have, do,* and *be*—in all of their forms—can also be used as main verbs.) Turn to 507.1 for a list of auxiliary verbs.

> **Underline** only the auxiliary verbs in the following sentences. You will find 21 words functioning as helping verbs.

1. Jocko the clown <u>has</u> <u>been</u> telling jokes all day.

2. Amiri <u>was</u> exposed to mumps.

3. Francine, <u>can</u> you finish your homework before supper?

4. Wise people <u>will</u> vote for the candidate with the best qualifications.

5. Mosha <u>does</u> not like potato soup.

6. Many cities <u>have</u> provided shelters for the homeless.

7. <u>Should</u> the flight be here by now?

8. The bald eagle <u>will</u> soon <u>be</u> removed from the endangered species list.

9. Oh, the bald eagle <u>has</u> already <u>been</u> removed.

10. Maybe we <u>should</u> celebrate!

11. I <u>have</u> always known that I am a good thinker.

12. The doctor said my stepfather <u>should</u> swim every day.

13. <u>Has</u> your little sister made banana splits again?

14. Tomeka, <u>may</u> I join your group?

15. I <u>do</u> like to do yoga twice a week.

16. Yoga <u>does</u> improve my flexibility.

17. It <u>has</u> also helped me feel more centered and calm.

18. We <u>will</u> <u>have</u> <u>been</u> playing cards for almost four hours.

Extend: Choose five helping verbs from the list at 507.1. Write sentences using your verbs as auxiliary verbs, not as main verbs. (Use a form of the verbs *have* and *do* at least once.)

Linking Verbs

Linking verbs (*be, am, is, are, sound, taste*) join subjects to words that rename (predicate noun) or describe (predicate adjective) the subjects. Turn to 507.3 in *Writers INC* for a list of linking verbs. (Also see 502.3 and 513.1 for information about predicate nouns and adjectives.)

> **My grandma's spaghetti is my favorite food.** (The linking verb *is* connects the subject *spaghetti* with *food*, a predicate noun that renames the subject.)

> **Wow, that spaghetti tasted great!** (The linking verb *tasted* connects the subject *spaghetti* with *great*, a predicate adjective that describes the subject.)

Complete the following sentences by adding a linking verb and either a predicate noun or a predicate adjective. Circle the linking verbs.

Answers will vary.

1. *(predicate noun)*

The new train ⟨is⟩ a monorail.

2. *(predicate adjective)*

Our old football uniforms ⟨look⟩ shabby.

3. *(predicate noun)*

The magic show ⟨will be⟩ a big hit!

4. *(predicate noun)*

Malcolm's new telephone ⟨is⟩ a technical wonder.

5. *(predicate noun)*

Emily's new computer ⟨became⟩ her gateway to the world.

6. *(predicate adjective)*

Brody's twice-baked potatoes ⟨taste⟩ delicious.

7. *(predicate adjective)*

This wool shirt ⟨feels⟩ itchy.

8. *(predicate adjective)*

The movie we saw last night ⟨was⟩ too violent.

Extend: Write five sentences about food. Use a linking verb and colorful predicate nouns and adjectives. (Turn to pages 130-131 in *Writers INC*.)

Present Tense Verbs & Third Person Pronouns

The form of most verbs changes only when a third-person singular pronoun is used with a verb in the present tense. (See the chart below.) Turn to 510.2 in *Writers INC*.

	Present Tense	
Person	**Singular**	**Plural**
1st person	I learn.	We learn.
2nd person	You learn.	You learn.
3rd person	He, She, It *learns*.	They learn.

Write sentences using the present tense verbs listed below; use pronouns as subjects. (The person and number are indicated for each pronoun.) Then rewrite each sentence using a third-person singular pronoun. Remember to adjust the verb.

Answers will vary.

1. *go*—(a) first person, plural (b) third person, singular

a. We go to the beach every summer.

b. He goes to the beach every summer.

2. *swim*—(a) third person, plural (b) third person, singular

a. They swim like tadpoles.

b. She swims like a tadpole.

3. *enjoy*—(a) first person, singular (b) third person, singular

a. I enjoy pizza, squid, and onion rings.

b. She enjoys pizza, squid, and onion rings.

4. *ski*—(a) second person, singular (b) third person, singular

a. You ski only on the bunny hill.

b. He skis only on the bunny hill.

5. *repair*—(a) first person, singular (b) third person, singular

a. I repair just about any broken appliance.

b. She repairs just about any broken appliance.

Extend: Write six sentences using the present tense of the verb *find*. In the first three sentences, use singular first-, second-, and third-person pronouns. In the other three, use plural forms of the three persons of a pronoun.

Active & Passive Voice

The voice of a verb determines if the subject is acting or being acted upon. Writing is generally most effective in the active voice. It's also important to avoid switching between active and passive voice in the same sentence. (Turn to 508.1 and 510.3 and the chart at the bottom of page 511 in *Writers INC* for more information.)

> **Earthquakes damage a tremendous amount of property.**
> (*Damage* is an active verb; the subject, *earthquakes,* is doing the acting.)

> **A tremendous amount of property is damaged by earthquakes.**
> (*Is damaged* is a passive verb; the subject, *a tremendous amount of property,* is being acted upon.)

Rewrite the following passive sentences so that they are active.

1. Most earthquakes are generated by shifting plates in the earth's outer shell.

Shifting plates in the earth's outer shell generate most earthquakes.

2. An earthquake's strength is measured with seismographs.

Seismographs measure an earthquake's strength.

3. Seismic waves that can travel for miles are created by an earthquake.

An earthquake creates seismic waves that can travel for miles.

4. Landslides, fires, and floods can also be caused by earthquakes.

Earthquakes can also cause landslides, fires, and floods.

5. Most deaths are caused by collapsing buildings.

Collapsing buildings cause the most deaths.

6. Tsunamis, enormous ocean waves, are produced by earthquakes beneath the ocean floor.

Earthquakes beneath the ocean floor produce tsunamis, enormous ocean waves.

Extend: Write a paragraph describing a recent event you experienced—a dance, a concert, a ball game, or some other activity. Use active voice in your description.

Present, Past, & Future Verb Tenses

Tense indicates time. The three simple tenses of a verb are present *(I eat)*, past *(I ate)*, and future *(I will eat)*. Turn to 511.1 in *Writers INC* for further explanation.

> **Rewrite** each sentence below, changing the verb to the tense indicated.

1. Learning to drive causes me much anxiety.

Past: *Learning to drive caused me much anxiety.*

Future: *Learning to drive will cause me much anxiety.*

2. Mr. Lonetree carves wooden whistles.

Past: *Mr. Lonetree carved wooden whistles.*

Future: *Mr. Lonetree will carve wooden whistles.*

3. High winds whipped the sea into a sailor's nightmare.

Future: *High winds will whip the sea into a sailor's nightmare.*

Present: *High winds whip the sea into a sailor's nightmare.*

4. The football players will take ballet classes.

Past: *The football players took ballet classes.*

Present: *The football players take ballet classes.*

5. New teachers needed knowledge and patience to succeed.

Present: *New teachers need knowledge and patience to succeed.*

Future: *New teachers will need knowledge and patience to succeed.*

6. Rappelling will require strength and courage.

Past: *Rappelling required strength and courage.*

Present: *Rappelling requires strength and courage.*

Extend: Turn to page 211 in *Writers INC*. The first paragraph in the student essay is written in the present tense. Rewrite it first in the past tense and then in the future tense. Note the changes you need to make to each verb to alter its tense.

Perfect Tense Verbs

The three perfect tenses are present perfect (*I have eaten*), past perfect (*I had eaten*), and future perfect (*I will have eaten*). Turn to 511.1 in *Writers INC* for more information.

> **Form** the perfect tense for each sentence below using the past participle of the verb in parentheses.

1. Many people _____ **have called** _____ Italy's Leaning Tower of Pisa one of the seven wonders of the modern world. (*call:* present perfect)

2. Depending on how you calculate it, the Leaning Tower _____ **has existed** _____ for 650 to 800 years. (*exist:* present perfect)

3. Built on sandy soil, it began to sink unevenly after workers _____ **had completed** _____ the first three stories. (*complete:* past perfect)

4. By the end of the sixteenth century, the Leaning Tower _____ **had become** _____ famous for Galileo's experiment on the effects of gravity. (*become:* past perfect)

5. Over the years, engineers _____ **have tried** _____ many schemes to stop the tower from sinking and leaning. (*try:* present perfect)

6. Until recently, visitors _____ **had been permitted** _____ to climb the 300 steps to the top. (*permit:* past perfect)

7. Soon engineers _____ **will have poured** _____ an entirely new concrete base for the tower. (*pour:* future perfect)

8. If the plan works, these scientists _____ **will have saved** _____ one of the oldest and most famous landmarks of Italy. (*save:* future perfect)

9. If you visit Italy without seeing the Leaning Tower, you _____ **will have missed** _____ seeing a unique structure. (*miss:* future perfect)

Extend: Write three sentences about a tourist attraction you've seen or heard about. Use each of the three perfect verb tenses.

Review: Verbs 1

> **Write** sentences that demonstrate your knowledge of verbs. Use verbs that meet all the requirements listed for each sentence.

Answers will vary.

1. action verb, present tense, active voice _The weather forecaster predicts sunshine today._

2. linking verb and predicate adjectives _Abraham Lincoln was tall and thin._

3. linking verb and predicate noun _Latisha is a firefighter._

4. action verb, passive voice _The ball was slam-dunked by the seven-foot center._

5. action verb, active voice _The committee will count the votes._

6. action verb, present perfect tense _Joshua has picked all the apples._

7. action verb, future perfect tense _He will have picked nearly 100 bushels before he's done._

8. action verb, past perfect tense _All the apples in the orchard had been picked._

9. linking verb and predicate adjective _The apples were great._

10. action verb, past tense, passive voice _The baskets were loaded by the pickers onto the waiting trucks._

Transitive & Intransitive Verbs

A transitive verb shows action and is always followed by an object that receives the action. An intransitive verb refers to an action that is complete in itself. It does not need an object to receive the action. (Turn to 508.1 and 507.2 in *Writers INC.*) Note that some verbs can be either transitive or intransitive, as in the following examples.

> **Raphael painted the *Alba Madonna,* the *Sistine Madonna,* the *Madonna of the Chair,* and the *Transfiguration.*** (The transitive verb *painted* is followed by multiple direct objects—*Alba Madonna, Sistine Madonna,* etc.)

> **Raphael Sanzio painted for a living.** (The intransitive verb *painted* expresses a complete action.)

Write a *T* in the blank if the underlined verb is transitive; write an *I* if it is intransitive.

_T_ **1.** Raphael, one of the great Renaissance painters, <u>influenced</u> artists as late as the early 1900s.

_T_ **2.** He <u>painted</u> altarpieces, frescoes (paintings on damp plaster), and portraits.

_I_ **3.** Raphael <u>was asked</u> by Pope Julius II to paint the Vatican Palace.

_I_ **4.** At the Vatican Palace, Raphael <u>worked</u> with Michelangelo, another great artist.

_T_ **5.** Raphael <u>painted</u> an entire ceiling with stories of Cupid and Psyche.

_T_ **6.** During this time, Raphael <u>created</u> many religious works, a common subject for painters of this period.

_I_ **7.** He traveled to many different countries and <u>learned</u> from the master artists along the way.

_T_ **8.** By 1516, Raphael <u>had painted</u> 10 large watercolors of the Apostles.

_I_ **9.** Raphael <u>died</u> in Rome at the age of 37.

_I_ **10.** Today, his works <u>appear</u> in museums all over the world.

Extend: Write five sentences in which you use transitive verbs. Explain why each verb is transitive.

Direct & Indirect Objects

Transitive verbs always take direct objects (and sometimes indirect objects). Intransitive verbs take neither. Turn to 508.1 in *Writers INC* for more information. (Remember that a verb must first have a direct object before it can take an indirect object.)

> **Lora took the candy.**
> (The transitive verb *took* has a direct object, *candy.*)

> **Tyler gave me the candy.**
> (The transitive verb *gave* has a direct object, *candy,* and an indirect object, *me.*)

Direct Object: *candy*	**Indirect Object:** *me*
(Tyler gave *what?*) *candy*	(Tyler gave candy *to whom?*) *me*

> **The candy melted.** (The intransitive verb *melted* has no objects.)

Create sentences using the patterns indicated. You may add modifiers to make your sentences interesting. Finally, answer questions 7 and 8.

1. *(subject + verb + direct object)*

The horse kicked the gate.

2. *(subject + verb)*

The gate swung open.

3. *(subject + verb + indirect object + direct object)*

The opened gate gave the horse a morning's freedom.

4. *(subject + verb + direct object)*

The clothes dryer always "eats" my socks.

5. *(subject + verb)*

Salmon swim upstream to spawn.

6. *(subject + verb + indirect object + direct object)*

Green apples give some people a stomachache.

7. Which sentences have transitive verbs? 1, 3, 4, 6

8. Which sentences have intransitive verbs? 2, 5

Gerunds, Infinitives, & Participles

Gerunds, infinitives, and participles are verbals. A verbal is derived from a verb, has the power of a verb, but acts as another part of speech. Turn to 508.2-509.2 in *Writers INC*.

Type of Verbal	Functions as		
	Noun	**Adjective**	**Adverb**
gerund (ends in *-ing*)	X		
infinitive (introduced by *to*)	X	X	X
participle (ends in *-ing* or *-ed*)		X	

> **Underline** the verbals in each of the sentences below. Write **G** above each gerund, **I** above each infinitive, and **P** above each participle.

      G
1. Talking to my sister gives me energy.

              I
2. I think we need to talk.

           P
3. The woman talking on the phone is my teacher.

                      G
4. Mr. Ramirez thanked us for delivering his package.

         P   *I*
5. The boy kicking the ball needs to score in a hurry.

            I
6. Ulla is about to kick a penalty shot that could win the game.

            I
7. I have an essay to finish tonight.

      G
8. Pushing the car out of the mud was impossible.

                P
9. The young campers, exhausted and sweaty, jumped into the stream.

           P   *I*
10. This pile of washed clothes needs to be sorted.

         I
11. Do I have to fold all the laundry?

        G   *G*
12. I plan on washing the car before going to the game.

         P   *I*
13. The stack of completed reports on the desk is going to fall over soon.

      G   *I*
14. Writing causes my hand to cramp up.

         I   *P*
15. I was tempted to eat all the ripened strawberries.

Extend: Write three sentences, each using one of the three kinds of verbals for the word *run*.

Verb Moods

The mood of a verb indicates the tone or attitude with which a statement is made. The *indicative mood* is used to state a fact or to ask a question. The *imperative mood* is used to give a command. The *subjunctive mood* is used to express a condition contrary to fact or an unreal condition. Turn to 512.1 in *Writers INC* for more information.

> *Can* frogs *breathe* underwater? No, but tadpoles *can breathe* underwater.
> (The indicative mood is used to ask a question or state a fact.)

> *Go* to your room immediately!
> (The imperative mood is used for a command.)

> If I *were* foolish, I'd never do my homework.
> (The subjunctive mood is used to express a condition contrary to fact.)

Write a sentence that contains a verb in the mood asked for in each instance below.

Answers will vary.

1. indicative mood (statement)

Niihau is one of the lesser-known Hawaiian islands.

2. imperative mood

Get down to the police station and pay your speeding ticket.

3. subjunctive mood to express a condition contrary to fact

If I were able to swim, I'd go to the pool party.

4. imperative mood

Turn off the engine.

5. indicative mood (question)

How much time must sharks spend searching for food each day?

6. subjunctive mood with *as though* or *as if* to express an unreal condition

She looked at us as if we were invisible.

7. indicative mood (question)

Are the students looking forward to the homecoming dance?

8. indicative mood (statement—answer the question in number 7)

The students are looking forward to the homecoming dance.

Irregular Verbs 1

Regular verbs form the past tense and past participle with an *-ed* ending. Irregular verbs form their past tense and past participle in other ways. Turn to the chart on page 509 in *Writers INC* for examples. (Always use a dictionary if you are unsure of a verb's principal parts.)

> **Change** the irregular verbs in the sentences below from present to past tense. All the sentences are taken from the writings of Raymond Chandler and one of his critics.

1. *went* *got* *drove*
   I go out back and get my convertible from the garage and drive it around front.

2. *drove* *did*
   I drive down to the library and do a little research.

3. *sat*
   I sit there and poisoned myself with cigarette smoke and listened to the rain
   thought
   and think about it.

4. *rode*
   I ride up to the seventh floor.

5. *laid*
   Captain Gregory of the Missing Persons Bureau lays my card down on his desk.
   thought
   "I think you could help me."

6. *left* *stood* *said* *was*
   He leaves. Ms. Grayle stands up and says she is very glad to have met me.

7. *took* *drank*
   I take a long untidy drink. I drink some more water.

8. *fought* *said*
   "You fight, you screamed, you had to be restrained. If you leave here," he says

   sharply, "you will be arrested at once."

9. *went*
   I go back to the sea steps and moved down them as cautiously as a cat on a wet

   floor.

10. *wrote*
    "Raymond Chandler writes like a slumming angel and invested the sun-

    blinded streets of Los Angeles with a romantic presence," said one of his critics.

Extend: Write a sentence using the past tense or past participle of each of the following verbs: *shrink, grow, break, swim, am,* and *wear.*

Irregular Verbs 2

Regular verbs form the past tense and past participle with an *-ed* ending. Irregular verbs form their past tense and past participle in other ways. Turn to the chart on page 509 in *Writers INC* for examples. (Always use a dictionary if you are unsure of a verb's principal parts.)

> **Use** the past participles of the irregular verbs listed below to fill in the blanks in the story. Choose the verb that best fits each sentence. Use each verb only once.

Answers may vary.

catch, choose, come, creep, drive, fall, feel, find, go, sit, see, spring, speak, take, write

1. Many writers had _____*written*_____ eerie tales for the *Strand Magazine*.

2. The following sentences have been _____*taken*_____ from those eerie tales.

3. The last time he came for a visit, Henry had _____*chosen*_____ a room at the Greyhound Inn.

4. Henry had _____*gone*_____ to bed a strong young man, but he had been poisoned!

5. Soon after lying down, he had _____*felt*_____ faint and feeble.

6. Out of the corner of his eye, Henry had _____*seen*_____ something moving.

7. He had _____*sprung*_____ from the bed and dived at the figure.

8. He did not understand what had _____*driven*_____ him to madness.

9. Before the incident, he had _____*spoken*_____ of his dead friend.

10. He had _____*sat*_____ still in the chair—so still that every muscle ached.

11. The loud, scraping sound had _____*come*_____ from behind him.

12. Henry had _____*caught*_____ Ivy just as she was about to faint.

13. They had _____*fallen*_____ down the stairs.

14. They had _____*found*_____ themselves alone and horrified in the catacombs.

15. To get through the narrow opening, they had _____*crept*_____ on their hands and knees.

Extend: Write three to five sentences using irregular verbs to describe a scary situation. First write in the present tense. Then rewrite the sentences in the past perfect tense. Which description sounds more effective?

Review: Verbs 2

Write sentences that follow the patterns listed below. Add other words as needed.

Answers will vary.

1. *(gerund + transitive verb + indirect object + direct object)*

   Running gave me cramps.

2. *(subject + linking verb + predicate adjective)*

   The old washing machine was loud.

3. *(subject + participle + transitive verb + direct object)*

   The bronco, snorting and rearing, broke the corral gate.

4. *(subject + auxiliary verb + main verb + adverb)*

   Our company has arrived early.

5. *(subject + transitive verb + indirect object + direct object)*

   Some parents give their children too little time.

6. *(subject + verb + infinitive)*

   Katia wants to learn Russian.

7. *(imperative mood: transitive verb + direct object)*

   Bring your camera.

8. *(subject + linking verb + predicate noun)*

   The kitchen is a mess.

Pretest: Adjectives & Adverbs

> **Insert** an effective adjective or adverb in the sentences below. Identify your choice by writing **ADJ** (adjective) or **ADV** (adverb) on the blank.

Answers will vary.

ADJ **1.** India is one of the _____*oldest*_____ civilizations in the world.

ADJ **2.** Sometime between the summer of 1999 and the spring of 2000, India's _____*enormous*_____ population exceeded 1 billion.

ADV **3.** India's population has _____*essentially*_____ doubled in the last 30 years.

ADJ **4.** Some Indians see reaching the 1-billion-people mark as cause for _____*great*_____ celebration.

ADJ **5.** "Nothing is _____*impossible*_____ when 1 billion Indians work together," exclaimed government-sponsored ads in newspapers.

ADJ **6.** "We shall overcome everything that stands between today's India and her _____*rightful*_____ place among the great nations of the world."

ADJ **7.** Only China's population is _____*greater*_____ than India's.

ADJ **8.** However, China's growth rate has been _____*lower*_____ than India's in recent years.

ADV **9.** Concerns about population growth have increased _____*considerably*_____ during the past several decades.

ADV **10.** This concern is _____*largely*_____ due to the extra demands that the additional population places on human and natural resources.

ADV **11.** Supplies of water, fuel, and food are all _____*tremendously*_____ strained by huge populations.

ADV **12.** Though some of India's leaders remain confident that India can manage its huge population, others are _____*extremely*_____ worried.

Identifying Adjectives

An adjective describes a noun or a pronoun. The articles *(a, an, the)* are also adjectives. Turn to 513.1 in *Writers INC* for information and examples.

> **Circle** the word in each of the following groups that would *most likely* be used as an adjective. In the blank, indicate whether it is a *common* adjective, a *proper* adjective, or an *article*. Finally, write a sentence using the adjective.

1. through, monkey, (bland,) cook ___*common*___

___Grandpa must eat bland food to keep his ulcer under control.___

2. very, brain, (an,) disc, sprint ___*article*___

___An egg is needed to make a cake.___

3. (shy,) trunk, doctor, remain, into ___*common*___

___The shy cat hid in the rafters.___

4. Tom, Germany, spot, Wisconsin, (Hawaiian) ___*proper*___

___The neighbors went on a Hawaiian vacation.___

5. rhumba, (wacky,) newspaper, accident, novel ___*common*___

___He was such a wacky comedian.___

6. (all,) cookie, skid, Texas, lock ___*common*___

___All mushrooms are not poisonous.___

7. book, since, (the,) sticker, electricity ___*article*___

___Please gift wrap the box.___

8. jump, Florida, pen, really, (Japanese) ___*proper*___

___Do you like Japanese food?___

Extend: Go back to each of the word groups above and find a different word that could work as an adjective. For example, in the first word group, *monkey* (which is usually a noun) is used as an adjective in the following sentence: *Some people think bananas are monkey food.* Your challenge is to select such a word in each group and use it as an adjective in a sentence.

Using Adjectives to Compare

Different forms of adjectives (positive, comparative, and superlative) are used to describe and compare nouns. Turn to 513.2 in *Writers INC* for information and examples.

Fill in the blanks with the correct form of each adjective.

	Positive	Comparative	Superlative
1.	cold	*colder*	*coldest*
2.	*low*	lower	*lowest*
3.	late	*later*	*latest*
4.	*beautiful*	more beautiful	*most beautiful*
5.	*happy*	happier	*happiest*
6.	*likely*	less likely	*least likely*
7.	much	*more*	*most*

Identify the underlined adjective in each sentence below. Use **P** for positive, **C** for comparative, and **S** for superlative.

_____P_____ **1.** Isaac Asimov is an enormously <u>popular</u> author of both fiction and nonfiction.

_____C_____ **2.** Readers of science fiction think that Asimov's novels are <u>better</u> than those of other authors.

_____C_____ **3.** His fans find his science fiction <u>more interesting</u> than that of other writers.

_____S_____ **4.** On topics ranging from astronomy to limericks, Asimov's books are some of the <u>best</u> books ever written.

_____S_____ **5.** When he died in 1992, the world lost one of the <u>most prolific</u> sci-fi writers who ever lived.

Extend: The following adjectives are irregular and their forms must be memorized: *good, better, best* and *bad, worse, worst*. Use each of these adjectives in a sentence.

Review: Adjectives

> **Label** the type (common, proper, article) of the underlined adjectives below.

1   *common*
     Many people say that you can't compare apples and oranges. Why not?

2   *common*   *common*
    Apples and oranges are both round fruits that grow on leafy trees. Apple trees

3   *article*   *proper*
belong to the Rosaceae family, and oranges are from the Rutaceae family. Why,

4   they're practically related!

5   *common*   *common*
    Orange trees are evergreens that grow about eight feet tall. Apple trees

6   *common*   *common*
are taller, unless they are dwarf trees. Fruit trees are among the hardest of

7   *common*   *proper*
all the trees to grow. They need more care than other trees need. United

8   *common*
States growers produce about 10 million metric tons of juicy oranges each year

9   *article*
and almost as many tons of apples. But apples are the most popular fruit of all

10   *common*
in this country.

> **Label** the form (positive, comparative, superlative) of the underlined adjectives below.

1   *comparative*
    Apple trees are grown in all 50 states but do better in colder places

2   where the temperature may drop below freezing for several months. The

3   *superlative*
most productive apple-growing states are Washington, New York, Michigan,

4   *positive*
California, Pennsylvania, and Virginia. There are many varieties of apples.

5   *comparative*
The Delicious apple is one of the more popular apples in the United States.

6   *positive*   *superlative*
    Oranges do not like the cold and only grow where it is warm. The best

7   states of all the orange-growing states are Florida, California, Texas, and

8   *positive*
Arizona. There are three types of oranges: sweet, sour, and mandarin oranges.

9   *superlative*
The navel orange is the sweetest orange in the Western states.

Identifying Adverbs

Adverbs modify verbs, adjectives, or other adverbs by telling *how, when, where, how often,* and *how much.* Turn to 514.1 in *Writers INC* for information and more examples.

> **Underline** the adverbs in the following paragraphs and label them *how, when, where, how often,* or *how much.* (*Note:* Do not underline prepositional phrases used as adverbs unless your teacher directs you to do so.)

$\quad$ **how often** $\qquad$ **how much**

1 $\quad$ <u>Oftentimes</u> people do <u>not</u> realize that their activities, hobbies, and interests

2 $\quad$ are preparing them for a particular future. For example, it seems unlikely that

3 $\quad$ T. E. Lawrence, born in Wales in 1888, knew he was preparing for his future

$\qquad\qquad\qquad\qquad\qquad$ **how** $\qquad\qquad\qquad$ **how much**

4 $\quad$ when he spent much of his childhood <u>happily</u> exploring castles. It's <u>also</u> unlikely

$\qquad\qquad\qquad\qquad\qquad\qquad\qquad\qquad\qquad$ **when**

5 $\quad$ that he knew his trek across the Middle East while in college would <u>later</u>

$\qquad$ **how much**

6 $\quad$ contribute <u>significantly</u> to his career.

$\qquad\qquad\qquad\qquad\qquad\qquad$ **how**

7 $\quad$ When World War I began, Lawrence <u>willingly</u> joined the British Army.

when $\qquad$ **how**

8 $\quad$ <u>Later</u>, he was <u>quietly</u> sent on a diplomatic mission into the heart of Arabia to

$\qquad\qquad\qquad\qquad\qquad$ **where** $\qquad\qquad\qquad$ **when**

9 $\quad$ meet warring tribesmen who lived <u>there</u>. Lawrence <u>eventually</u> convinced the

$\qquad\qquad\qquad$ **how** $\qquad\qquad\qquad$ **how**

10 $\quad$ tribes to work <u>together</u>. He became <u>passionately</u> devoted to the Arab cause.

when

11 $\quad$ <u>Next</u>, he helped to organize the Arab revolt against the Turkish Ottoman

12 $\quad$ Empire.

$\qquad\qquad\qquad\qquad\qquad\qquad$ **when**

13 $\quad$ After the war, Lawrence wrote his <u>now</u> famous autobiography, *The Seven*

$\qquad\qquad$ **when** $\qquad\qquad\qquad\qquad\qquad\qquad$ **how**

14 $\quad$ *Pillars of Wisdom.* <u>Shortly</u> after retiring from the army in 1935, he <u>tragically</u>

15 $\quad$ died in a motorcycle accident.

$\qquad\qquad\qquad$ **how much**

16 $\quad$ Lawrence was <u>not</u> famous until Hollywood produced the movie *Lawrence of*

$\qquad\qquad$ **when**

17 $\quad$ *Arabia* in the 1960s. <u>Now</u> many social studies and literature classes view this

18 $\quad$ movie to learn about Arabia, the Turkish Ottoman Empire, and the war

19 $\quad$ between them.

Extend: Write five sentences about another country, using at least one adverb in each sentence. Underline the adverbs and label them *how, when, where, how often,* or *how much.* (See the "Geography" section of *Writers INC* for some ideas.)

Using Adverbs

Adverbs modify a verb (or verbal), an adjective, or another adverb. Turn to 514.1 in *Writers INC* and the introductory information on page 514 for further explanation.

> **Fill in** each blank with an adverb that tells *how, when, where, how often,* or *how much,* as asked for in parentheses. Don't use any adverb more than once.

Answers will vary.

1. Where I live, we ___frequently___ *(how often)* have blizzards.

2. Streets, sidewalks, and cars get ___completely___ *(how much)* buried in snow.

3. ___Yesterday___ *(when)* my sister and I had to go ___out___ *(where)* and shovel the driveway.

4. I ___quickly___ *(how)* made a snowball and threw it at my sister.

5. While I built a snowman, she ___secretly___ *(how)* made a snowball.

6. My sister ___always___ *(how often)* aims ___accurately___ *(how)*.

7. Just as I put my scarf on the snowman, the sloppy snowball whopped me ___precisely___ *(how)* between the shoulder blades.

8. Running ___away___ *(where or how)* was my sister's best defense.

9. I chased her inside, where my dad had been ___calmly___ *(how)* making a pot of chili.

10. I ___suddenly___ *(how)* forgot about getting even with her.

11. After lunch, I ___happily___ *(how)* called my friends to go sledding.

12. We met ___later___ *(when)* to go sledding in Whitnall Park.

13. Our sleds sped ___smoothly___ *(how)* down the hills.

14. The hills were ___really___ *(how much)* steep.

15. ___Finally___ *(when)* we went home and warmed up with hot chocolate.

Extend: Read the first paragraph of "One Hot Night" on page 159 in *Writers INC*. On your own paper, list all the adverbs. Then ask yourself, which of the verb-adverb combinations could be replaced with a single vivid verb? Which verbs could be substituted?

Using Adverbs to Compare

Adverbs, like adjectives, have three forms: *positive*, *comparative*, and *superlative*. (Turn to 514.2 in *Writers INC.*) Use the comparative form to compare two things, the superlative to compare three or more. Most one-syllable adverbs take the endings *-er* or *-est* (*soon, sooner, soonest*) to create the comparative and superlative forms; but longer adverbs and almost all those ending in *-ly* use *more* and *most* or *less* and *least* (*more ambitiously, most ambitiously; less ambitiously, least ambitiously*).

> **Use** each of the following adverbs in a sentence. Use the form listed in parentheses.

Answers will vary.

1. often (comparative)

   Does Lori come here more often than John?

2. close (positive)

   We drove close to the ocean.

3. early (superlative)

   Of all my guests, Sean arrived earliest.

4. occasionally (positive)

   Rosa occasionally goes to visit her relatives.

5. well (comparative)

   It seems that you understand algebra better than I do.

6. smoothly (superlative)

   Of all the salespeople, Jack talked most smoothly.

7. swiftly (comparative)

   Gazelles run more swiftly than lions run.

8. slowly (superlative)

   Of all the animals in the parade, the cats moved most slowly.

Extend: Choose two adverbs, one that uses *-er* or *-est* and one that uses *less* or *least*, to form comparisons. Write sentences using each adverb in the three forms: positive, comparative, and superlative.

Review: Adverbs

> **Underline** the adverbs in the following paragraph.

1   <u>Yesterday</u> we received the weekly newscast that we <u>always</u> look <u>forward</u> to.
2 It is <u>really</u> <u>quite</u> decent of Ol' Man Pepy to bring our supplies and stay to let us
3 listen to the news on his truck's radio. It's <u>not</u> that we love the news—wars,
4 taxes, fires, murders, people acting <u>stupidly</u> in a thousand different ways—no,
5 what we love is the man who delivers the news. We imagine him sitting
6 <u>regally</u> in a fine office—lots of chairs; fancy, electric lights; a <u>very</u> large wooden
7 desk; a swivel chair for himself. He wears a suit (a piece of clothing we've
8 <u>never</u> <u>actually</u> seen) and a necktie. His voice soars across the entire nation,
9 dropping <u>profoundly</u>, rising <u>excitedly</u>, carrying us <u>along</u> on every word. He
10 speaks for <u>only</u> 15 minutes. It is our dream to leave <u>forever</u> the valley where
11 we live <u>so</u> <u>quietly</u>, leave this high range where we tend flocks throughout the
12 summer, to become newscasters.

> **Write** sentences according to the directions given below. Remember that a writer uses adverbs to add detail or color to a sentence.

Answers will vary.

1. Use an adverb that tells how someone does something.

He worked diligently on his report.

2. Use "substantially" to tell how much.

We had substantially increased our savings.

3. Use an adverb that tells time: when, how often, or how long.

I will love Bebe, my dog, forever.

4. Use an adverb to tell place: where, to where, or from where.

We walked backward as the snarling dog approached us.

5. Use the comparative form of "quietly."

We spoke more quietly after the baby fell asleep.

6. Use the superlative form of "fast."

The oldest horse ran fastest and won the race.

Pretest: Prepositions, Conjunctions, & Interjections

> **Underline** the prepositional phrases in the sentences below and circle the prepositions. Write **O** above the objects of the prepositions.

1. Both eagles and falcons began disappearing (during) the time DDT (a pesticide) was used extensively (in) this country.

2. (By) 1975, there were only 325 pairs (of) nesting peregrine falcons (in) North America, (down from) thousands just thirty years earlier.

3. (Before) that time, eagles and falcons were seen (in) abundance, nesting (on) river bluffs.

4. Although peregrine falcons are the swiftest birds (on) earth, speed is no protection (against) poison.

> **Underline** the interjections and conjunctions below. Write each one in the appropriate column at the bottom of the page

1. Well, DDT has been banned throughout the United States for years, and the results with regard to falcons have been dramatic.

2. Because we began protecting the peregrine falcon population, it has been on the rise, so in 1999, there were 1,650 nesting pairs of peregrine falcons.

3. Wow! That's a good argument for conservation, but we can do even better.

4. Either we protect our endangered species, or we will see more of them disappear from our world.

Interjections	Coordinating Conjunctions	Correlative Conjunctions	Subordinating Conjunctions
Well	and	Either, or	Because
Wow!	but		
	so		

Identifying Prepositions & Interjections

A prepositional phrase is made up of a preposition and an object (a noun or a pronoun that follows the preposition), plus any words that modify the object. For example, in the phrase "into the river," *into* is the preposition, *river* is the object, and *the* modifies *river.* Turn to page 515 and 516 in *Writers INC* for more information.

> **Underline** each prepositional phrase below, and write **O** above the objects of the prepositions. **Label the interjections with an *I*.**

                         I   *O*

1. Wow, Cher has had an amazing career <u>in show business</u>.

2. She has had recordings <u>on the top</u> <u>of the charts</u>, hosted a top-rated variety show <u>for a television network</u>, starred <u>in motion pictures</u>, and acted <u>in Broadway musicals</u>.

3. Gosh, accomplishing just one <u>of those things</u> would be enough <u>for most people</u>.

4. Cher is one <u>of those entertainers</u> <u>with an incredible ability</u> to reinvent herself.

5. She has said there are times when she needs to escape <u>from the pressure</u> <u>of fame</u>.

6. Well, Cher is never <u>out of public view</u> <u>for long</u>.

7. <u>In 1999</u>, she revived her recording career <u>with a top-selling album</u>, and her music videos are once again a staple <u>on TV</u>.

8. Few <u>of Cher's fans</u> are surprised <u>at her dramatic musical comeback</u>.

9. Her fans have grown accustomed <u>to the rapid reversals and changes</u> <u>of Cher's unpredictable career</u>.

10. Do you own any <u>of her recordings or movies</u>?

Extend: Phrasal prepositions are made up of more than one word: *along with, from among, in addition to, instead of, next to,* and *up to.* Use each of these phrasal prepositions in a sentence. Underline each prepositional phrase. You may write about a celebrity, a hero or heroine, or a topic of your choice.

Coordinating Conjunctions

Study the following examples to learn how to use coordinating conjunctions. Turn to 516.1 and the chart "Kinds of Conjunctions" in *Writers INC* for more examples and an explanation.

> **Kayaking can be a <u>fun</u> *and* <u>exciting</u> sport.**
> (The coordinating conjunction *and* connects two equal words.)

> **A good kayak should <u>glide swiftly</u> *yet* <u>turn easily</u>.**
> (The coordinating conjunction *yet* connects two phrases.)

> **<u>Kayaks are much like canoes</u>, *but* <u>they are enclosed to keep water out</u>.**
> (The coordinating conjunction *but* connects two clauses.)

Combine the sentences below with the coordinating conjunction listed in parentheses.

Answers may vary.

1. Some kayaks are built out of wood. Other kayaks are made of plastic. Kayaks can also be constructed of fiberglass. *(or)*

   Kayaks are built out of wood, plastic, or fiberglass.

2. Kayakers must be skilled with a double-bladed paddle. Kayakers need to make a variety of paddle strokes. *(for)*

   Kayakers must be skilled with a double-bladed paddle, for they

   need to make a variety of paddle strokes.

3. Kayakers must make forward strokes. Another stroke is the backstroke. Another type of stroke is the sweep stroke. *(and)*

   Kayakers must make forward strokes, backstrokes, and sweep

   strokes.

4. One stroke moves the kayak sideways. Another stroke turns the kayak around. *(and)*

   One stroke moves the kayak sideways, and another turns the

   kayak around.

5. One of the most popular kayaking strokes is the Eskimo roll. This stroke is one of the most difficult to master. *(yet)*

   One of the most popular kayaking strokes is the Eskimo roll, yet

   this stroke is one of the most difficult to master.

Extend: Write sentences about an activity that you enjoy. Try to use all seven coordinating conjunctions listed in the chart on page 516.

Correlative Conjunctions

Study the examples below to see how to use correlative conjunctions. Turn to 516.2 and the chart "Kinds of Conjunctions" in *Writers INC* for more examples and an explanation.

> **Mountain biking is *both* <u>exciting</u> *and* <u>dangerous</u>.** (The correlative conjunctions *both* and *and* connect two equal words.)

> **Mountain bikes are used *either* <u>on streets</u> *or* <u>on dirt trails</u>.** (The correlative conjunctions *either* and *or* connect two equal phrases.)

> ***Whether* <u>you ride to school</u> *or* <u>you compete in a race</u>, mountain bikes are fun.** (The correlative conjunctions *whether* and *or* connect two equal clauses.)

Combine the sentences below using the correlative conjunctions listed in parentheses.

Answers may vary.

1. The list of biker safety equipment includes a helmet. Reflectors are important, too. *(not only, but also)*

   The list of biker safety equipment includes not only a helmet but

   also reflectors.

2. You need strength to climb hills. You also need endurance. *(both, and)*

   You need both strength and endurance to climb hills.

3. Usually, street curbs don't stop a mountain biker. Also, fallen logs don't stop a mountain biker. *(neither, nor)*

   Usually, neither street curbs nor fallen logs stop a mountain biker.

4. When biking in the country, always have a spare tire. This is also true for traveling in the city. *(whether, or)*

   Whether biking in the city or in the country, always have a spare

   tire.

5. Touring in the backcountry is a great way to bike. It includes all the adventure of camping. *(not only, but also)*

   Not only is touring in the backcountry a great way to bike, but it

   also includes all the adventure of camping.

Extend: Write six sentences using the six pairs of correlative conjunctions listed in the chart on page 516 in *Writers INC*. You can write about camping, biking, or whatever other activity you like. Make your sentences pertain to one subject so you can write them as a paragraph.

Subordinating Conjunctions

Study the example below to review how a subordinating conjunction connects an independent clause to a dependent clause. Turn to 516.3 and the chart "Kinds of Conjunctions" in *Writers INC* for more information.

 We hiked all day although it was raining. (The clause *although it was raining* is dependent. It depends on the rest of the sentence to complete its meaning.)

> **Complete** the following sentences with a dependent clause that begins with the underlined subordinating conjunction.

1. She will not go swimming <u>because</u> _she is afraid of water._

2. We wouldn't be surprised to find out <u>that</u> _he won the lottery._

_____

3. The waiter did not come back to our table <u>until</u> _all our menus were_

placed facedown on the table.

4. <u>Since</u> _we watch television every night,_

_____ we seldom go to the movies.

5. He can sing at the prom <u>as long as</u> _he chooses an appropriate song._

_____

6. <u>If</u> _his nose hadn't gotten broken,_

_____ my favorite wrestler would have won the cage match.

7. Detectives sit in their car and eat <u>while</u> _they are on a stakeout._

_____

8. The librarian came to get my neighbor's books <u>after</u> _they had been_

overdue for six months.

9. I like growing up in a large city <u>where</u> _there are many things to do._

_____

Extend: Choose one of the sentences above and write a paragraph based on that sentence. Include at least two sentences that connect an independent and a dependent clause with a subordinating conjunction.

Review: Prepositions, Conjunctions, & Interjections

Underline each prepositional phrase. Then label each interjection in the sentences below with an *I* and each conjunction with a *C*.

1. [I] Wow, I just finished reading *The Complete Sherlock Holmes,* [C] and I discovered a lot <u>of facts</u> I never knew <u>about Holmes</u>.

2. Not [C] only was Holmes extremely moody, [C] but he also had some very weird habits.

3. He would get depressed [C] and lie around <u>for days</u>, scraping away <u>on his violin</u> [C] and driving Dr. Watson nearly <u>over the edge</u>.

4. [C] Although he could play the violin brilliantly [C] when he wished, Sherlock simply screeched <u>out of tune</u> <u>during his depressions</u>.

5. Holmes used his apartment wall <u>for target practice</u> [C] since leaving the apartment was too much <u>of a bother</u> <u>for him</u>.

6. He also kept his mail <u>in order</u> <u>in an unusual way</u>; Holmes stuck it safely <u>to the mantelpiece</u> <u>with his pocketknife</u>.

7. [C] When Holmes wanted to smoke his pipe, he had to get his tobacco <u>from the place</u> [C] where he stashed it—<u>in the toe</u> <u>of his Persian slippers</u>.

8. [I] Well, Sherlock was brilliant, [C] but his older brother, Mycroft, was brilliant <u>beyond belief</u>.

9. [C] Because Mycroft had no ambition, he left his room only <u>on rare occasions</u> [C] and then only <u>for a brief time</u>.

10. [C] Both Sherlock [C] and Mycroft were well <u>above average</u> <u>in intelligence</u>, [C] but they were also <u>on the eccentric side</u>.

Review: Language Activities

Complete the following statements.

1. A noun or a pronoun is in the objective case when it is used as a direct object, a(n) _indirect object_ , or a(n) _object of a preposition_ .

2. A(n) _interjection_ shows strong emotion or surprise.

3. A(n) _pronoun_ can be used in place of a noun.

4. Both nouns and pronouns have three cases: _nominative_ , objective, and _possessive_ .

5. *Who, whose, whom, which,* and *that* are relative _pronouns_ .

6. The _comparative_ form of adjectives and adverbs compares two persons, places, things, or ideas.

7. A(n) _verb_ expresses action or state of being.

8. *I see* is an example of _present_ tense.

9. In the sentence *Renaldo showed me his skateboard yesterday,* the word _skateboard_ is the direct object.

10. A gerund is a(n) _verb_ form that ends in *-ing* and is used as a noun.

11. An infinitive is usually introduced by the word _to_ .

12. A(n) _relative_ pronoun relates an adjective clause to the noun or pronoun it modifies.

13. Adverbs modify _verbs_ , _adjectives_ , or _adverbs_ .

14. A(n) _noun_ is a word that names a person, a place, a thing, or an idea.

15. In the sentence *Tarzan is smart,* the word *smart* is a predicate _adjective_ .

16. The _superlative_ form of adjectives compares three or more persons, places, things, or ideas.

17. In the sentence *David was snoozing,* the word *was* is a(n) _auxiliary (or) helping_ verb.

18. When a noun or a pronoun shows ownership, it is in the _possessive_ case.

19. In the phrase *behind the door,* the word *behind* is a(n) _preposition_ .

20. *And, but, or, for, nor, yet,* and *so* are coordinating _conjunctions_ .

21. A(n) _demonstrative_ pronoun points out people, places, or things without naming them.

22. *Since* is a(n) _subordinating_ conjunction.

23. A(n) _proper_ noun names a particular person, place, thing, or idea.

24. *I saw* is an example of _past_ tense.

25. A(n) _collective_ noun names a group or a unit.

26. The pronoun *our* is in the _first_ person.

27. Adjectives describe or modify _nouns_ or _pronouns_ .

28. *Who* is a(n) _interrogative_ or a(n) _relative_ pronoun.

29. In the sentence *Britt gave me a birthday present,* the word *me* is a(n) _indirect object_ .

30. A(n) _conjunction_ connects individual words or groups of words.

31. A(n) _noun_ or a(n) _pronoun_ is most often used as the subject of a sentence, but a gerund or an infinitive may also be used.

32. In the sentence *I admire her persistence,* the verb is in the _active_ voice.

33. The _third_ person is used to name the person or thing spoken about.

34. Many adverbs end in _-ly_ .

35. *Both/and* and *not only/but also* are _correlative_ conjunctions.

SENTENCE ACTIVITIES

The activities in this section cover three important areas: (1) the basic parts, types, and kinds of sentences as well as agreement issues; (2) methods for writing smooth-reading sentences; and (3) common sentence errors. Most activities include practice in which you review, combine, or analyze different sentences. In addition, the **Extend** activities provide follow-up practice with certain skills.

Pretest: Subjects & Predicates

Draw a line between the complete subject and the complete predicate in each sentence. Then underline the simple or compound subject once and the simple or compound predicate twice.

1. Athletes | hit the ball, leap the hurdle, and go the distance.

2. People of all ages and abilities | love sports.

3. More than 1 million athletes, representing 150 countries as well as all 50 American states, | participate in the Special Olympics.

4. The athletes who compete in the Special Olympics | are both like and unlike other athletes.

5. Like all Olympic contestants, Special Olympians | enjoy the thrill of competition and appreciate the special camaraderie of the games.

6. They | train hard to do their best.

7. Each Special Olympian | has some degree of mental retardation.

8. That single fact | does not prevent a Special Olympian from enjoying sports, however.

9. The public and the media | often overlook the heroic accomplishments of Special Olympians.

10. But these athletes | understand the joy of sports.

11. Winning | is important.

12. Bravery, determination, persistence, and good sportsmanship | count for even more.

Subjects & Predicates 1

A *sentence* must have a subject and a predicate that together express a complete thought. A *simple subject* is the subject without its modifiers; a *simple predicate* is the verb without its modifiers. *Complete subjects* and *complete predicates* contain all the modifiers, too. Turn to 519.1-519.2 in *Writers INC* for information and examples.

> **Draw** a line between the complete subject and the complete predicate. **Underline** each simple subject once and each simple predicate twice.

1. A <u>flock</u> of turkey vultures | <u><u>landed</u></u> in a pasture across the road yesterday.

2. <u>Tariq</u> | <u><u>wondered</u></u> why they had landed there.

3. <u>Carrion</u>—the decaying flesh of dead animals—<u><u>is</u></u> the main source of food for vultures.

4. Looking around the pasture, <u>Tariq</u> | <u><u>saw</u></u> no dead animals.

5. These big, ugly <u>birds</u> of prey | <u><u>were</u></u> perhaps <u><u>hunting</u></u> for a safe place to rest.

6. <u>Turkey vultures</u> | <u><u>are related</u></u> to birds even bigger and uglier than they are.

7. For instance, <u>vultures</u> living in the mountains of the Mediterranean region and in central Asia | <u><u>have</u></u> a wingspan of about nine feet!

8. Another <u>kind</u> of vulture, the California condor, | <u><u>boasts</u></u> an equally impressive wingspan of nine to ten feet.

9. The <u>California condor</u> | <u><u>is</u></u> an endangered species.

10. <u>Scientists</u> | <u><u>began breeding</u></u> these rare birds in captivity during the 1980s.

11. The <u>condor</u> | <u><u>is</u></u> slowly <u><u>making</u></u> a comeback, thanks to the efforts of scientists and environmentalists.

Extend: Write three or four basic sentences with a simple subject and a simple predicate. Expand the sentences, adding details to both the subject and the predicate. Turn to page 93 in *Writers INC* to see the five basic ways to expand a sentence.

Subjects & Predicates 2

A *compound subject* is composed of two or more simple subjects. A *compound predicate* is composed of two or more simple predicates. Turn to 519.1-519.2 in *Writers INC* for examples.

> **Draw** a line between the complete subject and the complete predicate. **Underline** any compound subjects or compound predicates.

1. <u>You</u> and <u>I</u> | are going to have to talk, Michael.

2. The orange ceramic <u>tiger</u> and the blue glass <u>dolphin</u> | are missing from your grandma's apartment.

3. They | could not <u>have disappeared</u> or <u>walked</u> away on their own.

4. Your <u>grandmother</u> and her upstairs <u>neighbor</u> | were quite fond of those figurines.

5. Grandma | <u>received</u> the dolphin from her father and <u>bought</u> the tiger at the 1939 World's Fair in New York.

6. <u>You</u> and <u>Bart</u> | were the last ones in the garage.

7. <u>Moving</u> or <u>breaking</u> the figurines | could have happened accidentally.

8. No, I | haven't <u>seen</u> or <u>heard</u> the upstairs neighbor's new cat.

9. Oh, this cat | <u>steals</u> things and <u>hides</u> them.

10. <u>You</u> and <u>Bart</u> | will help us look for the figurines, please.

11. Both <u>Bart</u> and <u>Michael</u> | <u>jump</u> in and <u>join</u> the search.

12. "Mom and Grandma, we | found the tiger and the dolphin under the sofa!"

13. I | <u>examined</u> them carefully and <u>put</u> them back on the shelf.

14. Neither the <u>tiger</u> nor the <u>dolphin</u> | is damaged.

15. <u>Grandma</u> and <u>I</u> | apologize for accusing you and Bart.

Extend: Using a friend and yourself as the compound subject, write three to five sentences that include compound predicates.

Review: Subjects & Predicates

> **Write** the correct term for each of the following definitions.

<u>subject</u>   **1.** the part of the sentence about which something is said

<u>sentence</u>   **2.** must have a subject and a predicate (but either the subject or the predicate may be "understood")

<u>complete subject</u>   **3.** simple subject and all the words that modify it

<u>simple predicate</u>   **4.** the verb without its modifiers

<u>sentence</u>   **5.** one or more words that express a complete thought

<u>complete predicate</u>   **6.** simple predicate and all the words that modify it

<u>predicate</u>   **7.** the part of the sentence that shows action or says something about the subject

> **Draw** a line between the complete subject and the complete predicate. Then underline the simple or compound subject once and the simple or compound predicate twice.

1. Maya and her sister | competed against each other in a chess tournament.

2. Hundreds of purple and yellow butterflies | darted carelessly through the meadow.

3. The teaching styles of high school teachers | are as different as their personalities.

4. The marching band, led by the drummers, | increased the pace and cranked up the volume.

5. Neither Red nor I | had ever seen or heard such a performance.

> **Write** a sentence with a complete subject and a compound predicate.

The fans at the hockey game between Boston College and UW Madison yelled, chanted, and pantomimed like happy children.

Pretest: Phrases

> **Identify** each italicized phrase in the sentences below. On the blanks, write **V** for verbal, **P** for prepositional, or **A** for appositive.

___V___ **1.** Would you like *to be a Blue Angel*?

___P___ **2.** Who hasn't heard *of the Blue Angels*?

___A___ **3.** The Blue Angels, *the most famous flight demonstration team in the world*, are Navy and Marine Corps pilots.

___V___ **4.** *To fly with speed and precision* is their goal.

___V___ **5.** *Being in A-1 physical condition* is a minimum requirement.

___P___ **6.** Their bodies, kept physically fit *by vigorous exercise*, must respond perfectly during every flight.

___P___ **7.** The pilots say that their 45-minute flight demonstrations require the effort and focus *of an 8-hour day*.

___A___ **8.** Their planes, *models equipped with special controls*, fly remarkably close to one another.

___V___ **9.** *Flying in tight formation*, the Blue Angels keep their wingtips just 18 to 36 inches apart.

___V___ **10.** *To imagine the intensity of the experience*, try holding your muscles contracted for 45 minutes.

___P___ **11.** The Blue Angels perform *for thousands of fascinated spectators* every year.

___A___ **12.** Their demonstrations, *precision ballets in the sky*, kept 15 million spectators in awe at 70 air shows in 1999.

Verbal Phrases

Gerunds, infinitives, and participles are verbals. A *verbal* is derived from a verb, has the power of a verb, but acts as another part of speech. Turn to 508.2-509.2 and 520.1 in *Writers INC* for examples and more information.

Type of Verbal	Functions as		
	Noun	Adjective	Adverb
gerund (ends in *-ing*)	X		
infinitive (introduced by *to*)	X	X	X
participle (ends in *-ing* or *-ed*)		X	

Identify the underlined verbal phrases in the following sentences. Write **G** for gerund, **I** for infinitive, and **P** for participial.

1. A person must decide whether or not <u>to use slang</u> in everyday situations. *I*

2. <u>Using slang</u> is not always appropriate. *G*

3. A formal paper <u>filled with slang terms</u> makes the writer appear uneducated. *P*

4. The decision <u>to use slang</u> can be the result of a desire <u>to appear cool</u>. *I   I*

5. Others use slang <u>to put people at ease</u>, <u>to express friendliness</u>, or <u>to be informal</u>. *I   I   I*

6. Slang terms <u>expressed in a humorous way</u> can make conversation much more entertaining. *P*

7. People sometimes use slang <u>to refer to painful or frightening events</u>. *I*

8. Before <u>taking a test</u>, a student might use a cliche like "It's time <u>to face the music</u>." *G   I*

9. Some slang is the result of <u>dropping one or more syllables from a longer word</u>, also called *clipping*. *G*

10. Slang words <u>created in this fashion</u> include *psycho*, short for "psychopath," and *rep*, short for "reputation" or "representative." *P*

Extend: Develop three to five sentences about the slang you use. Use a different type of verbal phrase in each sentence. Label each of your verbal phrases.

Prepositional & Appositive Phrases

A *prepositional phrase* consists of a preposition, its object, and any modifiers. An *appositive phrase,* which consists of a noun and its modifiers, follows another noun or pronoun and renames it. Turn to the top of page 521 in *Writers INC* for examples.

> **Write** an appositive phrase or a prepositional phrase as indicated to complete each sentence below.

Answers will vary.

1. I decided to go to the concert _____ **in the park** _____ .
   prepositional phrase

2. The performers, _____ **a new local band** _____ , seemed to be
   appositive phrase
   surprised at the size of the crowd.

3. _____ **Throughout the evening** _____ , the emcee had the hiccups.
   prepositional phrase

4. _____ **After the concert** _____ , I stopped for a steaming hot cup of coffee.
   prepositional phrase

5. I began reading an article _____ **in a magazine** _____
   prepositional phrase
   that someone had left on the table.

6. It was about the members of Pearl Jam, _____ **a popular rock group** _____ .
   appositive phrase

7. Sufi Kinjhon, _____ **an author with an upbeat style** _____ , wrote the article.
   appositive phrase

8. A man _____ **beside me** _____ politely inquired, "May I
   prepositional phrase
   sit here?"

9. I immediately recognized him as Jeff, _____ **my brother's friend** _____ .
   appositive phrase

10. My brother, _____ **a senior at Notre Dame** _____ , used to date Jeff's sister.
    appositive phrase

11. _____ **During our chat** _____ , Jeff and I discovered we had a lot in common.
    prepositional phrase

12. Jeff, _____ **a generally calm person** _____ , was excited about our chance meeting.
    appositive phrase

Extend: Write three or four sentences about a concert or musical performers. Include an appositive phrase or a prepositional phrase in each sentence.

Absolute Phrases

An *absolute phrase* consists of a noun and a participle (a word often ending in *-ing* or *-ed*); it acts as an adjective. Absolute phrases can also contain an object and/or modifiers. Study the examples below and turn to the top of page 521 in *Writers INC*.

How can you be certain you have composed an absolute phrase? Try adding *was* or *were* to each absolute phrase in the sentences below. If the addition of *was* or *were* makes a complete sentence, you can be certain you have an absolute phrase.

> The wolves chased the sheep. (basic sentence)

> <u>Mouths drooling</u>, <u>eyes shining</u>, the wolves chased the sheep. (absolute phrases)

> <u>Mouths drooling like rabid animals</u>, <u>eyes shining in anticipation</u>, the wolves chased the sheep. (absolute phrases containing modifiers)

Underline the absolute phrases in the following sentences. Next, write sentences using the models as patterns.

Answers will vary.

1. <u>Hands shaking</u>, <u>voice trembling</u>, the actor stepped onto the stage.

Feet flying, arms flailing, the skater fell.

2. The running back, <u>his legs churning powerfully</u>, slammed into the defensive line.

The lost child, his tears streaming silently, waited for his older sister.

3. The folders fell on the floor, <u>pages scattering in all directions</u>.

The leaves fell from the maples, millions of them drifting into huge piles.

4. <u>Its numbers dwindling from exhaustion and starvation</u>, the defeated army wandered westward.

Their faces glowing with pleasure and excitement, the curious Scouts trooped onward.

5. The victorious candidate, <u>her supporters cheering loudly</u>, tried to hear the reporters' questions.

The acrobatic clown, her somersaults spinning wildly, appeared to enjoy her strenuous workout.

Extend: Write three or four sentences that contain absolute phrases.

Using Phrases Like the Pros

Professional writers engage a reader with the skillful use of phrases, adding detail and variety to their sentences. To review the types of phrases, turn to 520.1 in *Writers INC*.

> **Create** sentences that imitate these examples from well-known works. Circle the phrases you use.

Answers will vary.

1. *(two gerund phrases)* I like sitting on the side and watching the band play . . .
   — Dick Gregory, "Not Poor, Just Broke"

   Dad suggested (swimming in the river) and (watching the moon rise.)

2. *(one prepositional phrase and two participial phrases)* The dogs' feet fell heavily on the trail, jarring their bodies and doubling the fatigue of a day's travel.
   —Jack London, *The Call of the Wild*

   The wind came unexpectedly (from the east,) (numbing our faces) and

   (biting through our thin coats.)

3. *(seven prepositional phrases)* In the corner of the sofa, there was a cushion, and in the velvet which covered it, there was a hole, and out of the hole peeped a tiny head with a pair of frightened eyes in it.
   —Frances Hodgson Burnett, *The Secret Garden*

   (At the edge) (of the forest,) there stood a hut, and (in the doorway,)

   there was a girl, and (next to the girl) sat a shaggy dog (with a collar)

   (of shimmering blue stones) (around its neck.)

4. *(two infinitive phrases connected with a conjunction)* Bannerman looked as though he didn't know whether to laugh at Johnny or to deal him a good swift kick. —Stephen King, *The Dead Zone*

   Sometimes I don't know whether (to throttle you or to kiss you.)

5. *(one participial phrase and three prepositional phrases)* The boy, regaining his balance, dragged Sounder off the porch and to the corner of the cabin.
   —William H. Armstrong, *Sounder*

   My uncle, (regaining his composure,) pulled himself (to his feet) and

   walked (to the gate of the corral.)

Extend: Using one of your sentences as a topic sentence, write a paragraph. Use a variety of phrases in your sentences.

Review: Phrases

> **Write** sentences following the directions given below.

Answers will vary.

1. Use an appositive phrase and underline it.

Michigan's arboretums, <u>Leila Arboretum in Battle Creek and Nichols Arboretum in Ann Arbor</u>, have fine collections of plants, shrubs, and trees.

2. Use a gerund phrase as a subject and underline it.

<u>Learning American slang words</u> was difficult for the foreign exchange student.

3. Use a gerund phrase as the object of a preposition and underline it.

We learned a lot about <u>banding birds</u> on our field trip.

4. Use an infinitive phrase as a subject and underline it.

<u>To help the park rangers band birds</u> made me feel useful.

5. Use prepositional phrases and underline them.

Tired and pleased <u>with ourselves</u>, we talked all the way home <u>about becoming park rangers</u>.

6. Use prepositional phrases and underline them.

We also talked <u>about bird-watching</u> <u>in our own backyards</u>.

7. Use an absolute phrase and underline it.

<u>Enthusiasm growing</u>, class members asked to go on another field trip.

Pretest: Clauses

> **Identify** each underlined clause, using *I* for independent and *D* for dependent. For each dependent clause, identify it as an adjective clause (*ADJ*), an adverb clause (*ADV*), or a noun clause (*N*).

1. Many eyes in the world focused on the last solar eclipse of the twentieth century, *D/ADJ* <u>which occurred on August 11, 1999</u>.

2. Although it was primarily visible in Europe, *I* <u>the 1999 event was one of the most widely seen eclipses in history, thanks to television's coverage.</u>

3. We looked only indirectly at the eclipse, *D/ADV* <u>although we were wearing sunglasses</u>.

4. *D/ADV* <u>Since looking directly at an eclipse can cause blindness</u>, viewers should shield their eyes properly.

5. *I* <u>A solar eclipse occurs</u> when the moon passes between the sun and the earth, casting a shadow.

6. If the solar eclipse is total, *I* <u>the sun completely disappears from view in some places on earth.</u>

7. Scientists have studied *D/N* <u>what happens during a solar eclipse</u>.

8. In seconds, day becomes night and temperatures plummet, *D/ADJ* <u>which is a direct result of the absence of sunlight.</u>

9. *I* <u>In 1999, thousands of Europeans cheered</u> as the moon's shadow fell upon them.

10. *D/N* <u>Whoever watched from Romania</u> observed the longest period of darkness: 2 minutes and 23 seconds.

11. People used to be terrified of eclipses *D/ADV* <u>because they didn't know why the sun disappeared</u>.

12. A solar eclipse is a natural phenomenon *D/ADJ* <u>that can help scientists learn more about our red-hot power source, the sun.</u>

Independent & Dependent Clauses

A *clause* is a group of related words that has both a subject and a predicate. An *independent clause* can stand alone as a sentence, while a *dependent clause* cannot. Turn to 521.1 in *Writers INC* for examples.

> **Underline** each independent clause once and each dependent clause twice.

1. Bombay, which has a population of more than 12 million, is the largest city in India.

2. Because it is an island city, several bridges link Bombay with the mainland.

3. Most people live in cheap housing in outlying neighborhoods, although wealthy residents occupy modern apartments in the central city.

4. Almost a million people live in dilapidated shanties without proper sanitation, while thousands of others are homeless.

5. Since overcrowding is such a serious problem, the government has been developing a new industrial and residential area on the mainland near Bombay.

6. The principal religion is Hinduism, though Islam has many followers as well.

7. This enormous city, which boasts numerous banks and insurance companies, is a major financial center.

8. Bombay is also a major producer of cotton textiles and leather, which are exported all over the world.

9. Before Bombay became part of India, it was a commerce post founded by Portuguese traders in the 1530s.

10. When King Charles II of England married a Portuguese princess in 1661, he received Bombay as a wedding gift!

Extend: Living in a city of 12 million people must present a number of challenges to everyday life. Write four (or more) sentences describing how you'd overcome these challenges. Include dependent clauses in your sentences.

Adverb, Adjective, & Noun Clauses

There are three types of dependent clauses: *adverb clauses*, beginning with subordinating conjunctions (*when, since, if,* etc.); *adjective clauses,* beginning with relative pronouns (*who, which, that,* etc.); and noun clauses, beginning with *what, whatever, that, who,* or *whoever.* (Turn to 503.4, the chart on page 504, 516.3, and 521.2 in *Writers INC* for further explanation.)

> *Adverb Clause:*
> **My mother took me shopping, because she wanted to cheer me up.**
> (The clause is used as an *adverb* to modify the verb *took*.)

> *Adjective Clause:*
> **She must be thinking I'm like my sister Sarah, who loves to shop.**
> (The clause is used as an *adjective* to modify the noun *Sarah*.)

> *Noun Clause:*
> **Shop until you drop is what Sarah likes to do.**
> (The clause is used as a *noun,* in this case a *predicate noun*.)

Underline the dependent clauses in the following sentences and identify them as *ADV* for adverb, *ADJ* for adjective, or *N* for noun.

1. Half of all people in the United States live in suburbs, while roughly a quarter [ADV] of them inhabit rural areas.

2. We could see that Althea was not a good swimmer. [N]

3. Some Moroccan musicians who were playing folk melodies in the park will be [ADJ] on the TV news tonight.

4. I'll use the parts that I salvaged from the old car to fix the new one. [ADJ]

5. After you sort the laundry, put a load in the washing machine. [ADV]

6. Whoever plans to go on the field trip should be on the bus at 8:00 a.m. sharp. [N]

7. Yes, you may take my car, as long as you've finished your homework. [ADV]

8. Eli, whose father is a pilot, travels frequently. [ADJ]

9. What the officer said surprised me. [N]

10. The fact that you like him is no reason to act so silly. [ADJ]

Review: Clauses

> **Identify** each underlined clause, using **D** for dependent and **I** for independent.

1. Viruses, <u>which are microscopic organisms</u> [D] that live inside the cells of other living things, are a major cause of disease.

2. Viruses are <u>primitive, lifeless particles</u> [I] that only become active inside a living cell.

3. They lack some of the substances <u>that they need for independence</u> [D], so they enter the cell of a living thing and use the cell's materials to live and reproduce.

4. Most viruses can be seen only with an electron microscope <u>because their size ranges from .01 to .3 microns.</u> [D]

5. <u>Viruses cause disease by damaging the cells of an organism</u> [I], although a virus sometimes lives in a cell without harming it.

> **Identify** each dependent clause underlined below as **ADJ** for adjective, **ADV** for adverb, and **N** for noun.

1. A cell <u>that is infected by a virus</u> [ADJ] produces proteins <u>that the virus needs.</u> [ADJ]

2. <u>After the virus uses these proteins</u> [ADV], the chemical composition of the cell is changed; as a result, the cell may be damaged or killed.

3. <u>Because the cell proteins are available to the virus</u> [ADV], it can reproduce itself hundreds of times.

4. Research has clearly shown <u>that the newly produced viruses leave the cell and infect other cells.</u> [N]

5. Most drugs <u>that are able to kill or damage a virus</u> [ADJ] also damage healthy cells.

6. <u>Because doctors cannot stop a virus from causing disease</u> [ADV], they merely attempt to control the symptoms.

Pretest: Sentences

Insert end punctuation in the following sentences. On the first blank, identify each sentence as **S** for simple, **CD** for compound, **CX** for complex, or **CD-CX** for compound-complex. On the second blank, identify each sentence as **D** for declarative, **IN** for interrogative, **IM** for imperative, or **E** for exclamatory.

_S_ _IN_ **1.** Why is Alfred Hitchcock called the master of suspense?

_CD-CX_ _D_ **2.** If you have to ask that question, you probably haven't seen any of his films, or you haven't thought much about them.

_CD_ _IM_ **3.** Turn to any list of the greatest movie directors of all time, and you will see Alfred Hitchcock's name near the top.

_CD-CX_ _IN_ **4.** Have you seen the chilling attack in _The Birds,_ when the actress Tippi Hedren fends off murderous gulls, or have you seen the thrilling chase in _North by Northwest,_ when Cary Grant tries to outrun a crop duster?

_CX_ _E_ **5.** Yikes, I'd almost forgotten that those scenes were so scary!

_CX_ _IN_ **6.** Have you seen reruns of Hitchcock's weekly TV shows, which he introduced with a dignified walk and a sinister comment?

_CD_ _D_ **7.** Audiences found Hitchcock mysterious and entertaining, and they found his movies and TV shows riveting.

_CX_ _D_ **8.** The real Alfred Hitchcock was a kind, loyal, sensitive, hardworking man who was devoted to his wife and daughter.

_S_ _E_ **9.** You've got to be kidding!

_CD-CX_ _D_ **10.** Truth is stranger than fiction, and everyone admits that Alfred Hitchcock was fond of strangeness.

Kinds of Sentences

The four kinds of sentences are declarative, interrogative, imperative, and exclamatory. A sentence might make a statement, ask a question, give a command, or make an exclamation. Turn to 522.1 in *Writers INC* for examples.

> **Identify** the following sentences with a **D** for declarative, **IN** for interrogative, **IM** for imperative, or **E** for exclamatory. Add end punctuation.

__D__ **1.** Last summer, my family drove to the East Coast for a vacation.

__E__ **2.** What a disaster it was!

__IN__ **3.** Have you ever sat in a traffic jam for well over an hour?

__D__ **4.** We did, and then the car's radiator overheated.

__D__ **5.** We finally got to see the Atlantic Ocean, but it was not what we expected.

__IN__ **6.** Who would have predicted that it would be only 60 degrees in July?

__IM__ **7.** Don't swim in the ocean when it's so chilly on the beach.

__IM__ **8.** Instead, look for seashells.

> **Write** four of your own sentences (one of each kind). Don't forget the end punctuation.

Answers will vary.

1. Declarative: Lenin State Library in Moscow is one of the largest libraries in the world.

2. Imperative: Always return your books before they become overdue.

3. Interrogative: Have you ever visited the Library of Congress in Washington, D.C.?

4. Exclamatory: The Library of Congress owns more than 84 million items!

Extend: Write three interrogative sentences on a sheet of paper, leaving room for answers. Exchange with a classmate, and answer the questions using one declarative, one imperative, and one exclamatory sentence.

Types of Sentences 1

The best writing contains a variety of sentence types: *simple, compound, complex,* and *compound-complex.* Practice creating these four types of sentences. Turn to 522.2 in *Writers INC.*

> **Write sentences following the directions given below.**

Answers will vary.

1. Write a simple sentence using this compound subject: *pizza and ice cream.*

   Pizza and ice cream are my favorite foods.

2. Write a compound sentence. Use the sentence you wrote above and connect it to another sentence with a coordinating conjunction: *and, but, or, for, yet, nor, so.*

   Pizza and ice cream are my favorite foods, but my brother prefers tacos and apple pies.

3. Write a complex sentence starting with this independent clause: *many people prefer to eat favorite foods.* Add a dependent clause that begins with *that.*

   Many people prefer to eat favorite foods that they loved as young children.

4. Write a compound-complex sentence. (Try to combine the ideas from your second and third sentences.)

   Pizza and ice cream are my favorite foods, but my brother prefers tacos and apple pies that he loved as a young child.

5. Write a compound sentence about your neighborhood. Combine the two independent clauses with a semicolon, or with a comma and a coordinating conjunction.

   Our neighborhood is full of older people now; they prefer quiet streets, quiet cars, and quiet neighbors.

Types of Sentences 2

You can determine the structure of a sentence (*simple, compound, complex,* or *compound-complex*) by looking at the number of dependent and independent clauses. Turn to 522.2 in *Writers INC* for more information.

> **Identify** the structure of the following sentences.

<u>*simple*</u>　　**1.** My family loves to go to restaurants for dinner.

<u>*simple*</u>　　**2.** The word *restaurant* comes from a Latin word meaning *to restore.*

<u>*complex*</u>　　**3.** It makes sense that people need to be "restored" after a long, hard day.

<u>*compound*</u>　　**4.** School and work demand a lot of time; we become exhausted.

<u>*compound-complex*</u>　**5.** Sometimes we work for hours, and we forget to eat, despite hunger pangs that are trying to tell us something.

<u>*compound-complex*</u>　**6.** We get comfort and nourishment from food—but it sure makes life easier when someone else makes and serves it.

> **Write** four of your own sentences, using a different structure for each one.

1. Simple: <u>*The sunrise glowed over the mountains.*</u>

2. Compound: <u>*We waited beside the lake, and finally we saw the boat coming.*</u>

3. Complex: <u>*The two campers whose canoe had capsized waited to be rescued.*</u>

4. Compound-Complex: <u>*We were worried until we saw the rescue boat coming, but it moved slowly through the choppy water.*</u>

Extend: Write the first draft of a paragraph. You may describe how you keep your head while living an active life or you may choose another topic. Use a variety of sentence structures.

Modeling a Sentence 1

Writers learn how to arrange sentences so they can achieve sentence variety and add details. One way to achieve variety is to put the main clause in different positions—at the beginning, in the middle, or at the end. Turn to 523.1 and page 92 in *Writers INC*.

> **Study** the following sentences, excerpted from the short story "a list of ten things" by student writer Loubel Cruz (handbook pages 170-172). Write your own version of each sentence, imitating the model part by part. The main clause in each sentence is underlined.

1. The next day I tried to find Davis, but at the same time, I tried to avoid him.

Occasionally I like to eat out, but most times, I like to eat at

home.

2. I looked over at Davis to see if he would give me one of his this-is-such-a stupid-class looks.

I questioned Juliet to discover why she borrowed my get-dressed-

up-and-go-out shoes.

3. Through my tears, I opened the envelope to read what Davis had written.

During the evening, I checked my e-mail to see what my friends

were up to.

4. Despite my tears, I found myself laughing.

Without her glasses, she found herself squinting.

5. I turned and saw a guy running toward me, panting.

He stopped and heard a sound piercing the air, shrieking.

Extend: Read the student essay "Leaving the Garden" on page 157 in *Writers INC*. Select three sentences from the essay and write your own imitations of them.

Modeling a Sentence 2

Writers often write sentences with a lot of personality, rhythm, balance, and variety. They emphasize a point, a detail, a word. To learn the names for different sentence arrangements, turn to 523.1 and page 92 in *Writers INC*.

> **Study** the following sentences. Underline the main clause in each sentence. Then write your own version of each one, imitating the model part by part.

1. An iguana hissed at us as it skittered across the gravel walkway, heading for cover under a flowering bush.

    The squirrel made clicking noises as it raced across the expansive lawn, launching itself up a maple tree.

2. Since I am one of U2's biggest fans, I made sure that I was first in line for concert tickets, knowing they would sell out quickly.

    As long as I can remember, I liked the boy who was the narrator of the school play in first grade, noticing he was slyly signaling me.

3. David and Monica bounded into the room, waving their driver's licenses and whooping excitedly.

    Mom and Dad attended the performance, recording my part and whispering loudly.

4. Despite the impending storm, the team continued its soccer practice, wanting to get in a few more plays before the rain started.

    Instead of a complete practice, they cut short their calisthenics, needing to save time for a scrimmage on the soccer field.

5. Drawing upon his years of experience as an instructor and businessman, he gently suggested that the staff member's efforts were inadequate for the job at hand.

    Clearing items from her car after the funeral procession, she finally understood that her aunt's attempt at humor was medicine for their aching hearts.

Review: Sentences

Fill in the blanks to complete the following sentences correctly.

1. A simple sentence has only one _____*independent*_____ clause and no
   _____*dependent*_____ clauses.

2. A compound sentence consists of two _____*independent*_____ clauses.

3. A complex sentence has one _____*independent*_____ clause and at
   least one _____*dependent*_____ clause.

4. A compound-complex sentence contains at least two _____*independent*_____
   clauses and at least one _____*dependent*_____ clause.

5. _____*Declarative*_____ sentences make a statement and use a period.

6. _____*Interrogative*_____ sentences ask a question and need a question mark.

7. _____*Imperative*_____ sentences make a command and use a period.

8. _____*Exclamatory*_____ sentences communicate strong emotion or surprise.

Write an example of the four different kinds of sentences.

1. Simple _____*James Longstreet was a Confederate general in the Civil War.*_____

2. Compound _____*Longstreet fought in most of the major battles in*_____
   Virginia, and Robert E. Lee counted on him throughout the war.

3. Complex _____*His troops called him "Old Pete" because he was not*_____
   aggressive in battle.

4. Compound-Complex _____*Longstreet, who was born in South Carolina, also*_____
   fought in the Mexican War, and in 1880 he was appointed minister
   to Turkey.

Pretest: Subject-Verb Agreement

Circle the verb that agrees with the subject in each of the following sentences.

1. There *(are, is)* many types of athletic competitions that require intensive training.

2. Training, discipline, and hard work *(is, are)* necessary for any serious athlete.

3. The Ironman competition, whose most famous location may be Kailua-Kona, Hawaii, *(consist, consists)* of 2.4 miles of swimming, 112 miles of cycling, and 26.2 miles of running.

4. *(Has, Have)* anyone heard of an event called the Double Ironman?

5. All participants in the Double Ironman *(swim, swims)* 4.8 miles, *(bike, bikes)* 224 miles, and *(run, runs)* 52.4 miles.

6. Tina Bishoff, one of the world's top athletes, *(is, are)* a world-record holder, having set a time of 22 hours and 7 minutes for this event in 1994.

7. What kind of a training schedule *(do, does)* a person have to follow to prepare for the Double Ironman?

8. Two New Yorkers, Patricia Buttenheim and Ann Snoeyenbos, *(is, are)* training for the Double Ironman.

9. Neither rain nor sleet *(keep, keeps)* them from training.

10. Each of the women *(is, are)* determined to train safely and sanely.

11. Both of them *(bike, bikes)* 40 miles, *(do, does)* 1½ hours of yoga and strength training, and *(swim, swims)* or *(run, runs)* 2 hours—every day.

12. This *(is, are)* one of the sports I'd rather read about than participate in!

Subject-Verb Agreement 1

The following activity gives you practice in choosing verbs that agree with their subjects. Turn to 526.1-527.3 in *Writers INC* for more information.

Circle the verb that agrees with each subject in the following sentences.

1. The oldest tree in Washington County *(is,* are*)* dying and will have to be cut down.

2. The stately white ash *(stand,* stands*)* more than 70 feet high.

3. Leaves still *(*sprout,* sprouts)* from some of its branches.

4. But now rot *(gnaw,* gnaws*)* at its insides, and dead branches *(*rattle,* rattles)* against each other.

5. "The 250-year-old tree *(suffer,* suffers*)* from the complications of old age," *(say,* says*)* county forester Frank Smith, who adds, "It can't adapt to urban stresses."

6. But Smith *(*doesn't,* don't)* want this ancient tree to end up as firewood.

7. When the tree comes down, Smith *(plan,* plans*)* to save two or three slices of the tree's 12-foot trunk for educational purposes.

8. The rings on each cross section of the trunk *(*show,* shows)* the tree's actual age, and dates of historical events will be marked on the preserved slabs.

9. "This tree *(*was,* were)* a seedling when the Native Americans traveled through here, and luckily, they didn't step on it," *(joke,* jokes*)* Smith.

10. Throughout its long life, many people *(has,* have*)* passed this tree—maybe even George Washington, who *(*was,* were)* surveying forestland in the 1750s.

11. Who *(know,* knows*)* who rested under this venerable tree?

12. The territory *(*was,* were)* made a state when the tree reached its 100th birthday.

13. The old path turned into a paved road in the 1950s. Now the combination of age, heavy traffic, and car exhaust *(*is,* are)* putting the tree to rest.

Extend: Make a list of four to six nouns and four verbs. Use the words in your list to write two sentences with singular verbs and subjects and two sentences with plural verbs and subjects.

Subject-Verb Agreement 2 (Delayed & Compound Subjects)

Single subjects need single verbs. Plural subjects need plural verbs. When a subject is *delayed,* or when the subject is compound (joined with *and* or *or*), a writer may have trouble making subjects and verbs agree. Turn to 526.1-526.4 in *Writers INC* for more information.

> **Today there lurks among us an insidious threat.** (delayed subject)

> **Mercy and justice are needed in the classroom.** (compound subject joined with *and*)

> **Either Sarah or Sally is going to the dance with me.** (compound subject joined with *or*)

> **Mumps is a serious health threat again.** (plural noun but singular in meaning)

Underline the incorrect verb in the following sentences and write the correction **above it.**

---

1. The budget and the deadlines is established.
   are

2. The corncobs and the hay is going to be delivered here tonight.
   are

3. This year economics or mathematics are my toughest subject.
   is

4. There was a dozen buttons on the floor yesterday.
   were

5. Blue and green is still my favorite colors.
   are

6. Neither the wood chips nor the paper are catching fire in this rainy weather.
   is

7. The team and the umpires is turning in their uniforms Friday.
   are

8. Is the All Star players going to be named this weekend?
   Are

9. There is some players who will receive a trophy, a letter, and a plaque.
   are

10. Camping with my brothers in the Badlands or visiting New York City with my parents were my favorite vacation.
    was

11. The parents and teachers has contributed their time.
    have

12. Parents, teachers, and students has helped write the school's bylaws.
    have

13. Parents, teachers, or students is planning to distribute the flyers.
    are

14. Both my grades and my friendships needs more of my attention.
    need

Subject-Verb Agreement 3
(Indefinite Pronouns & Collective Nouns)

When used as a subject, some indefinite pronouns (*some, most, all*) may be either singular or plural. It depends on whether the object in the prepositional phrase that comes after the pronoun is singular or plural. Also, collective nouns (*team, crowd, pair*) may be either singular or plural. It depends on whether the collective noun refers to a group as a unit or refers to individuals in the group. Turn to 527.1-527.2 in *Writers INC* for more information.

Circle the verb that agrees with the subject in the following sentences.

1. A few of the American colonial laws (*was,* *were*) rejected by British officials, causing resentment in the colonies.

2. "British parliament (*has,* *have*) too much control over us," the colonists complained.

3. "That government (*do,* *does*) not have the right to rule us!"

4. "People of the colonies (*is,* *are*) getting weary of taxation without representation," they lamented.

5. The populace of the American colonies (*was,* *were*) further upset when it heard the British Parliament (*was,* *were*) going to tax sugar and molasses in the American colonies.

6. In Boston, citizens harassed the British soldiers, and the army troop at the Custom House (*was,* *were*) a favorite target.

7. When the Second Continental Congress met in 1775, colonial minutemen (*was,* *were*) battling with British forces.

8. The colonial army (*was,* *were*) 14,500 men strong when Washington wrote, "The men would fight very well . . . although they are an exceeding[ly] dirty and nasty people."

9. At Boston High, the faculty (*is,* *are*) lucky to have in its reference library a collection of letters written by famous Americans.

Review: Subject-Verb Agreement

> **Circle** the verb that agrees with the subject in the following sentences.

1. There *(is, are)* many interesting facts about each United States president.

2. Many presidents *(was, were)* soldiers or *(was, were)* involved in wars, but only three *(was, were)* graduates of military academies.

3. Andrew Johnson and Bill Clinton *(is, are)* the only two presidents who *(has, have)* been tried for impeachment. Neither *(was, were)* removed from office.

4. Scissors *(was, were)* a handy tool for Andrew Johnson. He *(was, were)* trained as a tailor and made his own clothes. Mathematics *(was, were)* a hobby for James Garfield. News *(was, were)* publisher Warren Harding's chief interest, and medicine *(was, were)* studied by William Henry Harrison.

5. The herd of horses in George Washington's stables *(was, were)* a pampered bunch; they had their teeth brushed every morning—perhaps because Washington had no teeth of his own. Some of his many sets of dentures *(was, were)* made of cow teeth, hippo teeth, and human teeth. Others *(was, were)* fashioned from ivory and lead. Contrary to legend, none of the teeth *(was, were)* made of wood.

6. A flock of sheep *(was, were)* seen grazing on the White House lawn during Woodrow Wilson's term. The wool *(was, were)* sold to raise money for the Red Cross during World War I.

7. *(Is, Are)* anyone amazed by President Taft's bathtub? Weighing more than 300 pounds, he used a bathtub big enough for four people.

8. *James (was, were)* the first name of six presidents.

9. Here is one of those facts that *(is, are)* hard to believe. Jimmy Carter *(was, were)* the first president born in a hospital.

Pretest: Pronoun-Antecedent Agreement

Circle the correct pronoun choice in each set of parentheses in the sentences below. Then underline the antecedent or antecedents for each pronoun.

1. Twenty years ago, portable tape players—the first in a long line of portable stereo systems—made (*its, their*) debut in this country.

2. Neither the inventor nor the manufacturers could have guessed how successful (*his, their*) product would be.

3. Shizuo Takashino and other engineers used (*his, their*) expertise to create the first portable tape players.

4. Both of my sisters get upset whenever (*she, they*) can't find (*her, their*) players.

5. In fact, most of the people I know would not think of going on (*their, his or her*) merry way without some kind of portable music.

6. Neither Christina nor Calvin feels fully dressed without (*her or his, their*) personal music player.

7. Each of the men at the barbershop wore (*his, their*) headset while waiting.

8. All personal stereos have changed greatly since (*its, their*) introduction to the public.

9. For one thing, they are now less expensive; (*its, their*) original price was $200.

10. Most of the personal stereos today have (*its, their*) prices set under $50.

11. Carlos and Mark have made hundreds of (*his, their*) own tapes and discs.

12. One of the five players in our house needs (*its, their*) batteries replaced.

Pronoun-Antecedent Agreement 1

Pronouns must agree with their antecedents in number, person, and gender. Turn to page 528 in *Writers INC* for more information. Also review indefinite pronouns at 527.2 and the chart of pronouns on page 504.

> **Underline** any pronoun that does not agree with its antecedent and write the correct pronoun above it.

1. Each of the 54 national parks has <u>their</u> own beauty. *its*

2. Anyone who enjoys watching whales should take <u>their</u> vacation in Maine's *his or her*

   Acadia National Park.

3. None of us could believe <u>their</u> eyes when we spied both a humpback and a *our*

   finback whale.

4. Anybody wishing to see an elk or a bison should drive <u>their</u> car through *his or her*

   Yellowstone National Park.

5. Many motorists hit <u>his or her</u> brakes whenever one of these big beasts shows *their*
   <u>their</u> face near a road. *its*

6. One of the country's most extraordinary parks, known for <u>their</u> wild beauty, is *its*

   Everglades National Park.

7. Nobody should pass up <u>their</u> chance to walk along the Everglades' Anhinga *his or her*

   Trail and see the alligators, snapping turtles, and wading birds.

8. One can easily see how Big Bend National Park earned <u>her</u> name; the park lies *its*

   on the Texas/Mexico border, where the Rio Grande makes one of <u>his</u> big turns. *its*

9. Few are prepared to make <u>his or her</u> trek through Big Bend, because <u>they're</u> *their* *it's*

   one of the most rugged areas in the country.

Extend: Describe a park or another interesting place and explain why people should visit it. Be sure your pronouns agree with their antecedents.

Pronoun-Antecedent Agreement 2

Antecedents joined by *and* are considered plural. Singular antecedents joined by *or* or *nor* take a singular pronoun. When one of the antecedents joined by *or* or *nor* is singular and one is plural, the pronoun must agree with the closer one. Turn to page 528 in *Writers INC*.

Circle the correct pronoun in each set of parentheses in the sentences below.

---

1. In 1804, Meriwether Lewis and William Clark led *(his,* (their)*)* Corps of Discovery into the wilderness.

2. Neither the leaders nor the other men knew what to expect on *(his,* (their)*)* journey.

3. As leaders of the expedition, either Lewis or Clark could have let power go to *(*(his,)* their)* head.

4. But both Lewis and Clark listened carefully to *(his,* (their)*)* sergeants, privates, and interpreters.

5. Neither Lewis nor the sergeants would be able to communicate much with Native Americans on *(his,* (their)*)* travels, so several interpreters were hired.

6. Lewis and Clark kept notes for almost every day of the trip in *(his,* (their)*)* journals.

7. History also shows that either Sergeant Patrick Gass or Sergeant John Ordway wrote in *(*(his,)* their)* own journal.

8. Neither French trapper Toussaint Charbonneau nor his Shoshone wife, Sacagawea, knew how important *(*(his or her,)* their)* particular language skills would be to the expedition.

9. Along the way, neither Lewis nor the men could believe *(his,* (their)*)* eyes as a son was born to Sacagawea.

Extend: Write three sentences about an experiment or a trip. Use *and, or,* and *nor* to join subjects in your sentences. Double-check your pronouns and antecedents for agreement.

Review: Pronoun-Antecedent Agreement

Circle the correct pronoun in each set of parentheses in the sentences below.

1   Many simple inventions have had a great impact. For example, anybody

2 who was an explorer or a soldier during the nineteenth century probably owes

3 (their, *his or her*) survival to Peter Durand. Durand, a British merchant,

4 invented the tin can. (*His,* Her) cans kept fresh foods from spoiling.

5   When Ezra Warner of Connecticut patented the first can opener in 1858,

6 (they, *it*) represented a major breakthrough. Before Warner's invention, people

7 had struggled to open (*their,* his or her) cans of food with a chisel and hammer.

8 However, a person using Warner's invention had to be very careful not to cut off

9 (their, *his or her*) fingers. Then in 1870, William Lyman introduced (*his,* her)

10 can opener, which was far less hazardous. But neither Warner nor Lyman

11 thought about powering (their, *his,* her) can opener with electricity. That

12 wouldn't happen until 1957.

13   During the 1870s another simple product eventually made (his, her, *its*)

14 owner's name famous. William Frisbie baked and sold pies in tin plates. Over

15 the next 80 years, students from nearby Yale University ate (*their,* his or her)

16 pies and then had fun tossing the empty metal tins. When Americans turned

17 (his or her, *their,* her) eyes to the skies to look for flying saucers in the '50s,

18 Walter Frederick designed (their, *his,* her) toy flying saucer. About the same

19 time, Wham-O toy company president Richard Knerr visited Connecticut.

20 When (*he,* she) saw everyone tossing (their, *his or her*) Frisbie pie pans, (she, *he,*

21 they) gave the toy saucer a new name—the Frisbee.

Pretest: Sentence Combining

> **Combine** the short sentences below into longer, more detailed sentences using the methods indicated. Add, delete, or rearrange words as needed.

Answers will vary.

- The homecoming football game started at 2:00 p.m.
- It was a special event.
- Three bands played and marched at halftime in the rain.
- By 3:00 it was pouring rain.
- The huge crowd got very wet.
- Lightning filled the air around 3:30.
- The game had to be called off.

1. Use a series. *The homecoming football game started at 2:00 p.m., the rain began to pour at 3:00, and lightning filled the air around 3:30.*

2. Use a relative pronoun. *The homecoming football game, which started at 2:00 p.m., had to be called off.*

3. Use an introductory clause or phrase. *Because it was pouring rain, the huge crowd got very wet.*

4. Use a participial phrase. *Marching at halftime in the rain, three bands played as the huge crowd got very wet.*

5. Use a semicolon. *By 3:00 it was pouring rain; by 3:30 lightning filled the air.*

6. Use correlative conjunctions. *Not only did the huge crowd get very wet, but the game had to be called off.*

7. Use an appositive (or an appositive phrase). *The special event, the homecoming football game, started at 2:00 p.m.*

8. Use a conjunctive adverb. *The game started at 2:00 p.m.; however, by 3:00 p.m. it was pouring rain.*

Sentence Combining 1

> **Study** the groups of sentences below. Combine each group of sentences using one of the ways demonstrated on page 91 in *Writers INC*. Tell which method you used.

Answers will vary.

1. The film featured several big stars. It used many special effects. It had an elaborate sound track.

The film featured several big stars, used many special effects, and had an elaborate sound track. (series)

2. The film grossed $400 million. It won the Academy Award for best picture.

Not only did the film gross $400 million, but it also won the Academy Award for best picture. (correlative conjunctions)

3. Many scenes were improvised. The actors' skills were tested.

Because many scenes were improvised, the actors' skills were tested. (introductory clause)

4. The director developed his own style. It allowed actors to be creative.

The director developed his own style, a style that allowed actors to be creative. (key word)

5. The movie producer wanted to be historically accurate. The movie producer hired a historian to evaluate the script.

Wanting to be historically accurate, the movie producer hired a historian to evaluate the script. (participial phrase)

6. The film was a critical success. It pleased moviegoers and reviewers alike.

The film, a critical success, pleased moviegoers and reviewers alike. (appositive)

Extend: Write 10 *short* sentences about a topic you are studying. Exchange sentences with a classmate. Combine the shorter sentences into longer, more detailed sentences using as many methods as possible.

Sentence Combining 2

Combining simple ideas into longer sentences provides variety, which is a characteristic of good writing. Study the eight ways to combine sentences on page 91 in *Writers INC*.

> **Combine** the following sentences using the method indicated. (You may have to reword some of the sentences.)

1. **Use a relative pronoun.** Mary Cassatt was a famous American artist. She lived during the nineteenth century.

   Mary Cassatt was a famous American artist who lived during the

   nineteenth century.

2. **Use an introductory phrase and a relative pronoun.** Mary Cassatt attended art school in Philadelphia. She decided to move to Paris. This was unusual for a woman of her time.

   After attending art school in Philadelphia, Mary Cassatt moved

   to Paris, which was unusual for a woman of her time.

3. **Use a semicolon.** While living in Paris, Mary Cassatt befriended many other artists. One of her closest friends was the artist Degás.

   Mary Cassatt befriended many artists while living in Paris; one of

   her closest friends was the artist Degás.

4. **Use a relative pronoun and a series.** Mary Cassatt is greatly admired for her graceful portraits of mothers with children. She is also admired for her peaceful domestic scenes. Scenes from everyday life are her most admired subjects. She is considered the most famous female Impressionist painter.

   Mary Cassatt, who is considered the most famous female

   Impressionist painter, is admired for her graceful portraits of

   mothers with children, her peaceful domestic scenes, and her

   scenes from everyday life.

Combine the following sentences using the method you think will work best.

1. *Little Girl in a Big Straw Hat and Pinafore* is one of Cassatt's best-known paintings. Another is *Mother About to Wash Her Sleepy Child.* A third is *The Mirror.*

   Some of Cassatt's best-known paintings are Little Girl in a Big

   Straw Hat and Pinafore, Mother About to Wash Her Sleepy

   Child, and The Mirror.

2. In 1893, Mary Cassatt was asked to paint a mural for the World's Fair. The World's Fair was held in Chicago. The mural was called *The Modern Woman.* This work helped make Cassatt famous in America.

   The Modern Woman, a mural that Mary Cassatt painted for the

   1893 World's Fair in Chicago, helped make her famous in America.

3. In 1905, Mary Cassatt began to lose her vision. By 1914, she had ceased painting. In 1926, she died at the age of 82.

   In 1905, Mary Cassatt began to lose her vision, in 1914 she had

   ceased painting, and in 1926 she died at the age of 82.

4. Some say that Mary Cassatt is the best-known American female painter. Interestingly, she spent most of her life abroad.

   Some say that Mary Cassatt is the best-known American female

   painter; interestingly, she spent most of her life abroad.

5. Cassatt worked tirelessly to help American collectors buy the finest examples of European art, by masters both old and new. She advised family, friends, and art dealers.

   Advising family, friends, and art dealers, Cassatt worked tirelessly

   to help American collectors buy the finest examples of European

   art, by masters both old and new.

Review: Sentence Combining

Use the ideas listed below, rewording as necessary, to write 10 smooth-reading sentences. Tell which combining method you used to produce each sentence. (You may use an idea more than once.)

Answers will vary.

Thunderstorm Safety
- Reduce the possibility of getting hit by lightning.
- Find shelter in a substantial building.
- Small picnic shelters are unsafe.
- Rain shelters on golf courses are unsafe.
- Get off high ground.
- Move away from tall trees.
- Stay away from large metal objects.
- Get out of the water.
- Do not fly a kite or ride a bike.
- Stay in your vehicle with the windows completely closed.
- Unplug the TV and computer.
- Follow these precautions.

1. *During a thunderstorm, get off high ground, move away from tall trees, and stay away from large metal objects. (series)*

2. *If you follow these precautions, you can reduce the possibility of getting hit by lightning. (introductory clause)*

3. *Both flying a kite and riding a bike are dangerous during a thunderstorm. (correlative conjunctions)*

4. *Find shelter in a substantial building; small picnic shelters and rain shelters on golf courses are unsafe. (semicolon)*

5. *Follow these precautions, which will reduce the possibility of getting hit by lightning. (relative pronoun)*

6. Move away from tall trees, away from water, away from any large metal objects. (key word)

_____

7. Getting off high ground, an important precaution, reduces the possibility of getting hit by lightning. (appositive)

_____

8. To reduce the possibility of getting hit by lightning, you should follow these safety precautions. (introductory phrase)

_____

9. If you want to reduce the possibility of getting hit by lightning, get out of the water and stay away from large metal objects. (introductory clause)

10. Following these precautions, you can reduce the possibility of getting hit by lightning. (participial phrase)

_____

Pretest: Sentence Problems

Label the problems in the following sentences. Use *F* for fragment, *CS* for comma splice, *RO* for run-on sentence, *RAMB* for rambling sentence, *WORDY* for wordiness, and *MM* for misplaced modifiers.

_____*F*_____ **1.** Only about 76 million Americans.

_____*F*_____ **2.** In the United States in 1900.

*WORDY* **3.** About 20 percent of the Americans had arrived, or you might prefer to say just gotten off the boat, between 1890 and 1900.

*RAMB* **4.** William McKinley was assassinated in 1901, and then Theodore Roosevelt became president, and that was the same year that Queen Victoria died, and she had served Britain for more than 60 years.

_____*RO*_____ **5.** Theodore Roosevelt was a highly energetic man he liked action and the great outdoors.

_____*CS*_____ **6.** During Roosevelt's administration, the Panama Canal was built, the national park system was established.

_____*F*_____ **7.** A rickety-looking contraption that Orville and Wilbur Wright actually flew for 59 seconds in 1903 at Kitty Hawk, North Carolina.

_____*CS*_____ **8.** The year 1903 was also the year of the first World Series, Boston won five games against Pittsburgh.

*RAMB* **9.** The 1904 World's Fair was in St. Louis, and the public saw the coming wonders of the world, and electricity was one one of them, and they saw airplanes and other gadgets.

_____*MM*_____ **10.** Consuming huge quantities of ice cream and hot dogs, the fast-food industry may have been started by the fairgoers.

Correct the problem sentences above by rewriting each, in the best possible way, on the lines below.

Answers will vary.

1. *Only about 76 million Americans lived in the United States in 1900.*

2. *In 1900, only about 76 million Americans lived in the United States.*

3. About 20 percent of the Americans had arrived between 1890 and 1900.

4. After William McKinley was assassinated in 1901, Theodore Roosevelt became president. That was the same year that Queen Victoria died after serving Britain for more than 60 years.

5. Theodore Roosevelt, a highly energetic man, liked action and the great outdoors.

6. During Roosevelt's administration, the Panama Canal was built, and the national park system was established.

7. Orville and Wilbur Wright actually flew a rickety-looking contraption for 59 seconds in 1903 at Kitty Hawk, North Carolina.

8. The year 1903 was also the year of the first World Series in which Boston won five games against Pittsburgh.

9. At the 1904 World's Fair in St. Louis, the public saw the coming wonders of the world—electricity, airplanes, and other gadgets.

10. Consuming huge quantities of ice cream and hot dogs, fairgoers may have started the fast-food industry.

Identifying Sentence Fragments

A *fragment* is a group of words incorrectly used as a sentence. Because it lacks a subject, a verb, or another key element, the thought is incomplete. Turn to page 83 in *Writers INC*.

> **Read** the following sentence fragments. In the space provided, write "missing a subject," "missing a verb," or "does not convey a complete thought," whichever is true. (Hint: Dependent clauses do not convey complete thoughts.)

1. while I was sleeping _does not convey a complete thought_

2. the rising sun _missing a verb_

3. brought the dawn _missing a subject_

4. birds in the trees _missing a verb_

5. sang their songs _missing a subject_

6. didn't like the bird songs _missing a subject_

7. pulled the covers over my head _missing a subject_

8. didn't want to hear the tweet, tweet, tweet _missing a subject_

9. when the birds annoyed me _does not convey a complete thought_

> **Label** each group of words below as either a **sentence** or a **fragment**. Add end punctuation when needed.

fragment **1.** The moon rising

sentence **2.** The sun rose.

fragment **3.** When the moon was rising

fragment **4.** The light shining on the water

sentence **5.** Did the light shimmer and glisten?

fragment **6.** As the wind whispered

fragment **7.** Across the water and through the trees

Extend: Use the nine fragments at the top of this page to write a paragraph. Make sure you turn all the fragments into complete sentences.

Fixing Sentence Fragments 1

Sentence fragments may sound like complete sentences, but they are missing one or more of the three essential sentence ingredients: a subject, a verb, or the expression of a complete thought. Turn to page 83 in *Writers INC*.

Label the following with **S** for sentence or **F** for fragment. Use your imagination and the information in the exercise to correct the fragments.

Answers will vary.

___F___ **1.** The Elizabethan theater of Shakespeare's day very different from today's modern theater.

The Elizabethan theater of Shakespeare's day was very

different from today's modern theater.

___F___ **2.** Often involves formal clothing and tickets purchased well in advance.

Today, going to the theater often involves formal clothing

and tickets purchased well in advance.

___F___ **3.** Evening shows in darkened auditoriums with comfortable seating.

Evening shows are performed in darkened auditoriums with

comfortable seating.

___S___ **4.** Elizabethan plays originally were performed in open-air theaters during daylight hours—a practice some Shakespeare companies continue today.

_____

_____

___F___ **5.** Bought tickets moments before the show for a penny apiece.

Theatergoers bought tickets moments before the show for a

penny apiece.

___F___ **6.** The audience sitting on the ground and even on the stage.

The audience sat on the ground and even on the stage.

_____

Fixing Sentence Fragments 2

> **Expand** and edit each fragment to create a complete sentence. Turn to page 83 in *Writers INC* for assistance.

1. after I exercised in the weight room

After I exercised in the weight room, I swam laps in the pool.

2. worn-out from studying for the test

The class was worn-out from studying for the test.

3. to have faith in yourself

To have faith in yourself gives you self-confidence.

4. because the room was so dark

The little children were scared because the room was so dark.

5. in order to save money

In order to save money, I don't buy CD's or videos anymore.

6. editing the final draft of her essay

Editing the final draft of her essay, Lisa realized she hadn't used

the spell checker.

7. a popular writer

Stephen King, a popular writer, appeals to various age groups.

Extend: Use one of your sentences above as the topic sentence for a first draft of a paragraph. Include details as explained on page 99 in *Writers INC.* (Make sure your paragraph does not contain any fragments.)

Fixing Comma Splices

A *comma splice* results when two independent clauses are connected ("spliced") with only a comma. The comma is not enough. A period, a semicolon, a comma with a coordinating conjunction (*and, but, or . . .*), or a semicolon and a conjunctive adverb (*however, moreover, besides . . .*) must be used. The more closely related the sentences are to one another, the more appropriate it is to use a semicolon; a semicolon emphasizes this relationship. Turn to page 84 in *Writers INC* for an example.

> **Fix** the comma splices in the following sentences. Use one of the methods mentioned above.

Answers may vary.

1. I really wanted to see a movie on Sunday, **but** my parents made me go weed-whack at Grandma's instead.

2. My dog hates going to the groomer **;** she won't get out of the car without a panting, slobbering struggle.

3. The park has picnic tables and shade canopies now **. W** we can go there for our picnic on Saturday afternoon.

4. Thanks for finally putting away your clothes **; however,** you tracked mud up the stairs when you did it.

5. There are now environmentally safe household cleaners **;** they're made out of vegetable by-products.

6. I could stop at the store on my way home, **or** you could shop for me.

7. The red splotches on my legs turned out to be a heat rash **. I** I got it from the space heater that my teacher uses in the classroom.

8. My mom wants Karen to go to medical school **; instead,** she has applied to the Arizona Institute for Disc Jockeys.

9. I pulled a muscle in my leg while moving a piano, **so** I couldn't participate in the walkathon this year.

Extend: With a classmate, write five sentences that are "spliced" together with commas. Then decide the best method to fix each sentence.

Revising Run-On Sentences

A *run-on sentence* is actually two or more sentences combined without the proper use of punctuation or conjunctions. Turn to page 84 in *Writers INC* for an example.

> **Correct** each run-on sentence. Add a semicolon, or a semicolon with a conjunctive adverb, or a comma with a coordinating conjunction to correct some sentences. Others will need to be broken into two sentences. (Select the best method.) One sentence is correct as written.

Answers may vary.

1. Border, airport, and seaport checks become top priority when preventing the
transportation of illegal drugs and explosives. Employing the help of animals has
become common police policy.

2. In the battle against drugs, narcotics traffickers outnumber police officers; however, the
police have a special weapon: drug-sniffing dogs.

3. With smell receptors 100 times more powerful than those of humans, dogs such
as labradors, collies, and spaniels make excellent search dogs.

4. One 12-week training course teaches a dog to recognize smells. A dog trainer,
also called a handler, places a sample of the smell in a training aid made from
a newspaper, a rolled-up rag, or some other object.

5. The handler hides the training aid and asks the dog to bring it back; he rewards
the dog with treats or affection for a successful retrieval.

6. The training aid changes regularly, but the sample smell remains the same, so the
dog can recognize drugs and explosives no matter where they're hidden.

7. Eventually other scents, such as perfumes, are added. This allows the dogs to
find the drugs even when criminals try to disguise the scent.

8. Highly trained dogs can recognize 12 types of explosives and 4 types of drugs.
The dogs are never fooled by people's tricks or disguises.

Extend: Choose one of the run-on sentences above and see how many different ways you can correct it. You can use a comma and a conjunction or change punctuation, or even rewrite a clause into a phrase, but be sure to retain the basic meaning of the sentence.

Revising Rambling Sentences

Trying to pack too many ideas into one sentence can lead to confusion. Rambling sentences often result from the overuse of *and*'s. To correct rambling sentences, remove some of the *and*'s or other conjunctions that allow the sentence to go on and on. Then fix the punctuation, and reword some parts, if necessary, to produce a better passage. Turn to page 84 in *Writers INC.*

> **Improve** the rambling sentences by removing unnecessary *and*'s. Add punctuation where necessary.

Answers will vary.

1. The Robinson family was poor but athletic. So Jackie Robinson played college sports. But on a scholarship, and his brother, Mack, finished second in the 1936 Olympic 200-meter race, behind Jesse Owens.

2. The year 1945 proved to be a time ripe for breaking the race barrier in major-league baseball. Some sportswriters supported talented Negro League players, and minority voters applied political pressure. The Boston Red Sox even held a tryout for minorities.

3. Branch Rickey saw racism in baseball firsthand as a college coach and later when he became president of the Brooklyn Dodgers. He set out to break the race barrier by recruiting from the Negro League.

4. A Dodger scout brought Jackie Robinson to the head office. That is where Mr. Rickey uttered one of his most famous lines. He said, "I'm looking for a ballplayer with guts enough not to fight back."

5. The interview lasted three hours. Rickey needed that time to convince Robinson to sign with the Dodgers, and he also needed to let him know exactly how difficult it would be for a black player in a white league. Rickey said perhaps he and Robinson could open the doors of the major leagues to all players.

Review: Sentence Problems 1

> **Label** the types of sentence problems below. Use *F* for a sentence fragment, *R* for a rambling sentence, and *RO* for a run-on sentence.   Rewrite the four sentences where lines are provided.

Answers will vary.

__RO__ **1.** The Korean War began on June 25, 1950, troops from North Korea invaded South Korea.

The Korean War began on June 25, 1950, when North Korean

troops invaded South Korea.

__RO__ **2.** The United Nations Security Council demanded that North Korean troops retreat the troops ignored the demand.

__R__ **3.** Sixteen countries sent troops to South Korea and forty-one countries sent supplies and the United States provided most of the troops and supplies.

Sixteen countries sent troops to South Korea; forty-one

countries sent supplies. The United States provided most

of the troops and supplies.

__F__ **4.** General Douglas MacArthur commander in chief of the Allied forces.

__R__ **5.** MacArthur believed that there was no substitute for total victory and President Truman feared that MacArthur's use of "all-out measures" might lead to a third world war and he relieved MacArthur of his command in April 1951.

MacArthur believed that there was no substitute for total

victory. President Truman feared that MacArthur's use of

"all-out measures" might lead to a third world war, so he

relieved MacArthur of his command in April 1951.

__F__ **6.** Truce talks from July 1951 until October 1952 without a settlement.

Truce talks took place from July of 1951 until October of

1952 without a settlement.

Misplaced Modifiers

When a modifier is placed incorrectly, it can change or confuse the meaning of a sentence. Turn to a humorous example of a misplaced modifier on page 86 in *Writers INC*.

> **Circle** the misplaced modifier in each of the following sentences. Draw an arrow from the misplaced modifier to the word(s) it should modify. One sentence is correct.

1. The surf crested, and the beach bustled with people (over 15 feet high.)

2. Yelling "Surf's up!" Ethan grabbed his board (with an excited grin) and headed for the water at a full sprint.

3. Hawaii always offers the perfect waves (with its tropical atmosphere) for surfing enthusiasts from the mainland.

4. However, the local surfers don't always appreciate foreigners on vacation surfing at the pristine beaches.

5. Ethan steered clear of the locals (paddling in another direction.)

6. He finally reached the seaward side of the breaking waves (with aching arms,) and paddled back toward shore as a big wave approached.

7. The wave swamped Ethan and rocketed him toward the shore (rolling with incredible strength.)

8. Luckily, Ethan had used a special wax to prepare his board (that was expensive but very sticky.)

9. The breathtaking ride was the highlight of the morning and ended too soon (on the neon-orange surfboard.)

10. (A place with top-notch beaches,) Ethan expected Hawaii to have great surfing, and he wasn't disappointed.

Extend: Misplaced modifiers are often funny. Look around your classroom and briefly list some of the details you observe. Use your list to compose three "misplaced modifier jokes." Example: *The teacher has a stack of detention slips for late students sitting on her desk.*

Dangling Modifiers

When a modifying phrase or clause does not clearly and sensibly modify a word in a sentence, the result is called a dangling modifier. Dangling modifiers may be difficult to recognize in your own writing, but they are often easy to fix. Turn to page 86 in *Writers INC*.

> **Underline** the dangling modifiers in the examples below and then rewrite the sentences.

Answers may vary.

1. Blasting hot water and steam 100 feet into the air, the park ranger showed us Old Faithful.

The park ranger showed us Old Faithful blasting hot water and

steam 100 feet into the air.

2. Three bears were spotted driving on Yellowstone National Park's twisting roads.

While driving on Yellowstone National Park's twisting roads, we

spotted three bears.

3. If lost in the forest, the sun can be used to determine direction.

If lost in the forest, you can use the sun to determine direction.

4. Erupting every 76 minutes, our tour guide explained the origin of the geyser's name, Old Faithful.

Our tour guide explained that, because the geyser erupts every 76

minutes, it was named Old Faithful.

5. Having never missed an eruption in 80 years, Yellowstone National Park attracts over a million tourists each year to see Old Faithful.

Having never missed an eruption in 80 years, Old Faithful attracts

over a million tourists each year to Yellowstone National Park.

6. While exploring Yellowstone, buffalo can often be seen on the road.

While exploring Yellowstone, tourists often see buffalo on the road.

Wordiness & Deadwood

The best writing is often simple writing. Wordiness and deadwood rob sentences of their clarity and simplicity without adding any significant meaning. Turn to pages 87 and 88 in *Writers INC.*

> **Rewrite** the sentences below, removing wordiness and deadwood.

Answers will vary.

1. To this day, today's historians are at a loss, unable to pinpoint the exact origin of the yo-yo, leaving the birth of the yo-yo a mystery.

Historians cannot pinpoint the origin of the yo-yo.

2. It's generally accepted by most historians that the earliest records of the first yo-yos date back to ancient China, 2,500 years ago.

The earliest records of yo-yos date back 2,500 years to ancient

China.

3. These Chinese yo-yos were basic toys with a crude design and made of common, everyday materials like wood and rock that were readily available.

Chinese yo-yos were crudely designed and made of materials like

wood and rock.

4. Paintings on Greek urns from 500 B.C.E. record the historical journey of the yo-yo, depicting ancient Greeks playing with yo-yos, continuing the yo-yo's legacy.

Paintings on Greek urns from 500 B.C.E. depict people playing with

yo-yos.

5. As the story goes, legends speak of Philippine hunters sitting in trees using yo-yos as hunting weapons on animals below, but in these skeptical times historians dispute the accuracy of such dubious stories.

Legends speak of Philippine hunters using yo-yos as weapons.

6. After all this time, throughout history, this simple toy still gives simple pleasure to millions even in this age of computer games and television.

Even in this age of computer games and television, this simple toy

still gives pleasure to millions.

Unparallel Construction 1

Parallel structuring is the repetition of similar words, phrases, or clauses. Inconsistent (unparallel) construction occurs when the kinds of words, phrases, or clauses change in the middle of a sentence. Turn to pages 90, 129, and 432 in *Writers INC*.

> **Underline** the parallel parts in the following sentences. On the lines, write the type of word or word group that is repeated in each sentence, explaining what is similar about them.

1. The driver was squeezing the steering wheel, watching oncoming traffic, and driving on the shoulder of the road.

    phrases beginning with the same verb form (-ing).

2. Rubiel likes boxing, swimming, and wrestling.

    gerunds

3. Annie likes Khono's optimism, Bob's cheerfulness, and Jan's helpfulness.

    possessive names with nouns

4. To pass this class you need to study, to think, and to remember.

    infinitives

5. Our team scored early, but faltered badly in the second half.

    past tense verbs followed by adverbs

6. Taking a test is simple; passing it is hard.

    similar clauses, each having a gerund subject linked by the verb is

    to a predicate adjective

7. Three of the most intelligent subhuman primates are the chimpanzee, the orangutan, and the baboon.

    nouns modified by the same article (the)

8. Jackie, a Chacma baboon, was probably the only monkey in history to become a corporal in the army and to earn a war medal.

    infinitive phrases

Extend: Demonstrate your understanding of parallel construction by writing three to five sentences about humans and primates. Use parallel forms in each sentence, and underline each set as you did above.

Unparallel Construction 2

Inconsistent (unparallel) construction occurs when the kinds of words or phrases being used change in the middle of a sentence. Turn to pages 90 and 129 in *Writers INC*.

> **Fill in** the blanks with words that make sense and are parallel in form.

Answers will vary.

1. My English teacher is not only generous with his free time, but he is also _____ _generous with his praise._

2. John had to decide whether to keep the wallet or _to give it back._

3. My mom thinks rap music would be better if _it were less vulgar_ and if _it were easier to understand._

4. For our holiday, my family decided to _stay home_ , _grill hamburgers_ , _and play games._

5. On Saturday morning I plan to _sleep late_ and _watch cartoons._

6. Both _a music program_ and _a new gymnasium_ would benefit my school.

7. To be computer literate, you should _use current software_ and _read computer magazines._

8. Neither _music_ nor _jokes_ could cure Brad's bad mood.

9. Starting with the very first day of school, I found that I _enjoyed_ _studying history_ and _despised_ _studying Latin._

Extend: Find two or three examples of parallelism in a magazine, a textbook, or another book you are reading. Share your samples with a classmate. Discuss what constructions are repeated in order to achieve the parallelism.

Review: Sentence Problems 2

> **Look** for misplaced and dangling modifiers, wordiness, and unparallel constructions in the following sentences. Rewrite each sentence, rewording parts if necessary.

Answers may vary.

1. Falling nearly 1,430 feet, Yosemite National Park contains the highest waterfall in the United States.

Falling nearly 1,430 feet, the highest waterfall in the United

States is located in Yosemite National Park.

2. My dad says there are often super-perfect, wonderfully good reasons for most and maybe almost all of the school rules.

My dad says there are good reasons for most of the school rules.

3. To be a true couch potato, you need a remote control, a couch would help, and lots of food, too.

To be a true couch potato, you need a remote control, a couch,

and lots of food.

4. Try to arrive on time and not be late.

Try to arrive on time.

5. Mom fixed several snacks for the children filled with healthful ingredients.

Mom fixed several healthful snacks for the children.

6. Buried during the avalanche, the dog rescued the skier.

The dog rescued the skier who was buried during the avalanche.

7. That painting is my favorite piece in the entire gallery with the fluorescent colors.

That painting with the fluorescent colors is my favorite piece in the entire gallery.

8. One of the things I enjoy is learning something new, but I also like to ski like I've been shot out of a cannon, and I like snooping in vintage clothing stores.

I enjoy learning something new, skiing like I've been shot out of a cannon, and snooping in vintage clothing stores.

9. Are you one of those people who take forever to say something and you just can't seem to find anyplace to stop once you get started and you take too long to make your point?

Are you one of those people who take forever to say something?

10. The textbook had many pictures, some maps, and you could look up words in the glossary.

The textbook had many pictures, some maps, and a glossary.

11. If you could talk with a famous politician and if you could have dinner with a favorite author and if to spend a day with a movie star is your dream, which three people would you choose?

If you could talk with a famous politician, have dinner with a favorite author, and spend a day with a movie star, which three people would you choose?

Pretest: Shifts in Construction

> **Edit** the sentences below, correcting shifts in construction (number, tense, person, and voice). Underline each incorrect word and write the correct word above it. *Note:* If subjects of sentences change (for example, from singular to plural), change the verbs to agree with their subjects.

1. In a recent poll, 30 percent of the people said they were happy, 60 percent said
   were
   they <u>are</u> pretty happy, and only 10 percent <u>says</u> they <u>are</u> unhappy.
   said   were

2. Nobody polled teens or <u>ask</u> <u>him or her</u> how they <u>feel</u> about the subject.
   asked them   felt

3. Of course, sad things happen, and everybody <u>had</u> bad days.
   has

4. For example, when you have a cold, when <u>a pop quiz was failed</u>, or when you
   you fail a pop quiz
   find your favorite shirt chewed up by your dog, <u>a person</u> probably <u>isn't</u> going to
   you   aren't
   be happy.

5. Many people exercise to improve how <u>he or she</u> <u>feels</u> physically, which affects
   they   feel
   how they <u>felt</u> mentally.
   feel

6. To get the greatest benefits from exercise, a person must exercise after <u>they</u>
   he or she
   properly <u>warm</u> up.
   warms

7. Happy people have learned to accept and to forgive <u>herself</u> and others.
   themselves
   <u>He or she</u> <u>has</u> learned to set realistic goals.
   They   have

8. A happy person is often one who makes others happy, and <u>they</u> often <u>have</u> lots
   he or she   has
   of friends.

9. What goals, dreams, and wishes do you believe will make you happy when <u>one</u>
   you
   <u>is</u> an adult? What simple things make you happy?
   are

10. I am happy when I laugh at a joke, when I read a book, when <u>a friend is</u>
    I hug
    <u>hugged by me</u>, or when <u>you</u> feel the sun on <u>your</u> face.
    a friend   I   my

Shifts in Verb Tense 1

Verbs that describe actions happening at the same time should be kept in the same tense. Turn to page 90 in *Writers INC*.

> **Underline** the verb that shifts tense improperly and write the correction above it. The desired tense is shown in parentheses at the end of each sentence.

1. While rain fell inland, the sun is shining on the coast. *(past)* [*shone*]

2. The plane made an emergency landing in a valley, and the crew waits for the rescue team. *(past)* [*waited*]

3. When the bell rings, the students fled the classroom. *(present)* [*flee*]

4. I will call you so you will have known when to pick me up. *(future)* [*will know*]

5. The horses bolted, and the race begins. *(past)* [*began*]

6. Because the days are so hot, the nights felt cooler. *(present)* [*feel*]

7. My writing group evaluates each piece of writing and will suggest changes. *(present)* [*suggests*]

8. Because the doorbell rings so infrequently, Mary hurried to see who it was. *(past)* [*rang*]

9. Jill read the book, and she enjoys it. *(past)* [*enjoyed*]

10. I did my homework and find it very difficult. *(past)* [*found*]

11. My writing almost always has some sentence problems that will include fragments. *(present)* [*include*]

12. If a runner does not pace herself, she will become exhausted and will lost the race. *(future)* [*lose*]

13. I realized you were ill, so I will call the nurse. *(past)* [*called*]

14. Soon the buzzer will sound, and then we stopped working. *(future)* [*will stop*]

15. We returned to the airport and are looking for our luggage. *(past)* [*looked*]

Extend: Rewrite the first two sentences in this exercise so that all the verbs are (1) present tense, and (2) future tense.

Shifts in Verb Tense 2

Verbs that describe actions happening at the same time should be kept in the same tense. Turn to page 90 in *Writers INC*.

> **Circle** the verb that correctly avoids a shift in tense.

1. The chef went to the market and *(buys,* (bought)*)* fresh vegetables.

2. When he hit the home run, he (*(tied,)* *will tie)* the score.

3. He hits the home run, and the crowd ((goes,) *went)* crazy!

4. Hopefully he will hit a home run, and we ((will win,) *won)* the series.

5. Please clean your shoes off before you ((come,) *have come)* in.

6. I have cleaned my shoes, so I ((have followed,) *followed)* your wishes.

7. It rained gently at first, so we *(keep,* (kept)*)* the windows open.

8. You wash our clothes and ((scrub,) *will scrub)* the floors.

9. Keeping his head down, Syd slid into the vacant seat and *(waits,* (waited)*)*.

10. The wind banged the shutters, the wolves *(howl,* (howled)*),* and Sharien ((felt,) *feels)* a shiver run up and down her spine.

11. She works full-time at the bank and ((runs,) *ran)* a pet-walking service, too.

12. The plane takes off and everyone ((cheers,) *cheered)*.

13. While fireworks lit up the sky, music *(fills,* (filled)*)* the stadium.

14. Play that song for your recital and ((choose,) *chose)* another for the concert.

15. Fabien spoke at our meeting before he ((left,) *leaves)*.

16. I will finish my project, and then I *(went,* (will go)*)* home.

17. Ms. Kilty baked pies for the bake sale, but we *(eat,* (ate)*)* them.

18. They cleaned the kitchen before they *(go,* (went)*)* home.

Extend: Rewrite the last three sentences in this exercise. Change the tense of the first verb in each sentence so that the word in parentheses that you did *not* choose works.

Pronoun Shifts 1

Shifts in construction often involve the improper use of pronouns. One of the most common errors, shift in number, is moving from third-person singular to third-person plural, or vice versa. Turn to page 90, the chart on page 506, and 528.1 in *Writers INC*.

> **A *person* needs *their* privacy.**
> (incorrect shift: *person* is singular and *their* is plural)

> **A *person* needs *his or her* privacy.**
> (correct: *person* and *his or her* are both singular)

Underline the words in the following sentences that represent a shift. Fix each shift by writing the correct pronoun above the error. (You may need to change other words to make the sentence completely correct.)

1. A pioneer needed to ration their supplies wisely.
   his or her

2. After freezing nights in the mountains, many longed for his or her homes back east.
   their

3. Everyone ought to think beyond the pay scale when they choose a career path.
   he or she chooses

4. A wise counselor once said, "Determined, focused students can blend his or her dreams with practical pursuits."
   their

5. "Anyone can learn to do calculus," boasted Marshall, "if they work at it."
   he or she works

6. Jack and Todd finished his work early.
   their

7. Both Sarah and Emily biked 110 miles to raise her share of donations for the American Lung Association.
   their

8. Neither of Paul's parents likes their eggs poached.
   his or her

9. Students are naturally very concerned about his or her environments and social conditions.
   their

10. Anyone concerned about the future of the environment needs to do their homework and become involved.
    his or her

Extend: Carefully read 530.1 in *Writers INC*. Reword the sentences in this exercise that use *his or her*. Make the pronouns and their antecedents plural instead.

Pronoun Shifts 2

Personal pronouns are either first, second, or third person. Indefinite pronouns such as *one* are all third person. Shifting from a second-person pronoun to a third-person pronoun or noun antecedent—or vice versa—is a common error. Turn to page 90, 505.2, and the chart on page 506 in *Writers INC*.

> **> *You* must drink water regularly or *one* will dehydrate.**
> (incorrect shift: *you* is second person and *one* is third person)

> **> *You* must drink water regularly or *you* will dehydrate.**
> (correct: both elements are second person)

> **> *Athletes* must drink water regularly or *they* will dehydrate.**
> (correct: both elements are third person)

Underline the words in the following sentences that represent a shift in person. Fix each shift by writing the correct pronoun above the error. (You may need to change other words to make the sentence completely correct.)

---

1. When <u>you</u> think of what that family endured, <u>one</u> can only shudder.   *you*

2. If <u>you</u> love to write, draw, paint, and act, <u>people</u> should probably not go into   *you*

   accounting.

3. You've entered the kitchen and spied the pie of <u>one's</u> dreams!   *your*

4. <u>One</u> naturally think~~s~~, or hope~~s~~, that the pie is for <u>you</u>.   *You*

5. Before feasting, <u>you</u> realize that this treat could ruin <u>one's</u> diet. "Oh, well," <u>one</u>   *your*   *you*

   sigh~~s~~.

6. Calculus can either stretch <u>one's</u> brain or burn out <u>your</u> circuits.   *your*

7. The soccer <u>team</u> knows that <u>you</u> can rest only after giving 100 percent to the   *they*

   game.

8. The <u>students</u> quickly realized that <u>you</u> needed patience to survive the class.   *they*

9. The <u>girls</u> went to the outlet mall because <u>you</u> needed new basketball shoes.   *they*

10. Most <u>people</u> like strawberry licorice better than <u>you</u> like the original black   *they*

    licorice.

Extend: Explain in your own words what a pronoun shift is and how a writer can correct a shift.

Shifts in Verb & Pronoun Construction

The careful writer must avoid shifting (changing) from one person, tense, number, or voice to another in the same sentence. Turn to page 90 in *Writers INC*.

> **Circle** the verb and pronoun shifts in each of the sentences below. **Rewrite each sentence on the lines provided. Watch for shifts in person, tense, number, and voice.**

1. Mark Twain grew up in Hannibal, Missouri, before he (moves) to St. Louis, New York City, and Philadelphia to work as a printer.

   Mark Twain grew up in Hannibal, Missouri, before he moved to St.

   Louis, New York City, and Philadelphia to work as a printer.

2. While on a voyage to Europe, Twain saw a painting of a girl named Olivia; upon seeing the picture, he (falls) in love with her and later (was married to her.)

   While on a voyage to Europe, Twain saw a painting of a girl named

   Olivia; upon seeing the picture, he fell in love with her and later

   married her.

3. The couple had four children; however, (he) lost (his) only son to a childhood disease.

   The couple had four children; however, they lost their only son to a

   childhood disease.

4. In 1870, Twain and (their) family moved to Connecticut where (his two most popular novels, *Tom Sawyer* and *Huckleberry Finn*, were written.)

   In 1870, Twain and his family moved to Connecticut where he wrote

   his two most popular novels, Tom Sawyer and Huckleberry Finn.

5. In the first of Twain's great novels, Tom Sawyer tricks a friend into whitewashing a fence for him and even (convinced) the friend to pay for the privilege.

   In the first of Twain's great novels, Tom Sawyer tricks a friend into

   whitewashing a fence for him and even convinces the friend to pay

   for the privilege.

Extend: Carefully examine a piece of your writing. Correct any shifts that you find.

Review: Shifts in Construction

Fill in the blanks. This is knowledge you need in order to avoid shifts in construction.

1. Gender indicates whether a pronoun is masculine, _____*feminine*_____, or neuter.

2. List three masculine pronouns: _____*he*_____ , _____*him*_____ , _____*his*_____ .

3. List two neuter pronouns: _____*it*_____ , _____*its*_____ .

4. _____*First*_____ person pronouns are used in place of the name of the speaker or speakers.

5. _____*Second*_____ person pronouns are used to name the person or persons spoken to.

6. _____*Third*_____ person pronouns are used to name the person or thing spoken about.

7. The _____*number*_____ of a pronoun refers to whether the pronoun is singular or plural.

8. Three examples of plural pronouns are _____*our*_____ , _____*they*_____ , and _____*them*_____ .

9. Three examples of singular pronouns are _____*I*_____ , _____*he*_____ , and _____*you*_____ .

10. A paragraph or longer piece of writing should use a dominant verb _____*tense*_____ : present, past, future, present perfect, past perfect, or future perfect.

11. A _____*verb (tense)*_____ shift is acceptable in a sentence (or paragraph) that states one action as happening before another action.

12. The verbs in this sentence—*I see you cleaned your room*—shift appropriately from _____*present*_____ to _____*past*_____ tense.

13. In this sentence—*Patrick shot the basketball and grabs the rebound before his brother had tied his shoelaces*—the three verb tenses shift from ___*past*___, to ___*present*___, to ___*past perfect*___.

14. Rewrite the sentence in question #13 to correct the shift in verb tense. ___*Patrick shot the basketball and grabbed the rebound before his brother tied his shoelaces.*___

15. In this sentence—*Our new puppy is going to obedience classes and desirable behaviors are being learned by him*—the voice shifts from ___*active*___ to ___*passive*___.

16. Rewrite sentence #16 so that the voice is consistent. ___*Our new puppy is going to obedience classes and learning desirable behaviors.*___

Draw one line under the personal pronouns that shift and two lines under the verbs that shift unnecessarily. Above each pronoun and verb, write the appropriate form, or cross out any unnecessary helping verb.

---

1   Blu-It was a "real" cattle dog. You couldn't keep him out of the cattle pens.
    He   *wanted*   *his*
2   She always wants to help. One part of his name came from her breed—Blue
                                                        started
3   Heeler. The other part he ~~has~~ earned. And he starts earning his title two
4   minutes after he arrived. Although a baby himself, he felt it was his duty to
                                          were
5   "herd" my little sisters whenever they are outside. He'd nip at their heels to
6   keep them in a little group. He'd get between them and the house so they
                                     grew
7   couldn't go inside. They have grown afraid of him. Dad made Blu a nice
                             ate
8   kennel, but he eats through the wire in several hours. Mother also grew afraid,
                   made
9   so Dad makes another pen under the kitchen window. Mom could open the
                                               his
10   window and drop Blu's food into her pen. It took him about three days to dig
                          said
11   out. That's when Dad says, "I guess we blew it."

Review: Sentence Activities

Write sentences following the patterns below.

Answers will vary.

1. *(subject + linking verb + predicate adjective)*

I am weary. / I feel wonderful. / I look goofy.

2. *(subject + linking verb + predicate noun)*

I am a woman. / John is his name. / We became cerebral warriors.

3. *(adverb clause + compound subject + action verb + direct object + prepositional phrase)*

After Barbara threw the water balloon, Tom and I pushed her into

the pool.

4. *(gerund phrase (subject) + linking verb + your choice)*

Running 10 miles is my exercise of choice.

5. *(participial phrase + subject + action verb + your choice)*

Seizing Robby's arm, Brenda demonstrated her favorite judo

throw.

Write an example sentence for each of the following kinds of sentences.

1. Declarative: A tornado ripped through town last night.

2. Interrogative: Which weather conditions produce a tornado?

3. Imperative: Go to the basement.

4. Compound: The wind is rising, and the tornado sirens are wailing.

5. Complex: Tornado winds, which spin like a vortex, smash everything

in their path.

> **Combine** the following pairs of sentences.

Answers will vary.

1. My brother has permission to leave the house. I cannot go with him.

My brother has permission to leave the house, but I cannot go

with him.

2. The sparrow hawk can travel at remarkable speeds. It can catch its prey in midair.

Traveling at remarkable speeds, the sparrow hawk can catch its

prey in midair.

> **Choose** the entry from column B that best describes the problem in each sentence below. Write the corresponding letter in Column A.

Column A

Column B

d **1.** I walked to the store because some grapes needed to be bought for the church picnic.

h **2.** I saw the car coming toward me and had run to the closest exit I could find.

a **3.** The apple tree produced very few apples, there was a problem with the pollination.

g **4.** If he would have been paying attention.

c **5.** The bear ran for the tent and it ripped open the door and grabbed the food and took off running and we were left hungry!

b **6.** I had to take the rope back to the store it was too short.

e **7.** While finding the keys to her car, the infant climbed out of the crib and down the stairs.

f **8.** The bright yellow sun shone on our cheerful, smiling faces as we approached the flower-flooded meadow in my friend's sun-filled yard.

a. Comma splice

b. Run-on sentence

c. Rambling sentence

d. Shift in voice

e. Dangling modifier

f. Wordiness

g. Fragment

h. Shift in tense

POSTTEST ACTIVITIES

The posttests help teachers and students assess what they have learned and what they still need to learn. The final posttest uses the PSAT format, providing learners an opportunity to become familiar with the PSAT format.

Language Posttests

Sentence Posttests

Final SkillsBook Posttest

Posttest: End Punctuation

> **Add** the correct end punctuation and capitalization to the following paragraphs.

1   <u>D</u>
     đr. Thor Heyerdahl, a Norwegian explorer and writer, wondered, "is it

2   possible to cross 4,300 miles of ocean in a small wooden boat" to answer

3   his own question, Thor Heyerdahl decided to set out from Peru in South

4   America to Raroia in the Polynesian Islands he wanted to test his theory

5   that ancient South American Indians settled the Polynesian Islands, not

6   travelers from southeast Asia after Dr. Heyerdahl had researched the

7   huge, mysterious statues on Easter Island, which is located between Peru

8   and Polynesia, he developed his theory he found carvings on the statues

9   similar to those in Peru and pondered, "does this mean that people from

10   Peru carved the statues on Easter Island" Heyerdahl had to prove that

11   lightweight Peruvian boats were capable of such a long journey, so he and

12   five men built balsa-wood boats and paddled across the Pacific some 101

13   days later, they made it Heyerdahl also wanted to prove that African

14   sailors reached America long before Leif Eriksson Heyerdahl and seven

15   men sailed 3,300 nautical miles from Safi, Morocco, to the island of

16   Barbados in a papyrus boat (papyrus is a solid-stemmed marsh plant) to

17   prove his second theory Heyerdahl successfully completed this journey after

18   57 days at sea

19   after completing such incredible quests, did Heyerdahl ever think, "I

20   could write a book about my adventures" if you've read *Kon-Tiki,* you

21   know he did *Kon-Tiki* and another book he wrote, *Aku-Aku,* explain his

22   theories and describe his voyages

Posttest: Commas

> **Add commas where they are needed below.**

1. Some handwriting experts are forensic-document examiners and some are graphologists.

2. Expert document examiners detect forgeries by studying loops spacing and slant as well as dotted *i*'s and crossed *t*'s in handwriting.

3. Graphologists on the other hand believe that handwriting reveals a person's "inner self."

4. Graphologists say handwriting can profile a person's intelligence achievements and work habits.

5. Wow graphologists claim they can predict how people will react under pressure or in a team situation.

6. It's possible that when clients hear what they want to hear they decide that graphology astrology and palm reading are genuine arts.

7. This is called the *Barnum Effect* in honor of the spirited indomitable circus promoter P. T. Barnum who made circus history when he said "There's a sucker born every minute."

8. Graphologists claim to be able to tell whether a writer is male or female but even laypeople can guess this correctly 70 percent of the time.

9. Do you think handwriting that is uneven and erratic indicates that a person is troubled depressed or just a little sloppy?

10. Forensic-document examiners and not graphologists work for law firms the CIA the FBI and other organizations both private and public.

Posttest: Semicolons & Colons

Insert semicolons and colons where they are needed in the following message. Do not change capitalization or other punctuation.

1   From   Jenny O'Halleran, Business Manager, Wayside School District

2   Date   Monday, February 14, 2000

3   To   Henry Barry, Principal, Armstrong Elementary School

4   Time   116 P.M.

5   Subject   Playground Equipment

6   Dear Mr. Barry

7   The playground equipment has been ordered from Metal-Play, Inc. I

8   ordered six items two spiral slides, one corkscrew climber, two tube slides,

9   and an elevated rung climber.

10   The physical education teacher requested a knotted, heavy-duty nylon rope

11   10 feet long she says it will help build cardiovascular strength. I tried to

12   order the teeter-totter you requested however, our insurance will not allow

13   it.

14   Armstrong School's budget will have to be adjusted I hope you notified the

15   PTA. Section 7 of Article IV outlines the procedure. Call me if you have

16   any questions.

17   Sincerely,

18   *Jenny O'Halleran*

19   Jenny O'Halleran

Posttest: Hyphens & Dashes

> **Place** dashes and hyphens correctly in the following sentences. Do not change any capitalization and do not add other types of punctuation.

1. My father in law knows a lot of facts about feet because he's a podiatrist.

2. There are fifty two bones in your feet, which amounts to about one quarter of all the bones in your body.

3. Footwear has become very technical; some shoes have tri level construction.

4. If your shoes get wet, you should give them 12 24 hours to dry thoroughly.

5. Buy shoes in the midafternoon; tired, worn out feet are always larger than early morning feet.

6. Women experience many more foot problems than men do usually after years of wearing two or three inch heels.

7. Your feet have 250,000 sweat glands, producing up to a cupful of sweat in a twenty four hour period.

8. Your feet carry a heavy burden and take a lot of steps 8,000 to 10,000 each day.

9. Dr. Sanmoy, the well known foot care specialist, is always looking for models foot models, that is.

10. His company is located in Liberty Corner, New Jersey 079380276.

11. The average person walks 115,000 miles in a lifetime which is like circling the globe nearly five times!

12. If you would like to hear more about foot care, call 18005551111.

Posttest: Quotation Marks & Italics (Underlining)

> **Add** the missing quotation marks and italics (underlining).

1. Tea was so important to the Chinese that a three-volume work called The Classic of Tea was written more than 1,000 years ago!

2. Eisai, founder of Rinzai Zen, introduced tea to Japan with his book Kissa Yojoki.

3. My cousin, a sociology major at the University of Illinois, wrote recently, I'm even taking a course devoted entirely to the tea ceremony!

4. The course catalog states, Students are introduced to Japanese culture and to new ways of thinking and viewing the world.

5. Tea Hyakka magazine has documented the tea ceremony's formal rituals in its article titled Encyclopedia of the Japanese Tea Ceremony.

6. Sen Rikyu, the sixteenth-century tea master, identified the four spirits of tea in his book The Way of Tea.

7. They are kei, wa, sei, and jyaku, which in English mean respect, harmony, purity, and tranquility.

8. Japanese tearooms have low ceilings and a nijiriguchi, or crawl-through doorway, so that everyone enters without ego.

9. Rojii, meaning dewy ground, is fresh water sprinkled on the garden and/or sidewalk to purify the entryway for teahouse guests.

10. Recently, the cruise ship Queen of the Seas introduced formal teas.

11. Their pamphlet, Tea on the Queen, suggests proper attire and etiquette.

Posttest: Apostrophes

Add apostrophes where they are needed in the following sentences. (In some cases, you may need to add an apostrophe and an **s.**)

1. The African Zulus culture predates Western recorded history.

2. Therefore, this ancient peoples language and traditions are older than our written word.

3. The Zulus dont have an alphabet with *A*s and *Z*s.

4. Instead, culture and folklore are handed down, in part, through each familys history and artwork.

5. Beaded jewelry often communicates a womans history.

6. The arrangement of the beads—as well as the jewelrys color and geometric patterns—represent different facts, proverbs, and morals.

7. Most of the jewelrys patterns are based upon the triangle and a combination of seven colors.

8. White beads in the jewelry accent another colors positive meaning; black beads carry a negative meaning.

9. A woman wont wear a diamond-shaped pattern unless shes married.

10. The diamond represents the union of an unmarried females triangle (pointing up) and an unmarried males triangle (pointing down).

11. My neighbors, Mr. and Mrs. Byss, often travel to Africa with young peoples groups and sometimes visit a shop owned by Nikiva, Rossi, and Oona.

12. Much of Mrs. Byss jewelry comes from Nikiva, Rossi, and Oonas shop in Capetown, South Africa.

13. One of the Byss sons-in-law is interested in South Africas fruit orchards, which gives the family another reason for returning to Africa.

Posttest: Punctuation

> **Add** end punctuation, commas, semicolons, colons, apostrophes, dashes, hyphens, quotation marks, and underlining (italics).

1. Did you know that telephones didnt always have *Q*s and *Z*s on the dial or keypad

2. Since each button held only three letters the two least used letters *Q* and *Z* were often left off (at least on old phones)

3. Early phone companies thought seven digit phone numbers would be too hard for people to remember

4. For example, a number like 5551234 was originally KL51234 the KL stood for *Klondike*

5. Before direct dialing parents used to say Dont dial zero or the operator will answer

6. Numbers beginning with 900 are toll calls which are often expensive calls to make

7. Have you ever wondered what the *M*s stand for on a package of M&Ms

8. During World War II Forrest Mars Sr founder of the Mars Candy Co and William Murray president of the Hershey Candy Co formed a partnership

9. The new product M&Ms was named using the first letter of each mans last name

10. Did you know that the first novel ever composed entirely on a typewriter was Mark Twains Tom Sawyer

11. Heres what Twain once said about his stories Part of my plan has been to pleasantly remind adults of what they once were themselves

Posttest: Capitalization

Cross out each incorrect use of a lowercase letter and write the capital letter above it.

1. African american soldiers fought in washington's army during the american revolution against great britain.

2. There were black heroes in that war: during the battle of bunker hill, peter salem and salem poor distinguished themselves.

3. African american soldiers served with andrew jackson at new orleans in 1815.

4. In 1861, during the civil war, colonel t. w. higginson took command of the first regiment of south carolina.

5. It was the first entirely african american regiment in the united states.

6. In june of 1866, congress created six more such regiments that protected the pioneers and settlers of the west.

7. One of the first black heroes of the civil war was robert smalls, who sailed a confederate ship out of charleston harbor and turned it over to the union.

8. The emancipation proclamation of 1863 encouraged many more african americans to join the union forces.

9. They were called *buffalo soldiers* out of respect for the fighting spirit of the native american's sacred symbol.

10. During the spanish-american war, the buffalo soldiers accompanied teddy roosevelt on his charge up san juan hill.

11. Nearly a million african americans served in the u.s. armed forces during ww II.

12. Benjamin O. Davis and his son benjamin o. davis, jr., became the first African american generals in the u.s. army and air force.

Posttest: Plurals & Spelling

Underline the correctly spelled word in each pair of words below.

1. receive, recieve
2. piece, peice
3. wieght, weight
4. omited, omitted
5. beginning, begining
6. ocurr, occur
7. reference, referance
8. believe, beleive
9. reign, riegn
10. committed, commited
11. acceptible, acceptable

12. admited, admitted
13. regretted, regreted
14. resistent, resistant
15. controlable, controllable
16. wrapped, wraped
17. decieving, deceiving
18. vien, vein
19. liveable, livable
20. using, useing
21. ninty, ninety
22. wierd, weird

Write the correct plural for each word or phrase below.

1. grandchild _____
2. leaf _____
3. beach _____
4. hero _____
5. mouthful _____
6. fungus _____
7. wharf _____
8. gentleman _____
9. injury _____

10. boss _____
11. country _____
12. sandwich _____
13. life _____
14. sleigh _____
15. editor in chief _____
16. tomato _____
17. disc _____
18. reef _____

Posttest: Numbers & Abbreviations

> **Underline** each improper use of numbers and abbreviations. Write the correction above it.

1. The elections were held on Nov. ninth, nineteen ninety-eight.

2. All three thousand, two hundred fifty-seven voters in that Wyo. town with a pop. of 3,942 people turned out to vote for the city's new mayor.

3. The votes came in at 4 to one for Bartodella Roberts.

4. Her campaign workers celebrated the victory with 23 pizzas, fifteen gals. of milk, and 9 lbs. of chocolate.

5. They also had ten ten-foot sub sandwiches.

6. Mrs. Houghton sent her eighteen-year-old daughter, Becky, 18 balloons for her birthday and asked the florist to deliver them ASAP.

7. Becky wasn't in class when the balloons were delivered at ten-thirty ante meridiem and, sure enough, the attendance office called her mom at work.

8. Mrs. Houghton's coworkers voted twenty-three to four against imposing a punishment.

9. Becky returned to school after 2 hrs., but she hadn't been truant.

10. Everyone had forgotten her "special assignment": she had driven fifty-two mi. to take two foreign exchange students to another high school in Conn. to speak to an assembly of about one thousand one hundred students.

11. She had received a speeding ticket on Highway Seventy-Five, so her mother's coworkers decided to give her a birthday present.

12. They paid the seventy-five dollar and fifty cent ticket. (Happy Birthday!)

Posttest: Using the Right Word

Circle the correct word for each sentence below.

1. I will *(accept, except)* your apology.

2. All the guests came *(accept, except)* Ms. Tilly.

3. The *(affects, effects)* of the tornado were heartbreaking.

4. Yes, I'm *(already, all ready)* to go.

5. Is it *(alright, all right)* to use the truck?

6. Have you seen the *(amount, number)* of flags he's collected?

7. Yikes, how many *(ants, aunts)* are in the sugar bowl?

8. They are replacing the *(base, bass)* on the monument in the park.

9. Are you one of the choir members in the *(base, bass)* section?

10. Mom said, "Please, *(bring, take)* your raincoat to school with you."

11. Please *(bring, take)* the watermelon to the picnic when you come.

12. Yes, the *(capital, capitol)* of North Dakota is Bismarck.

13. I wonder if its *(capital, capitol)* is the tallest building in the state?

14. *(Farther, Further)* assistance is needed in the earthquake region.

15. The *(principal, principle)* needs more information from you.

16. My journals are full of *(personal, personnel)* memories.

17. *(Lay, Lie)* your fears aside.

18. Where did the woman *(lay, lie)* down?

19. *(Like, As)* the mothers talked, the children got into mischief.

20. We seem to be missing a *(peace, piece)* for the puzzle.

21. What is the *(weather, whether)* forecast for Saturday?

22. *(Your, You're)* the one who knows best.

Final Proofreading Posttest—Part 1

> **Put** capital letters where they are needed in the following sentences.

1. Abraham lincoln's gettysburg address begins, "four score and seven years ago, our fathers . . . . "

2. The mets won the world series in 1969.

3. Many years ago, richard j. daley was mayor of chicago, illinois; later his son, richard, jr., was elected to the same post.

4. *To sir with love* is a movie about a courageous teacher.

5. In the christian bible, jesus says to the pharisees, "render to caesar what is caesar's and to god what is god's."

6. My aunt has a job with the state of wisconsin's department of transportation.

7. "Hey, mom, why does grandma buy only allegro vans?" asked my brother, joey.

8. If I pass physics 301, i will graduate on june 8.

9. The statue of liberty, sculpted by frederic-auguste bartholdi, was a gift to the american people from the french people.

10. It was erected on bedloe island in new york harbor.

> **Write** the name of each punctuation mark described below.

_____ 1. sets off a nonrestrictive clause from the rest of the sentence

_____ 2. creates contractions

_____ 3. sets off a word, phrase, or clause for

_____ emphasis (Supply two answers.)

_____ 4. indicates foreign words

_____ **5.** follows an interrogative sentence

_____ **6.** joins single-letter prefixes to words

_____ **7.** separates groups of words that already contain commas

_____ **8.** forms some compound words

_____ **9.** indicates the title of a novel

_____ **10.** separates equal adjectives

Punctuate the following paragraphs. Insert end punctuation, commas, quotation marks, apostrophes, and hyphens. Also capitalize when necessary.

---

1   Have you ever heard of the Talking Oven Mitt It looks like an

2   ordinary oven mitt but if you check your baked potatoes with it you

3   might hear it say ready to eat or some other surprising message its

4   inventor Ted Selker who is a researcher at Massachusetts Institute of

5   Technology (MIT) created more than just the Talking Oven Mitt he also

6   invented the little red "mouse" button for laptop computers

7   When MITs researchers start thinking and inventing anything can

8   happen they are working to make your kitchen smarter mom and dad

9   your groceries will be ordered directly over the Internet the refrigerator

10   and cabinets will be programmed to do the ordering themselves scales

11   that are built into countertops will weigh food and count calories would

12   you like a talking laundry detergent box for instance a microchip on a

13   box could answer age old questions about laundry such as How do I get a

14   ketchup stain off my good shirt

15   What new fascinating things would you like to see invented If you

16   have some good ideas send them to MIT Or maybe youd prefer working

17   on the invention yourself

Final Proofreading Posttest—Part 2

Write a short sentence using both words correctly.

1. chose, choose   *I chose yesterday, so you can choose today.*

_____

2. your, you're   _____

_____

3. leave, let   _____

_____

4. good, well   _____

_____

5. loose, lose   _____

_____

6. lend, borrow   _____

_____

7. set, sit   _____

_____

8. lay, lie   _____

_____

9. who's, whose   _____

_____

10. its, it's   _____

_____

Circle the correctly spelled word in each pair.

1. vein, vien

2. beleiver, believer

3. reference, referance

4. truely, truly

5. guidence, guidance

6. easyly, easily

7. reigning, riegning

8. omitted, omited

9. referral, referal

10. nerveous, nervous

11. liveable, livable

12. attornies, attorneys

13. peices, pieces

14. begining, beginning

15. forgettable, forgettible

16. loveing, loving

17. useing, using

18. buryed, buried

Write plurals for the following words.

1. tomato _____

2. deer _____

3. alley _____

4. criterion _____

5. solo _____

6. wharf _____

7. fix _____

8. life _____

9. mother-in-law _____

10. pinch _____

11. mosquito _____

12. faculty _____

Write out the words for the following abbreviations.

1. m.p.h. _____

2. oz. _____

3. kg _____

4. ft _____

5. AK _____

6. mi. _____

7. cm _____

8. lb _____

9. KS _____

10. wt. _____

11. tbsp _____

12. misc. _____

Posttest: Nouns

Function				Case		Number
subject	S	direct object	DO	nominative	N	singular
predicate noun	PN	indirect object	IO	objective	O	plural
object of preposition	OP	possessive	POS	possessive	POS	

> **Underline** the nouns in the sentences below. Next, list them on the numbered lines in the same order that they appear in the sentences. Fill in the information required for each noun, using the symbols from the chart and words for *singular* and *plural*.

- **NASA** sent the astronauts messages.
- **Circuses must provide excellent care for their animals.**
- **Mrs. Tilly's antique table is a family treasure.**

	NOUN	FUNCTION	CASE	NUMBER
1.	NASA	S	N	S
2.				
3.				
4.				
5.				
6.				
7.				
8.				
9.				

> **Use** each noun below (in the case indicated) in a sentence.

1. elephant *(possessive)* _____

2. garden *(objective)* _____

3. baby *(nominative)* _____

Posttest: Pronouns

Write a sentence using each type of pronoun called for below. Circle the requested pronoun in your sentences so it stands out from any others.

1. *(1st person, plural, possessive case)* (Our) time has come. _____

    _____

2. *(interrogative pronoun)* _____

    _____

3. *(reflexive pronoun)* _____

    _____

4. *(2nd person, singular or plural, nominative)* _____

    _____

5. *(3rd person, singular, objective)* _____

    _____

6. *(demonstrative pronoun)* _____

    _____

7. *(relative pronoun)* _____

    _____

8. *(1st person, singular, objective)* _____

    _____

9. *(intensive pronoun)* _____

    _____

10. *(3rd person, singular, nominative)* _____

    _____

11. *(3rd person, plural, possessive)* _____

    _____

Posttest: Verbs

Identify the number, person, voice, and tense of each verb.

VERB	NUMBER	PERSON	VOICE	TENSE
1. Joe sings.	_singular_	_3rd_	_active_	_present_
2. You were chosen.				
3. I have grown.				
4. Su had won.				
5. We drove.				
6. They play.				
7. The bells will have been rung.				
8. You will pass.				

Rewrite the following sentences, changing the passive voice to active voice.

1. The snow had been plowed by the street department.

   The street department plowed the snow.

2. The money was deposited in the First National Bank by the committee.

   _____

   _____

3. Her hair had been lightened by the sun.

   _____

4. The Cool Cucumber band was booked by the agent to perform at the dance.

   _____

   _____

Posttest: Adjectives & Adverbs

Circle the adjectives and draw an arrow to the words they modify. **Underline the adverbs and draw an arrow to the words they modify. (Do not circle the articles *a, an,* or *the* or the possessive pronouns *their* or *his*.)**

1. Carthage, a North African seaport, was one of the most powerful cities in ancient times.

2. When the Romans began their endless struggle for more territory, the people of Carthage watched carefully.

3. The Romans captured the island of Sicily, located at the "toe" of the Italian "boot," during the First Punic War.

4. From Sicily, the Romans had only a short jump to Carthage itself.

5. Carthage watched nervously as the Roman Empire grew more dominant.

6. Eventually, the Second Punic War began.

7. Hannibal, a Carthaginian general, carefully planned his strategy.

8. He did not attack Rome by sea with his powerful navy.

9. Instead, he led his troops on and painfully fought his way through Spain, into southern France, and over the Swiss Alps into Italy.

10. Surprisingly, he brought 43 African elephants with him.

11. In the third century B.C.E., European soldiers had never seen such huge beasts before, and many fled at the sight.

12. The Romans again defeated Carthage, even though the Carthaginian soldiers fought well.

Posttest: Prepositions, Conjunctions, & Interjections

> **Underline** the prepositional phrases once and the conjunctions twice in the sentences below. Circle the interjections.

1. (Yikes,) in captivity, some flamingos live to be 50 years old, but that is the exception.

2. In their natural surroundings, flamingos live from 15 to 20 years.

3. The American flamingo has deep scarlet on its head, neck, and wings, while lighter shades of pink appear on its back and under its tail.

4. The beautiful color comes from the bird's diet of small, pinkish shellfish.

5. Flamingos are extremely social, although they are known to peck and squabble with each other quite often.

6. Incredible! Flamingo colonies can have thousands of members!

7. They build unique nests on the hot, salty mudflats where they live.

8. The flamingos carry mouthfuls of mud in their large beaks, piling the layers until a one- to three-foot-tall cone is formed.

9. A shallow indentation at the top of the cone holds the single egg.

10. The tall nest provides insurance against rising waters and hot temperatures on the alkaline ground.

11. Holy smokes! It can be 30 degrees cooler at the top of the cone—and an unhatched chick on the nest is probably grateful for the protection.

12. The parents take turns sitting on the egg.

13. Young flamingos leave the nest after five days, but the adults continue to feed them for two weeks.

Final Language Posttest—Part 1

Draw one line under each noun and two lines under each verb in the sentences below.

1. Which senators will visit Tokyo?

2. Harvey's daughter washed his car so she could borrow it later.

3. The faculty requests were not noticed by the superintendent.

4. That Chinese store sells bicycles and live chickens to its customers.

5. The cat cleaned her newborn kittens, one after another, and then nursed them.

6. "Have you been voting in the city's elections?" my mother asked.

7. "Becki, you polished that desk until it gleamed! Thank you," said Ms. Kim.

8. The Smiths attended their first Neighborhood Watch meeting.

Underline each adjective once and each adverb twice in the phrases below.

1. brightly colored flag

2. soft fur

3. walked more quickly

4. gazed wistfully

5. they were intelligent

6. washed thoroughly

7. yearly banquet

8. crops grown yearly

9. French bread

10. shirt was always clean

Underline each verbal and label it as a gerund (*G*), an infinitive (*I*), or a participle (*P*).

1. We need to study if we want to pass this chemistry test.

2. To pass chemistry is my goal; to pass English would be nice, too.

3. The coach stared at the team's tattered and muddied uniforms.

4. The driver received a warning for parking too close to the hydrant.

> **Underline** the prepositional phrases once and the conjunctions twice in the following sentences. Circle the interjections.

1. The pitcher waited <u>for the catcher's signal</u> <u><u>while</u></u> the batter crouched <u>in anticipation</u>.

2. The fastball roared over the plate just as the batter swung to strike it.

3. Kapow! The ball exploded off the aluminum bat and headed toward the fence.

4. The fans leaped out of their seats, spilling their sodas and popcorn.

5. Although the ball was curving down the foul line, it stayed inside the field of play.

6. Holy cow! That's the third home run for Sammy.

7. The Gators are going to have to either hit one, too, or find some other way to score.

> **Write** sentences using the types of words called for in italics. Then circle those words in your sentence.

1. *coordinating conjunction, gerunds* (Shopping) at the farmer's market (and) (cooking) fresh food are Mom's hobbies.

2. *possessive pronoun (third person, singular), adjectives* _____

   _____

3. *active verb, indefinite pronoun* _____

   _____

4. *prepositions, adverb* _____

   _____

5. *relative pronoun, direct object* _____

   _____

Final Language Posttest—Part 2

> **Fill** in the blanks below with the word that correctly completes each statement.

1. A/An _____ *linking* _____ verb links an adjective or a noun to the subject.

2. A/An _____ is a verbal that is usually introduced by *to* and may be used as a noun, an adjective, or a/an _____ .

3. The _____ tense of a verb expresses action that is happening at the present time, happens continually, or happens regularly.

4. A/An _____ describes a noun or a pronoun.

5. A/An _____ describes or modifies a verb, an adjective, or another _____ .

6. These words—*into, on, to, before*—are often _____ .

7. The three kinds of conjunctions are coordinating, _____ , and _____ .

8. In the following clause, *the members who have turned in their assignments,* the _____ pronoun is *who.*

9. The _____ form of an adjective or an adverb compares two things.

10. *We sang while we washed dishes* has a _____ conjunction showing a relationship between two clauses that are not equal.

11. The first noun or pronoun following a preposition is its _____ .

12. The three moods of a verb are _____ , _____ , and _____ .

Underline each pronoun in the following sentences.

1. Mother went to her meeting, but it had been canceled.

2. No, that is not our Border collie; however, you can leave it with us until you find its owners.

3. I like zucchinis and tomatoes, but you prefer turnips and rutabagas.

4. They are not popular vegetables.

5. Does anybody here like kohlrabies or parsnips?

6. Occasionally I permit myself a special treat of green beans and almonds.

7. Your tastes are different from my tastes.

8. Although Manny was talented, she herself didn't like his kind of music.

9. Will you take me to the library?

10. That reckless driver should be arrested before he kills someone!

List the personal pronouns in sentences 1-10 in the proper column below.

	Nominative	Possessive	Objective
1.	it	her	
2.			
3.			
4.			
5.			
6.			
7.			
8.			
9.			
10.			

Posttest: Subjects & Predicates

Draw a line between the complete subject and the complete predicate. Identify each subject as simple subject (**SS**) or compound subject (**CS**). Identify each predicate as simple predicate (**SP**) or compound predicate (**CP**).

1. *SS* | *SP* The Amish | are a small group of the Pennsylvania Deutsch (German) settlers.

2. The Amish arrived in Lancaster, Pennsylvania, and settled there during the 1720s.

3. The Amish teach separation from the modern world.

4. They work hard at keeping their lives simple and their families together.

5. They meet in each other's homes every two weeks for worship.

6. The Amish speak English at school and use a German dialect at home.

7. Some Amish drive horses and buggies.

8. They do not have electricity in their homes, and they send their children to private, often one-room schoolhouses.

9. Progressive Amish and many Mennonites do attend public high school and even go on to college.

10. Most Amish women and girls wear modest dresses with long sleeves and full skirts.

11. Men and boys wear broad-brimmed straw hats and dark-colored suits without lapels.

12. Their clothing is not a costume; it is an expression of their beliefs.

13. They believe in simplicity and demonstrate its advantages.

14. Amish communities are now found in 23 states and in Ontario, Canada.

Posttest: Phrases

> **Write** sentences using the following phrases. Use each phrase as designated in parentheses.

1. to cut the tall grass *(infinitive phrase used as a subject)* _To cut the tall_ _grass was very difficult._

_____

2. hiding in the tall grass *(participial phrase)* _____

_____

_____

3. a tiny, furry baby rabbit *(appositive phrase)* _____

_____

_____

4. ears quivering *(absolute phrase)* _____

_____

_____

5. mowing the grass *(gerund phrase used as a direct object)* _____

_____

_____

6. to mow the grass *(infinitive phrase used as a direct object)* _____

_____

_____

7. in the tulip garden *(prepositional phrase)* _____

_____

_____

Posttest: Clauses

Underline the dependent clauses. Label each adverb clause (**ADV**), each adjective clause (**ADJ**), and each noun clause (**N**).

1. The Arizona Poison and Drug Information Center, <ins>which is located in Tucson,</ins> *ADJ* handles about 15,000 cases per year.

2. Rattlesnakes, scorpions, and spiders—these are the species that are among North America's "most toxic."

3. Many people know that these poisonous species live in Arizona and near Tucson.

4. As Tucson's population continues to grow, expanding neighborhoods and new subdivisions invade these creatures' natural habitats.

5. Whatever is constructed becomes "home away from home" for snakes, which don't know what else to do or where else to go.

6. Ninety percent of adult males are bitten on the hand, arm, or face when they encounter a rattler.

7. The Poison Center considers most of these bites "illegitimate" because snakes can't jump.

8. The Center staff know that the person probably saw the snake, knew it was dangerous, but picked it up anyway.

9. Did you know that a number of species of scorpions are crawling around in the state of Arizona? Among these species is one that's a hairy, five-inch-long desert giant.

10. If you are stung by a scorpion, don't panic.

11. The dangerous exception is the inch-and-a-half-long *bark* scorpion that may be deadly to children or to adults with heart problems.

12. What you need to remember is wash the wound, ice it, and take some aspirin.

Posttest: Kinds & Types of Sentences

Identify each sentence by the kind of statement it makes: declarative *(D)*, interrogative *(IT)*, imperative *(IM)*, or exclamatory *(E)*. Next, identify the sentence's structure: simple *(S)*, compound *(CD)*, complex *(CX)*, or compound-complex *(CD-CX)*.

_____D___ ___CX___   **1.** Scientists place metal bands around the legs of birds so that they can study the birds' flight patterns.

_____   **2.** Banding research began in 1899 when a Danish schoolteacher crafted his own metal bands and placed them on starlings.

_____   **3.** Today almost 6,000 "banders" work together to solve the mysteries of bird biology and migration.

_____   **4.** Did you know that bird scientists are called *ornithologists*?

_____   **5.** The numbered leg bands are important to ornithologists.

_____   **6.** America wants to conserve its wildlife for future generations, and accurate banding helps supply critical information.

_____   **7.** What kinds of research data are collected?

_____   **8.** Research has revealed that the red knot shorebird flies 3,000 miles nonstop from Argentina before it reaches Delaware Bay; once there it must double its weight so that it can fly another 2,500 miles nonstop to the Arctic.

_____   **9.** Be careful when you band birds!

_____   **10.** Many species have beaks and talons that are extremely sharp and can cause injury.

Choose three to four facts from the sentences above. Arrange them into a sentence.

_____

_____

Posttest: Subject-Verb Agreement

> **Underline** the subject and circle the correct verb choice in the following sentences.

1. <u>Speech</u> *(**is**, are)* a required course in most schools.

2. The first days of speech class *(is, are)* often a little frightening.

3. Each of the students *(is, are)* required to give six speeches each semester.

4. Of the six speeches, the first *(is, are)* the easiest to write and the most difficult to present.

5. Five different topics *(is, are)* suggested for the first speech.

6. All of the speakers *(is, are)* to be prepared on the same day.

7. Neither Bert nor Arthur *(is, are)* anxious to give his first speech.

8. The instructor *(understand, understands)* the nervousness of students giving their first speeches.

9. Either Janna or Joy *(is, are)* to give her first speech today.

10. Both Janna and Joy *(is, are)* well prepared.

11. "Economics for Small Businesses" *(is, are)* the title of Janna's speech.

12. Someone in the class *(is, are)* snickering as Janna is giving her speech.

13. Janna does a good job in spite of the distraction and *(hope, hopes)* to receive a superior grade.

14. Each member of the class *(write, writes)* a critique of each presentation.

15. The teaching staff *(establishes, establish)* the criteria for its evaluation.

16. Preparation and research *(is, are)* two of the components of a good speech.

17. Most of the students *(pick, picks)* subjects that are interesting to them.

18. Alex or Katia, I forgot which one, *(is, are)* researching a speech called "Biofeedback and the Rhesus Monkey."

Posttest: Pronoun-Antecedent Agreement

> **Correct** the pronouns in the following sentences so that each agrees in number, person, and gender with its antecedent. Underline the errors and write the correct words above.

1. One of the computers is missing <u>their</u> mouse.
its

2. Judy chained his bicycle to the parking meter in front of the library.

3. People who vote in the election should be the only one allowed to complain to their representatives.

4. Neither Dr. Jekyll nor Mr. Hyde could rid their nature of evil.

5. Either Kevin or Maria left their jacket in the auditorium.

6. Neither my mother nor my sisters golfed her best.

7. Someone in the art class ruined the press, but they won't confess.

8. The air force wants to beef up their image with faster planes.

9. Both Greg and Bill are going to get his education at a state university.

10. Each of the teams had their own strategy for winning the potato-sack race.

11. "Those pieces of pie?" he asked. "I ate it."

12. One of my brothers forgot their watch.

13. Did everyone remember their handbook?

14. The assembly voted to raise its annual salaries.

15. Both of the girls gave her presentations today.

16. The book club has changed their meeting place.

17. Each person must clean up their mess.

18. Both the salad makers and the pastry chefs keep his or her best recipes to themselves.

19. Either the instrumentalists or the soprano vocalist missed their cue.

20. Nobody can find their coat.

Posttest: Combining Sentences

Combine the following sentences using the methods stated. You may use the same ideas in several sentences, and add or delete words as necessary.

Ancient Egyptian obelisks were single pieces of solid granite.

Ancient Egyptian obelisks weighed up to 440 tons.

Large teams of laborers spent years carving the obelisks.

Laborers placed the obelisks on timber sleds.

The Egyptian obelisks were lashed to the sleds with ropes.

Humans hauled the Egyptian obelisks up earthen ramps.

Ancient Egyptian obelisks were erected using levers.

Laborers tugged the obelisks upright to 90 degrees with brute force.

1. series _Ancient Egyptian obelisks were placed on timber sleds, lashed with ropes, and hauled up earthen ramps._

2. relative pronoun _____

_____

3. introductory phrase or clause _____

_____

4. a gerund phrase or a clause _____

_____

5. semicolon _____

_____

6. key word or words _____ _____

_____

7. correlative conjunctions _____

_____

8. appositive _____

_____

Posttest: Sentence Problems 1

> **Edit** the following sentences to eliminate fragments, comma splices, and run-ons. Also correct any rambling sentences. Use editing and proofreading marks when possible. Rewrite sentences that need extensive editing on the blank lines below.

1. Scientists ~~handling~~ *handled* the chemicals safely.

2. I hunted through the Yellow Pages to find a new pizzeria, the deliveries from the old place kept taking longer and longer.

3. After she worked all day.

4. I tried to tie my sister's hair with a ribbon, both got tangled around my fingers.

5. The movie theater was very comfortable it had reclining seats and cup holders.

6. The dolphins loved performing and they loved the treats they received and they kissed their trainer and the audience applauded enthusiastically.

7. The cat stretched his legs and his claws extended and his back arched and he yawned and then he curled up on top of my newspaper.

_____

_____

_____

_____

_____

_____

_____

_____

_____

Posttest: Sentence Problems 2

Edit the following sentences to eliminate wordiness, unparallel constructions, and misplaced or dangling modifiers. Use editing and proofreading marks when possible. Rewrite sentences that need extensive changes on the blank lines below.

1. Washing dishes is okay, but ~~to dry~~ *drying* them is boring.

2. Your interview went badly and you did not answer the interviewer's questions at all well so it was not what you'd call a good interview; otherwise you might have gotten the job.

3. Wait for me until I arrive so we can go together with each other to the movies.

4. When only ten years old, my father taught me how to drive the tractor.

5. Hurrying up the stadium steps, the baseball flew past us.

6. The clowns rode past the tigers on unicycles.

7. When I talk, you don't seem to hear what I am saying because you don't listen to me when I speak to you.

8. Jake likes playing the fiddle and he likes to play the harmonica, too.

_____

_____

_____

_____

_____

_____

_____

_____

_____

Final Sentence Posttest

Draw a line between the complete subject and the complete predicate in the following sentences. Label a simple subject *(S)* and a compound subject *(CS)*. Label a simple predicate *(P)* and a compound predicate *(CP)*.

1. Border collies and other working dogs | herd sheep.

2. The sheepdogs fetch, drive, and pen the sheep.

3. Their handlers twitter, whistle, and shout commands.

4. The dogs look like wolves to the sheep.

5. Sheepdogs cannot move too quickly or get too close to the sheep herd.

6. Then the sheep may run wildly.

7. Dogs have worked sheep for centuries, but the first sheepdog trial didn't take place until 1873.

8. Border collies now dominate other canine competitions, too—such as World Frisbee and Flyball.

Underline the phrases in the sentences below and identify them as gerund, infinitive, participial, prepositional, or appositive.

_____ 1. Grilling the steak made it tasty.

_____ 2. The person grilling the steak is our pastor.

_____ 3. Put the steak on the grill.

_____ 4. The chef, Monsieur Crasie, grilled the steak.

_____ 5. We started to grill the steak.

_____ 6. The carefully aged and grilled steak tasted delicious.

Identify each sentence as declarative (*D*), interrogative (*I*), imperative (*IM*), or exclamatory (*E*). Add end punctuation. Then underline each dependent clause and identify its type: noun (*N*), adjective (*ADJ*), or adverb (*ADV*).

_D_ _ADJ_ **1.** The distance between the rails on American train tracks is precisely 4 feet 8.5 inches, <u>which is a peculiar measurement.</u>

___ ___ **2.** Wouldn't you think that the engineers would have designed the rails to be an even 4 feet or 5 feet apart

___ ___ **3.** Tracks have an unusual width because American railroads were originally designed and built by British engineers and workers

___ ___ **4.** To design our tracks, they used the same patterns that were used to build horse-drawn trolley lines in Britain

___ ___ **5.** In turn, those trolley patterns matched the measurements that wagon makers had used

___ ___ **6.** Are you wondering why old wagon wheels had that particular spacing

___ ___ **7.** It's because British roads already had deep ruts that far apart

___ ___ **8.** The first ruts were made by Roman war chariots, which were built to match the width of two horses side-by-side

Underline each verb or pronoun that does not agree with the subject or with its antecedent. Write the correction above.

1. Some of the city's homes was destroyed in the flood.

2. Each of the new cars have a price sticker on their side window.

3. The news are grim no matter how you looks at it.

4. The quartet carried its instruments onto the stage.

5. Jack sold her mother's cow to buy magic beans.

6. Negative four plus positive seven equal positive three.

7. I hear O'Reilly's are selling its usual Irish imports.

8. Neither detergent nor bleach are going to clean that stain.

9. Everyone are invited to attend the bonfire after the game.

> **Rewrite** each sentence to eliminate fragments, run-on and rambling sentences, unparallel structure, wordiness, and misplaced or dangling modifiers.

1. I read that in 1871 a great fire destroyed Chicago in my new history book.

_____

_____

2. This summer I plan to visit my grandparents, plant a vegetable garden, and I will be working full-time.

_____

_____

3. The mouse ran past the tiger frantically squeaking.

_____

4. I am totally, like, bummed out and upset and stuff, because my mom told me to like, clean up the family room and, like, all my friends and I did was watch some videos and spill a little popcorn, and she really freaked when she found some gummy bears like, stuck, to the sofa. Can you, like, even believe it?

_____

_____

_____

_____

5. Don't touch that chair it has just been painted.

_____

_____

Final SkillsBook Posttest
Part 1: Identifying Common Errors

Test your knowledge of usage, grammar, spelling, and other common errors by answering the standardized test questions below. Each sentence below is either correct—or one of its underlined sections contains an error. (No sentence contains two errors.)

Circle the letter corresponding to the incorrect section. If the sentence has no error, circle the **E**.

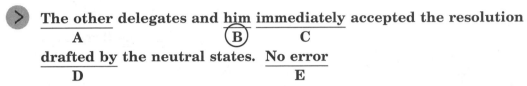

The other delegates and him immediately accepted the resolution
  A   B   C
drafted by the neutral states.   No error
  D   E

Note: The answer is B. This pronoun is part of the subject; it should be the nominative case *he*, not the objective case *him*.

1. "I'm not sure whether its serious if
          A   B
Leah misses her target on her first
              C   D
attempt," replied Chris.   No error
                            E

2. In spite of how bad he had begun the
       A   B
race, Isaiah caught up with the other
              C
runners and finished third.   No error
              D   E

3. I knew that Elvis was planning
       A   B
to appear, so I brought my camera.
   C   D
No error
   E

4. They're wasn't a trace of blood
       A   B
anywhere, so how did the evidence
          C
technician reach his or her conclusion?
                    D

No error
   E

5. Cleopatra wanted to ask Caesar for
his support but she knew the palace
       A
guards would deny her entry; so she
                        B
rolled herself up in a carpet that
her servant Apollodorus boldly
            C
carried past the guards and
                    D
presented to Caesar.   No error
                        E

6. Rayne emigrated from his home,
            A
a village in war-torn Bosnia,
            B
because he wanted to leave some very
          C
painful memories behind.   No error
                    D   E

7. The exact opposite of Julio and me,
           A   B
Scott and her are always very well-
          C   D
groomed.   No error
            E

8. A <u>dependable pair</u> of boots <u>have been</u>
        A   B
   crucial to a <u>cowboy's</u> well-being for
               C
   <u>more than</u> a century. <u>No error</u>
     D   E

9. <u>After choosing</u> the <u>most</u> expensive of
        A   B
   the two <u>options, Lisa</u> found <u>herself</u>
            C   D
   once again in the thick of controversy.
   <u>No error</u>
     E

10. In fact, <u>every writer</u> I know
          A
   <u>would be flattered</u> to have <u>their</u> short
        B   C
   story accepted by a major literary
   magazine <u>as prestigious</u> as the *New*
               D
   Yorker. <u>No error</u>
           E

11. Being quite <u>athletic</u>, <u>Bruno my</u>
     A   B
   <u>best friend excels</u> at swimming,
         C
   <u>soccer, and</u> tennis. <u>No error</u>
     D   E

12. <u>Despite</u> his poor performance today,
     A
   the pitcher <u>who lost</u> the game is not
           B
   <u>nearly</u> as incompetent as he
    C
   <u>appeared to be.</u> <u>No error</u>
      D   E

13. <u>Momentarily</u> forgetting <u>who</u> she
      A   B
   was, the <u>usually sophisticated</u> actress
              C
   began talking <u>loud</u> with a mouth full
              D
   of food. <u>No error</u>
          E

14. In the <u>movie</u> *A Room with a View,*
          A
   <u>one of the Americans</u> <u>are</u> portrayed as
        B   C
   a well-meaning man who is less
   civilized <u>than his</u> British counterparts.
           D
   <u>No error</u>
     E

15. After Kadeem planned the
   parent-teacher <u>banquet, he</u> called the
            A
   treasurer of the student <u>council</u> to
                 B
   find out the <u>course</u> of action
           C
   suggested by the <u>principal.</u> <u>No error.</u>
             D   E

16. "Just what are you <u>implying</u> by
               A
   telling me that <u>it's</u> your grandmother
            B
   who wore army <u>boots</u>"? asked the
             C
   company's director of <u>personnel.</u>
               D
   <u>No error</u>
     E

17. When Mom cooks <u>rattlesnake</u> I
             A
   always wish she would make more of
   the <u>delectable, sweet</u> <u>meat that</u> many
           B   C
   people compare with the
   <u>white, delicate</u> meat of chicken.
        D
   <u>No error</u>
     E

18. Alicia's great-uncle <u>leads</u> a more
      A   B
active life <u>then</u> many people <u>who</u>
         C   D
are considerably younger than he is.

<u>No error</u>
  E

19. Neither Dorothy <u>or</u> her dog Toto
             A
<u>expected</u> to experience <u>such a strange</u>
   B   C
variety of characters and adventures

<u>in Oz.</u> <u>No error</u>
  D   E

20. Why do you <u>think that</u> such a large
            A
<u>amount</u> of <u>professional basketball</u>
  B   C
players come from the <u>Midwest?</u>
                    D

<u>No error</u>
  E

21. I have a friend <u>whose</u> parents
             A
<u>insist on giving</u> him a subscription to
     B
the *Weekly Reader* even though he
        C
gets all the news he wants from the

New York Times. <u>No error</u>
    D   E

Part 2: Improving Sentences

Read the following sentences, paying careful attention to the underlined sections. Beneath each sentence you will find five ways of phrasing the underlined part. Choice **A** repeats the original; the other four are each different.

Circle the answer that best expresses the meaning of the original sentence. If you think the original is best, circle **A**. Your selection should produce the most effective sentence—clear and precise, without awkwardness, ambiguity, or errors.

 Laura Ingalls Wilder published her first book <u>and she was 65 years old then.</u>

   (A) and she was 65 years old then.
   (B) when she was 65 years old.
   (C) at age 65 years old.
   (D) upon reaching 65 years of age.
   (E) at the time when she was 65.

Note: The correct answer is *B.* The original, and *A,* are awkward, as is *E.* Both *C* and *D* are wordy.

1. The ticket agent could not determine <u>the destination to which the woman intended to travel.</u>

   (A) the destination to which the woman intended to travel.
   (B) where the woman wanted to travel to.
   (C) the woman's intended destination.
   (D) where did the woman want to travel?
   (E) to where did the woman wanted to travel.

2. If Carmen had correctly estimated <u>the amount of problems she could do per hour,</u> she would not have had to finish them on Sunday.

   (A) If Carmen had correctly estimated the amount of problems she could do per hour,
   (B) If Carmen had correctly estimated the amount of problems she could have done per hour,
   (C) If Carmen had correctly estimated the number of problems she could do per hour,
   (D) If Carmen would have correctly estimated the number of problems she could do per hour,
   (E) If Carmen would of correctly estimated the number of problems she could do per hour,

3. To successfully complete his mission, Eric the Red knew he needed <u>accurate maps, a good crew, and to have adequate provisions.</u>

(A) accurate maps, a good crew, and to have adequate provisions.

(B) accurate maps, to have a good crew, and to have adequate provisions.

(C) accurate maps and a good crew, as well as adequate provisions.

(D) accurate maps, have a good crew, and have adequate provisions.

(E) accurate maps, a good crew, and adequate provisions.

4. Herbie and I think that Kim is <u>neither the best or the worst person for this assignment.</u>

(A) neither the best or the worst person for this assignment.

(B) neither the best nor the worst person for this assignment.

(C) not either the best or the worst person for this assignment.

(D) for this assignment neither the best nor the worst person.

(E) not the best but not the worst person for this assignment.

5. <u>Who do you think wanted the pale purple convertible—my mother or my father?</u>

(A) Who do you think wanted the pale purple convertible—my mother or my father?

(B) Whom do you think wanted the pale purple convertible—my Mother or my Father?

(C) Who do you think wanted the pale purple convertible? My mother or my father?

(D) Whom do you think wanted the pale purple convertible—my mother or my father?

(E) Who do you think wanted the pale purple convertible: my Mother or Father?

6. Mathias usually <u>chose candidates on the basis of his or her</u> position on environmental issues.

(A) chose candidates on the basis of his or her

(B) selected candidates on the basis of his or her

(C) chose candidates on the basis of their

(D) chose a candidate on the basis of their

(E) has chosen candidates on the basis of their

7. Sara willingly brought the oily rags out to the trash <u>barrel, then she made</u> the mistake of trying to burn them.

(A) barrel, then she made

(B) barrel; then she made

(C) barrel, she then made

(D) barrel, afterwards she made

(E) barrel; then she went on to make

8. <u>Akira was upset and the other members of the team were perplexed.</u>

(A) Akira was upset and the other members of the team were perplexed.

(B) Akira was upset and the other members of the team also was perplexed.

(C) Akira and the other members of the team were respectively upset and perplexed.

(D) Akira was upset; at the same time, the other members of the team were perplexed.

(E) Akira was upset, and the other members of the team were perplexed.

9. Annie Oakley entered the crowded circus arena on a magnificent stallion firing both of her six-guns.

(A) Annie Oakley entered the crowded circus arena on a magnificent stallion firing both of her six-guns.

(B) Annie Oakley entered, firing both of her six-guns, the crowded circus arena on a magnificent stallion.

(C) On a magnificent stallion, Annie Oakley, firing both of her six-guns, entered the crowded circus arena.

(D) Firing both of her six-guns, Annie Oakley rode a magnificent stallion into the crowded circus arena.

(E) Entering the crowded circus arena on a magnificent stallion, Annie Oakley, fired both of her six-guns.

10. Leah enjoyed physical education almost as much as to have her wisdom teeth pulled or fixing a flat tire on a cold, rainy night.

(A) almost as much as to have her wisdom teeth pulled or fixing a flat tire

(B) almost as much as having her wisdom teeth pulled or a flat tire

(C) almost as much as having her wisdom teeth pulled or fixing a flat tire

(D) nearly as much as having her wisdom teeth pulled or a flat tire

(E) almost as much as wisdom teeth being pulled or fixing a flat tire

11. The homecoming football game, which started at 2:00 p.m., had to be called off; because, not only did it begin to rain and soak the huge crowd, but also lightning began to terrify everyone and make it dangerous to be outside.

(A) The homecoming football game, which started at 2:00 p.m., had to be called off; because, not only did it begin to rain and soak the huge crowd, but also lightning began to terrify everyone and make it dangerous to be outside.

(B) Starting at 2:00 p.m., the homecoming football game had to be called off since it began to rain and soak the huge crowd, while lightning terrified everyone.

(C) The homecoming football game, which started at 2:00 p.m., had to be called off because rain had soaked the huge crowd and lightning had terrified everyone.

(D) Calling off the homecoming football game, which had started at 2:00 p.m., was necessary because not only did it rain and soak the huge crowd, but lightning was terrifying everyone.

(E) When lightning terrified everyone and rain had been soaking the huge crowd at the homecoming football game, which started at 2:00 p.m., it had to be called off.

12. Despite her immense talent, <u>Natalie desiring for glory led to a tragic turn of events.</u>

(A) Natalie desiring for glory led to a tragic turn of events.

(B) Natalie's desire for glory led to a tragic turn of events.

(C) because Natalie desired glory, it led to a tragic turn of events.

(D) Natalie's desiring glory led to a tragic turn of events.

(E) Natalie desired glory; this led to a tragic turn of events.

13. The summer choir, <u>made up chiefly of altos and basses, have been making</u> a valiant attempt to compensate for their missing members.

(A) The summer choir, made up chiefly of altos and basses, have been making

(B) Made up of chiefly altos and basses, the summer choir have been making

(C) The summer choir, which usually has altoes and basses, has been making

(D) Made up of chiefly altos and basses, the summer choir has been making

(E) The summer choir, chiefly made up of altos and basses, have been making

14. <u>Has she or will she ever find</u> true happiness in digging for night crawlers?

(A) Has she or will she ever find

(B) Has her ever, or will her ever find

(C) Has she yet, or will she ever find

(D) Has she found or will she ever find

(E) Has she or will she find

15. If anyone finds the missing lapis lazuli necklace, <u>they will have solved</u> a 30-year-old family mystery.

(A) they will have solved

(B) he or she will have solved

(C) they would have solved

(D) they have solved

(E) he or she has solved

16. <u>Brenda Sue and Glenda Lou, who are twins, are my cousins and they are also my best friends.</u>

(A) Brenda Sue and Glenda Lou, who are twins, are my cousins and they are also my best friends.

(B) Brenda Sue and Glenda Lou who are twins, are my cousins and they are also my best friends.

(C) My cousins Brenda Sue and Glenda Lou, who are twins are also my best friends.

(D) Brenda Sue and Glenda Lou are twins, are my cousins, and are my best friends.

(E) My twin cousins, Brenda Sue and Glenda Lou, are my best friends.

17. Foreign languages generally mystified <u>Brendan, but</u> his fluency in Latin was <u>remarkable.</u>

(A) Brendan, but

(B) Brendan: however

(C) Brendan—but

(D) Brendan; yet

(E) Brendan; but

18. One of the very few laws that Uma and Cherise obeyed <u>were the laws of gravity.</u>

(A) were the laws of gravity.

(B) was the law of gravity.

(C) were that of gravity.

(D) was the ones about gravity.

(E) were those of gravity.

Part 3: Improving Paragraphs

Read the following essay—a first draft in need of editing. Do not correct the text directly. Instead, answer the questions listed after the essay to identify and fix mistakes. Circle the letter next to the answer you think is best.

(1) A mysterious ancient monument known as Stonehenge is located in southwestern England. (2) You approach it by a broad avenue. (3) It consists of a series of huge, standing stones surrounded by an earthwork. (4) A circular trench about 320 feet in diameter, with a bank on the inner side, encloses the monument. (5) Inside the bank is a circle of 56 holes with a diameter of 288 feet.

(6) The mammoth stones are set in four series: two large outer circles, a horseshoe, and an oval. (7) The outermost circle of rocks, almost 100 feet in diameter, consists of sandstone rocks nearly 15 feet high and averaging 25 tons. (8) A continuous circle of smaller blocks stood on top of them. (9) The next circle consists of about 60 smaller stones. (10) An oval setting is inside that, with an altar stone in the center.

(11) The purpose of Stonehenge is a mystery. (12) Most archaeologists believe that it was used for religious ceremonies. (13) The exact nature of the religious ceremonies is not known. (14) Modern astronomers' discoveries have led them to believe that the stones and layout of Stonehenge were used as a calendar of the seasons and signal eclipses of the sun and moon.

(15) Over the centuries, some of the stones fell and others were moved a short distance or even removed and used to build dams and bridges. (16) Restoration of Stonehenge began in 1922, and it is now carefully maintained by the government.

1. Which sentence in the first paragraph shifts to a second-person pronoun and interferes with the unity of the paragraph?
   (A) Sentence 1
   (B) Sentence 2
   (C) Sentence 3
   (D) Sentence 4
   (E) Sentence 5

2. Which of the following is the best way to revise the underlined portion of sentence 8 in order to keep the verbs consistent throughout the paragraph?
   (A) circle of smaller blocks stood
   (B) circle of smaller blocks is standing
   (C) circle of smaller blocks stands
   (D) circle of smaller blocks has stood
   (E) circle of smaller blocks had stood

3. Reread the entire second paragraph carefully. Which of the following sentences should be added between sentence 9 and 10 to maintain the organization of the paragraph?

(A) Even though these are smaller, they are still quite large.

(B) The horseshoe shape is next, and that has really large stones.

(C) These are called bluestones, because of their color.

(D) Why the next shape is a horseshoe, no one really knows.

(E) Inside that is a horseshoe-shaped configuration of enormous stones—up to 22 feet tall and weighing 30 to 40 tons.

4. What is the best way to combine sentences 12 and 13?

(A) Most archaeologists believe that it was used for religious ceremonies, the exact nature of the religious ceremonies is not known.

(B) Most archaeologists believe that it was used for religious ceremonies, yet the exact nature of the religious ceremonies is not known.

(C) Most archaeologists believe that it was used for religious ceremonies, and the exact nature of the religious ceremonies is not known.

(D) Although most archaeologists believe that it was used for religious ceremonies, the exact nature of those ceremonies is not know.

(E) Believing that it was used for religious ceremonies, archaeologists don't know the exact nature of the religious ceremonies.

5. Which is the best way to correct the unparallel construction in sentence 14?

(A) Modern astronomers' discoveries have led them to believe that the stones and layout of Stonehenge were used as a calendar to predict the seasons and signaling eclipses of the sun and moon.

(B) Modern astronomers' discoveries have led them to believe that the stones and layout of Stonehenge were used as a calendar to predict the seasons and to signal eclipses of the sun and moon.

(C) Discoveries have led modern astronomers into believing that the stones and layout of Stonehenge were used as a calendar predicting the seasons and signaling eclipses of the sun and moon at Stonehenge.

(D) Stonehenge was used to predict the seasons and for signaling eclipses of the sun and moon according to beliefs held by modern astronomers.

(E) Stonehenge was predicting the seasons and signaling eclipses of the sun and moon according to the beliefs held by modern astronomers.

6. To conclude the final paragraph in the best way, which of the following sentences should be added after sentence 16?

(A) It is just one of many interesting places to visit in England.

(B) The admission fee is very reasonable.

(C) However, not all the stones were found.

(D) Today this mysterious monument is one of England's most popular tourist destinations, attracting more than one million visitors a year.

(E) What a fascinating place!

POSTTEST
ANSWER KEY

Language Posttests

Sentence Posttests

Final SkillsBook Posttest

Posttest: End Punctuation

Add the correct end punctuation and capitalization to the following paragraphs.

1   *D* Dr. Thor Heyerdahl, a Norwegian explorer and writer, wondered, "*I* Is it

2   possible to cross 4,300 miles of ocean in a small wooden boat?" *T* To answer

3   his own question, Thor Heyerdahl decided to set out from Peru in South

4   America to Raroia in the Polynesian Islands. *H* He wanted to test his theory

5   that ancient South American Indians settled the Polynesian Islands, not

6   travelers from southeast Asia. *A* After Dr. Heyerdahl had researched the

7   huge, mysterious statues on Easter Island, which is located between Peru

8   and Polynesia, he developed his theory. *H* He found carvings on the statues

9   similar to those in Peru and pondered, "*D* Does this mean that people from

10   Peru carved the statues on Easter Island?" Heyerdahl had to prove that

11   lightweight Peruvian boats were capable of such a long journey, so he and

12   five men built balsa-wood boats and paddled across the Pacific. *S* Some 101

13   days later, they made it! Heyerdahl also wanted to prove that African

14   sailors reached America long before Leif Eriksson. Heyerdahl and seven

15   men sailed 3,300 nautical miles from Safi, Morocco, to the island of

16   Barbados in a papyrus boat (papyrus is a solid-stemmed marsh plant) to

17   prove his second theory. Heyerdahl successfully completed this journey after

18   57 days at sea.

19   *A* After completing such incredible quests, did Heyerdahl ever think, "I

20   could write a book about my adventures?" *I* If you've read *Kon-Tiki,* you

21   know he did. *Kon-Tiki* and another book he wrote, *Aku-Aku,* explain his

22   theories and describe his voyages.

Posttest: Commas

Add commas where they are needed below.

1. Some handwriting experts are forensic-document examiners, and some are graphologists.

2. Expert document examiners detect forgeries by studying loops, spacing, and slant as well as dotted *i*'s and crossed *t*'s in handwriting.

3. Graphologists, on the other hand, believe that handwriting reveals a person's "inner self."

4. Graphologists say handwriting can profile a person's intelligence, achievements, and work habits.

5. Wow, graphologists claim they can predict how people will react under pressure or in a team situation.

6. It's possible that when clients hear what they want to hear, they decide that graphology, astrology, and palm reading are genuine arts.

7. This is called the *Barnum Effect* in honor of the spirited, indomitable circus promoter P. T. Barnum, who made circus history when he said, "There's a sucker born every minute."

8. Graphologists claim to be able to tell whether a writer is male or female, but even laypeople can guess this correctly 70 percent of the time.

9. Do you think handwriting that is uneven and erratic indicates that a person is troubled, depressed, or just a little sloppy?

10. Forensic-document examiners, and not graphologists, work for law firms, the CIA, the FBI, and other organizations, both private and public.

Posttest: Semicolons & Colons

> **Insert** semicolons and colons where they are needed in the following message. Do not change capitalization or other punctuation.

1   From: Jenny O'Halleran, Business Manager, Wayside School District

2   Date: Monday, February 14, 2000

3   To: Henry Barry, Principal, Armstrong Elementary School

4   Time: 1:16 P.M.

5   Subject: Playground Equipment

6   Dear Mr. Barry:

7   The playground equipment has been ordered from Metal-Play, Inc. I

8   ordered six items: two spiral slides, one corkscrew climber, two tube slides,

9   and an elevated rung climber.

10   The physical education teacher requested a knotted, heavy-duty nylon rope

11   10 feet long; she says it will help build cardiovascular strength. I tried to

12   order the teeter-totter you requested; however, our insurance will not allow

13   it.

14   Armstrong School's budget will have to be adjusted; I hope you notified the

15   PTA. Section 7 of Article IV outlines the procedure. Call me if you have

16   any questions.

17   Sincerely,

18   *Jenny O'Halleran*

19   Jenny O'Halleran

Posttest: Hyphens & Dashes

Place dashes and hyphens correctly in the following sentences. Do not change any capitalization and do not add other types of punctuation.

1. My father in law knows a lot of facts about feet because he's a podiatrist.

2. There are fifty two bones in your feet, which amounts to about one quarter of all the bones in your body.

3. Footwear has become very technical; some shoes have tri level construction.

4. If your shoes get wet, you should give them 12 24 hours to dry thoroughly.

5. Buy shoes in the midafternoon; tired, worn out feet are always larger than early morning feet.

6. Women experience many more foot problems than men do usually after years of wearing two or three inch heels.

7. Your feet have 250,000 sweat glands, producing up to a cupful of sweat in a twenty four hour period.

8. Your feet carry a heavy burden and take a lot of steps 8,000 to 10,000 each day.

9. Dr. Sanmoy, the well known foot care specialist, is always looking for models foot models, that is.

10. His company is located in Liberty Corner, New Jersey 07938 0276.

11. The average person walks 115,000 miles in a lifetime which is like circling the globe nearly five times!

12. If you would like to hear more about foot care, call 1 800 555 1111.

Posttest: Quotation Marks & Italics (Underlining)

> **Add** the missing quotation marks and italics (underlining).

1. Tea was so important to the Chinese that a three-volume work called <u>The Classic of Tea</u> was written more than 1,000 years ago!

2. Eisai, founder of Rinzai Zen, introduced tea to Japan with his book <u>Kissa Yojoki</u>.

3. My cousin, a sociology major at the University of Illinois, wrote recently, "I'm even taking a course devoted entirely to the tea ceremony!"

4. The course catalog states, "Students are introduced to Japanese culture and to new ways of thinking and viewing the world."

5. <u>Tea Hyakka</u> magazine has documented the tea ceremony's formal rituals in its article titled "Encyclopedia of the Japanese Tea Ceremony."

6. Sen Rikyu, the sixteenth-century tea master, identified the four spirits of tea in his book <u>The Way of Tea</u>.

7. They are <u>kei</u>, <u>wa</u>, <u>sei</u>, and <u>jyaku</u>, which in English mean "respect," "harmony," "purity," and "tranquility."

8. Japanese tearooms have low ceilings and a <u>nijiriguchi</u>, or crawl-through doorway, so that everyone enters without ego.

9. <u>Rojii</u>, meaning "dewy ground," is fresh water sprinkled on the garden and/or sidewalk to purify the entryway for teahouse guests.

10. Recently, the cruise ship <u>Queen of the Seas</u> introduced formal teas.

11. Their pamphlet, <u>Tea on the Queen</u>, suggests proper attire and etiquette.

Posttest: Apostrophes

> **Add** apostrophes where they are needed in the following sentences. (In some cases, you may need to add an apostrophe and an **s**.)

1. The African Zulus' culture predates Western recorded history.

2. Therefore, this ancient peoples' language and traditions are older than our written word.

3. The Zulus don't have an alphabet with A's and Z's.

4. Instead, culture and folklore are handed down, in part, through each family's history and artwork.

5. Beaded jewelry often communicates a woman's history.

6. The arrangement of the beads—as well as the jewelry's color and geometric patterns—represent different facts, proverbs, and morals.

7. Most of the jewelry's patterns are based upon the triangle and a combination of seven colors.

8. White beads in the jewelry accent another color's positive meaning; black beads carry a negative meaning.

9. A woman won't wear a diamond-shaped pattern unless she's married.

10. The diamond represents the union of an unmarried female's triangle (pointing up) and an unmarried male's triangle (pointing down).

11. My neighbors, Mr. and Mrs. Byss, often travel to Africa with young people's groups and sometimes visit a shop owned by Nikiva, Rossi, and Oona.

12. Much of Mrs. Byss's jewelry comes from Nikiva, Rossi, and Oona's shop in Capetown, South Africa.

13. One of the Byss's sons-in-law is interested in South Africa's fruit orchards, which gives the family another reason for returning to Africa.

Posttest: Punctuation

> **Add** end punctuation, commas, semicolons, colons, apostrophes, dashes, hyphens, quotation marks, and underlining (italics).

1. Did you know that telephones didnt always have Qs and Zs on the dial or keypad

2. Since each button held only three letters the two least used letters Q *(or)* and Z *(or)* were often left off (at least on old phones)

3. Early phone companies thought seven digit phone numbers would be too hard for people to remember

4. For example, a number like 555 1234 was originally KL5 1234 the KL stood for *Klondike*

5. Before direct dialing parents used to say Dont dial zero or the operator will answer

6. Numbers beginning with 900 are toll calls which are often expensive calls to make

7. Have you ever wondered what the Ms stand for on a package of M&Ms

8. During World War II Forrest Mars Sr. founder of the Mars Candy Co. and William Murray president of the Hershey Candy Co. formed a partnership

9. The new product M&Ms was named using the first letter of each mans last name

10. Did you know that the first novel ever composed entirely on a typewriter was Mark Twains Tom Sawyer

11. Heres what Twain once said about his stories Part of my plan has been to pleasantly remind adults of what they once were themselves

Posttest: Capitalization

> **Cross out** each incorrect use of a lowercase letter and write the capital letter above it.

1. African american soldiers fought in washington's army during the american revolution against great britain.
   (corrections above: A over american, W over washington's, A over american; R over revolution, G over great, B over britain)

2. There were black heroes in that war: during the battle of bunker hill, peter salem and salem poor distinguished themselves.
   (corrections above: D over during, B over battle, B over bunker, H over hill, P over peter; S over salem, S over salem, P over poor)

3. African american soldiers served with andrew jackson at new orleans in 1815.
   (corrections above: A over american, A over andrew, J over jackson, N over new, O over orleans)

4. In 1861, during the civil war, colonel t. w. higginson took command of the first regiment of south carolina.
   (corrections above: C over civil, W over war, C over colonel, T over t., W over w., H over higginson, F over first; R over regiment, S over south, C over carolina)

5. It was the first entirely african american regiment in the united states.
   (corrections above: A over african, A over american, U over united, S over states)

6. In june of 1866, congress created six more such regiments that protected the pioneers and settlers of the west.
   (corrections above: J over june, C over congress; W over west)

7. One of the first black heroes of the civil war was robert smalls, who sailed a confederate ship out of charleston harbor and turned it over to the union.
   (corrections above: C over civil, W over war, R over robert, S over smalls; C over confederate, C over charleston, H over harbor, U over union)

8. The emancipation proclamation of 1863 encouraged many more african americans to join the union forces.
   (corrections above: E over emancipation, P over proclamation, A over african; A over americans, U over union)

9. They were called *buffalo soldiers* out of respect for the fighting spirit of the native american's sacred symbol.
   (corrections above: N over native, A over american's)

10. During the spanish-american war, the buffalo soldiers accompanied teddy roosevelt on his charge up san juan hill.
    (corrections above: S over spanish, A over american, W over war, T over teddy; R over roosevelt, S over san, J over juan, H over hill)

11. Nearly a million african americans served in the u.s. armed forces during ww II.
    (corrections above: A over african, A over americans, US over u.s., WW over ww)

12. Benjamin O. Davis and his son benjamin o. davis, jr., became the first African american generals in the u.s. army and air force.
    (corrections above: B over benjamin, O D over o. davis, J over jr.; A over american, US over u.s., A over army, A over air, F over force)

Posttest: Plurals & Spelling

Underline the correctly spelled word in each pair of words below.

1. <u>receive</u>, recieve
2. <u>piece</u>, peice
3. wieght, <u>weight</u>
4. omited, <u>omitted</u>
5. <u>beginning</u>, begining
6. ocurr, <u>occur</u>
7. <u>reference</u>, referance
8. <u>believe</u>, beleive
9. <u>reign</u>, riegn
10. <u>committed</u>, commited
11. acceptible, <u>acceptable</u>

12. admited, <u>admitted</u>
13. <u>regretted</u>, regreted
14. resistent, <u>resistant</u>
15. controlable, <u>controllable</u>
16. <u>wrapped</u>, wraped
17. decieving, <u>deceiving</u>
18. vien, <u>vein</u>
19. liveable, <u>livable</u>
20. <u>using</u>, useing
21. ninty, <u>ninety</u>
22. wierd, <u>weird</u>

Write the correct plural for each word or phrase below.

1. grandchild *grandchildren*
2. leaf *leaves (or) leafs*
3. beach *beaches*
4. hero *heroes*
5. mouthful *mouthfuls*
6. fungus *fungi (or) funguses*
7. wharf *wharves (or) wharfs*
8. gentleman *gentlemen*
9. injury *injuries*

10. boss *bosses*
11. country *countries*
12. sandwich *sandwiches*
13. life *lives*
14. sleigh *sleighs*
15. editor in chief *editors in chief*
16. tomato *tomatoes*
17. disc *discs*
18. reef *reefs*

Posttest: Numbers & Abbreviations

Underline each improper use of numbers and abbreviations. Write the correction above it.

1. The elections were held on Nov. ninth, nineteen ninety-eight.
November 9   1998

2. All three thousand, two hundred fifty-seven voters in that Wyo. town with a
3,257   Wyoming
pop. of 3,942 people turned out to vote for the city's new mayor.
population

3. The votes came in at 4 to one for Bartodella Roberts.
1

4. Her campaign workers celebrated the victory with 23 pizzas, fifteen gals. of
15   gallons
milk, and 9 lbs. of chocolate.
pounds

5. They also had ten ten-foot sub sandwiches.
10

6. Mrs. Houghton sent her eighteen-year-old daughter, Becky, 18 balloons for her
18
birthday and asked the florist to deliver them ASAP.
as soon as possible

7. Becky wasn't in class when the balloons were delivered at ten-thirty
10:30
ante meridiem and, sure enough, the attendance office called her mom at work.
A.M.

8. Mrs. Houghton's coworkers voted twenty-three to four against imposing a
23   4
punishment.

9. Becky returned to school after 2 hrs., but she hadn't been truant.
two hours

10. Everyone had forgotten her "special assignment": she had driven fifty-two mi.
52 miles
to take two foreign exchange students to another high school in Conn. to speak
Connecticut
to an assembly of about one thousand one hundred students.
1,100

11. She had received a speeding ticket on Highway Seventy-Five, so her mother's
75
coworkers decided to give her a birthday present.

12. They paid the seventy-five dollar and fifty cent ticket. (Happy Birthday!)
$75.50

Posttest: Using the Right Word

> **Circle** the correct word for each sentence below.

1. I will (**accept,** except) your apology.

2. All the guests came (accept, **except**) Ms. Tilly.

3. The (affects, **effects**) of the tornado were heartbreaking.

4. Yes, I'm (already, **all ready**) to go.

5. Is it (alright, **all right**) to use the truck?

6. Have you seen the (amount, **number**) of flags he's collected?

7. Yikes, how many (**ants,** aunts) are in the sugar bowl?

8. They are replacing the (**base,** bass) on the monument in the park.

9. Are you one of the choir members in the (base, **bass**) section?

10. Mom said, "Please, (bring, **take**) your raincoat to school with you."

11. Please (**bring,** take) the watermelon to the picnic when you come.

12. Yes, the (**capital,** capitol) of North Dakota is Bismarck.

13. I wonder if its (capital, **capitol**) is the tallest building in the state?

14. (Farther, **Further**) assistance is needed in the earthquake region.

15. The (**principal,** principle) needs more information from you.

16. My journals are full of (**personal,** personnel) memories.

17. (**Lay,** Lie) your fears aside.

18. Where did the woman (lay, **lie**) down?

19. (Like, **As**) the mothers talked, the children got into mischief.

20. We seem to be missing a (peace, **piece**) for the puzzle.

21. What is the (**weather,** whether) forecast for Saturday?

22. (Your, **You're**) the one who knows best.

Final Proofreading Posttest — Part 1

> **Put capital letters where they are needed in the following sentences.**

1. Abraham lincoln's gettysburg address begins, "four score and seven years ago,

   our fathers . . . . "

2. The mets won the world series in 1969.

3. Many years ago, richard j. daley was mayor of chicago, illinois; later his son,

   richard, jr., was elected to the same post.

4. *To sir with love* is a movie about a courageous teacher.

5. In the christian bible, jesus says to the pharisees, "render to caesar what is

   caesar's and to god what is god's."

6. My aunt has a job with the state of wisconsin's department of transportation.

7. "Hey, mom, why does grandma buy only allegro vans?" asked my brother, joey.

8. If I pass physics 301, i will graduate on june 8.

9. The statue of liberty, sculpted by frederic-auguste bartholdi, was a gift to the

   american people from the french people.

10. It was erected on bedloe island in new york harbor.

> **Write the name of each punctuation mark described below.**

_____ comma _____   1. sets off a nonrestrictive clause from the rest of the sentence

_____ apostrophe _____   2. creates contractions

_____ dash _____   3. sets off a word, phrase, or clause for

_____ colon _____   emphasis (Supply two answers.)

_____ italics _____   4. indicates foreign words

question mark **5.** follows an interrogative sentence

hyphen **6.** joins single-letter prefixes to words

semicolon **7.** separates groups of words that already contain commas

hyphen **8.** forms some compound words

italics **9.** indicates the title of a novel

comma **10.** separates equal adjectives

Punctuate **the following paragraphs. Insert end punctuation, commas, quotation marks, apostrophes, and hyphens. Also capitalize when necessary.**

1   Have you ever heard of the Talking Oven Mitt? It looks like an

2   ordinary oven mitt, but if you check your baked potatoes with it, you

3   might hear it say "ready to eat" or some other surprising message. Its

4   inventor, Ted Selker, who is a researcher at Massachusetts Institute of

5   Technology (MIT), created more than just the Talking Oven Mitt; he also

6   invented the little red "mouse" button for laptop computers.

7   When MIT's researchers start thinking and inventing, anything can

8   happen. They are working to make your kitchen smarter. Mom and dad,

9   your groceries will be ordered directly over the Internet. The refrigerator

10 and cabinets will be programmed to do the ordering themselves. Scales

11 that are built into countertops will weigh food and count calories. Would

12 you like a talking laundry-detergent box? For instance, a microchip on a

13 box could answer age-old questions about laundry such as, "How do I get a

14 ketchup stain off my good shirt?"

15 What new, fascinating things would you like to see invented? If you

16 have some good ideas, send them to MIT. Or maybe you'd prefer working

17 on the invention yourself.

Final Proofreading Posttest—Part 2

Write a short sentence using both words correctly.

1. chose, choose   *I chose yesterday, so you can choose today.*

2. your, you're   *You're going to go hunting with your dad.*

3. leave, let   *Let me leave now.*

4. good, well   *That was a good job done well.*

5. loose, lose   *She will soon lose that loose tooth.*

6. lend, borrow   *I'll lend you this shirt if I can borrow your sweater.*

7. set, sit   *Set the table before you sit down to rest.*

8. lay, lie   *Lay the book down before you lie down.*

9. who's, whose   *Who's going to whose parties?*

10. its, it's   *It's about time the team got its act together.*

Circle the correctly spelled word in each pair.

1. (vein,) vien
2. beleiver, (believer)
3. (reference,) referance
4. truely, (truly)
5. guidence, (guidance)
6. easyly, (easily)

7. (reigning,) riegning
8. (omitted,) omited
9. (referral,) referal
10. nerveous, (nervous)
11. liveable, (livable)
12. attornies, (attorneys)

13. peices, (pieces)
14. begining, (beginning)
15. (forgettable,) forgettible
16. loveing, (loving)
17. useing, (using)
18. buryed, (buried)

Write plurals for the following words.

1. tomato _tomatoes_
2. deer _deer_
3. alley _alleys_
4. criterion _criteria_
5. solo _solos_
6. wharf _wharves (or) wharfs_

7. fix _fixes_
8. life _lives_
9. mother-in-law _mothers-in-law_
10. pinch _pinches_
11. mosquito _mosquitoes_
12. faculty _faculties_

Write out the words for the following abbreviations.

1. m.p.h. _miles per hour_
2. oz. _ounce_
3. kg _kilogram_
4. ft _foot (or) feet_
5. AK _Alaska_
6. mi. _mile (or) mill_

7. cm _centimeter_
8. lb _pound_
9. KS _Kansas_
10. wt. _weight_
11. tbsp _tablespoon_
12. misc. _miscellaneous_

Posttest: Nouns

Function				Case		Number
subject	**S**	direct object	**DO**	nominative	**N**	singular
predicate noun	**PN**	indirect object	**IO**	objective	**O**	plural
object of preposition	**OP**	possessive	**POS**	possessive	**POS**	

> **Underline** the nouns in the sentences below. Next, list them on the numbered lines in the same order that they appear in the sentences. Fill in the information required for each noun, using the symbols from the chart and words for *singular* and *plural*.

- <u>NASA</u> sent the <u>astronauts</u> <u>messages</u>.
- <u>Circuses</u> must provide excellent <u>care</u> for their <u>animals</u>.
- <u>Mrs. Tilly's</u> antique <u>table</u> is a family <u>treasure</u>.

	NOUN	FUNCTION	CASE	NUMBER
1.	NASA	S	N	S
2.	astronauts	IO	O	P
3.	messages	DO	O	P
4.	Circuses	S	N	P
5.	care	DO	O	S
6.	animals	OP	O	P
7.	Mrs. Tilly's	POS	POS	S
8.	table	S	N	S
9.	treasure	PN	N	S

> **Use** each noun below (in the case indicated) in a sentence.

1. elephant *(possessive)* _The elephant's ears were scarred._

2. garden *(objective)* _In my garden I planted zinnias._

3. baby *(nominative)* _The baby cooed and giggled._

Posttest: Pronouns

> **Write** a sentence using each type of pronoun called for below. Circle the requested pronoun in your sentences so it stands out from any others.

Answers will vary.

1. *(1st person, plural, possessive case)* (Our) time has come. _____

_____

2. *(interrogative pronoun)* (Who) are you? _____

_____

3. *(reflexive pronoun)* I could kick (myself.) _____

_____

4. *(2nd person, singular or plural, nominative)* (You) should ride the bus. _____

_____

5. *(3rd person, singular, objective)* Francesca gave (him) a shove onto the _____

stage. _____

6. *(demonstrative pronoun)* (This) is my story. _____

_____

7. *(relative pronoun)* The man (who) is standing over there looks sad. _____

_____

8. *(1st person, singular, objective)* She asked (me) for a dollar. _____

_____

9. *(intensive pronoun)* Penelope (herself) isn't likely to attend, but her _____

brother will be there. _____

10. *(3rd person, singular, nominative)* (She) is my best friend. _____

_____

11. *(3rd person, plural, possessive)* They were asked to move (their) cars. _____

_____

Posttest: Verbs

Identify the number, person, voice, and tense of each verb.

VERB	NUMBER	PERSON	VOICE	TENSE
1. Joe sings.	singular	3rd	active	present
2. You were chosen.	singular/plural	2nd	passive	past
3. I have grown.	singular	1st	active	present perfect
4. Su had won.	singular	3rd	active	past perfect
5. We drove.	plural	1st	active	past
6. They play.	plural	3rd	active	present
7. The bells will have been rung.	plural	3rd	passive	future perfect
8. You will pass.	singular/plural	2nd	active	future

Rewrite the following sentences, changing the passive voice to active voice.

1. The snow had been plowed by the street department.

The street department plowed the snow.

2. The money was deposited in the First National Bank by the committee.

The committee deposited the money in the First National Bank.

3. Her hair had been lightened by the sun.

The sun lightened her hair.

4. The Cool Cucumber band was booked by the agent to perform at the dance.

The agent booked the Cool Cucumber band to perform at the dance.

Posttest: Adjectives & Adverbs

Circle the adjectives and draw an arrow to the words they modify. Underline the adverbs and draw an arrow to the words they modify. (Do not circle the articles *a, an,* or *the* or the possessive pronouns *their* or *his.*)

1. Carthage, a North African seaport, was one of the most powerful cities in ancient times.

2. When the Romans began their endless struggle for more territory, the people of Carthage watched carefully.

3. The Romans captured the island of Sicily, located at the "toe" of the Italian "boot," during the First Punic War.

4. From Sicily, the Romans had only a short jump to Carthage itself.

5. Carthage watched nervously as the Roman Empire grew more dominant.

6. Eventually, the Second Punic War began.

7. Hannibal, a Carthaginian general, carefully planned his strategy.

8. He did not attack Rome by sea with his powerful navy.

9. Instead, he led his troops on and painfully fought his way through Spain, into southern France, and over the Swiss Alps into Italy.

10. Surprisingly, he brought 43 African elephants with him.

11. In the third century B.C.E., European soldiers had never seen such huge beasts before, and many fled at the sight.

12. The Romans again defeated Carthage, even though the Carthaginian soldiers fought well.

Posttest: Prepositions, Conjunctions, & Interjections

> **Underline** the prepositional phrases once and the conjunctions twice in the sentences below. Circle the interjections.

1. (Yikes,) in captivity, some flamingos live to be 50 years old, but that is the exception.

2. In their natural surroundings, flamingos live from 15 to 20 years.

3. The American flamingo has deep scarlet on its head, neck, and wings, while lighter shades of pink appear on its back and under its tail.

4. The beautiful color comes from the bird's diet of small, pinkish shellfish.

5. Flamingos are extremely social, although they are known to peck and squabble with each other quite often.

6. (Incredible!) Flamingo colonies can have thousands of members!

7. They build unique nests on the hot, salty mudflats where they live.

8. The flamingos carry mouthfuls of mud in their large beaks, piling the layers until a one- to three-foot-tall cone is formed.

9. A shallow indentation at the top of the cone holds the single egg.

10. The tall nest provides insurance against rising waters and hot temperatures on the alkaline ground.

11. (Holy smokes!) It can be 30 degrees cooler at the top of the cone—and an unhatched chick on the nest is probably grateful for the protection.

12. The parents take turns sitting on the egg.

13. Young flamingos leave the nest after five days, but the adults continue to feed them for two weeks.

Final Language Posttest—Part 1

> **Draw** one line under each noun and two lines under each verb in the sentences below.

1. Which senators will visit Tokyo?

2. Harvey's daughter washed his car so she could borrow it later.

3. The faculty requests were not noticed by the superintendent.

4. That Chinese store sells bicycles and live chickens to its customers.

5. The cat cleaned her newborn kittens, one after another, and then nursed them.

6. "Have you been voting in the city's elections?" my mother asked.

7. "Becki, you polished that desk until it gleamed! Thank you," said Ms. Kim.

8. The Smiths attended their first Neighborhood Watch meeting.

> **Underline** each adjective once and each adverb twice in the phrases below.

1. brightly colored flag

2. soft fur

3. walked more quickly

4. gazed wistfully

5. they were intelligent

6. washed thoroughly

7. yearly banquet

8. crops grown yearly

9. French bread

10. shirt was always clean

> **Underline** each verbal and label it as a gerund (**G**), an infinitive (**I**), or a participle (**P**).

1. We need to study *(I)* if we want to pass *(I)* this chemistry test.

2. To pass *(I)* chemistry is my goal; to pass *(I)* English would be nice, too.

3. The coach stared at the team's tattered *(P)* and muddied *(P)* uniforms.

4. The driver received a warning *(G)* for parking *(G)* too close to the hydrant.

> **Underline** the prepositional phrases once and the conjunctions twice in the following sentences. **Circle** the interjections.

1. The pitcher waited <u>for the catcher's signal</u> <u>while</u> the batter crouched <u>in anticipation</u>.

2. The fastball roared <u>over the plate</u> just <u>as</u> the batter swung to strike it.

3. (Kapow!) The ball exploded <u>off the aluminum bat</u> <u>and</u> headed <u>toward the fence</u>.

4. The fans leaped <u>out of their seats</u>, spilling their sodas <u>and</u> popcorn.

5. <u>Although</u> the ball was curving <u>down the foul line</u>, it stayed <u>inside the field</u> <u>of play</u>.

6. (Holy cow!) That's the third home run <u>for Sammy</u>.

7. The Gators are going to have to <u>either</u> hit one, too, <u>or</u> find some other way to score.

> **Write** sentences using the types of words called for in italics. **Then circle** those words in your sentence.

Answers will vary.

1. *coordinating conjunction, gerunds* (Shopping) at the farmer's market (and) (cooking) fresh food are Mom's hobbies.

2. *possessive pronoun (third person, singular), adjectives* (Her) (apple) pies win (blue) ribbons.

3. *active verb, indefinite pronoun* The judges (give) an award or ribbon to (everyone.)

4. *prepositions, adverb* We waited (patiently) (in) line (for) a ride (on) the Ferris wheel.

5. *relative pronoun, direct object* I bought (cotton candy,) (which) I love.

Final Language Posttest—Part 2

Fill in the blanks below with the word that correctly completes each statement.

1. A/An _____ *linking* _____ verb links an adjective or a noun to the subject.

2. A/An _____ *infinitive* _____ is a verbal that is usually introduced by *to* and

   may be used as a noun, an adjective, or a/an _____ *adverb* _____ .

3. The _____ *present* _____ tense of a verb expresses action that is happening

   at the present time, happens continually, or happens regularly.

4. A/An _____ *adjective* _____ describes a noun or a pronoun.

5. A/An _____ *adverb* _____ describes or modifies a verb, an adjective, or

   another _____ *adverb* _____ .

6. These words—*into, on, to, before*—are often _____ *prepositions* _____ .

7. The three kinds of conjunctions are coordinating, _____ *correlative* _____ , and

   _____ *subordinating* _____ .

8. In the following clause, *the members who have turned in their assignments,* the

   _____ *relative* _____ pronoun is *who.*

9. The _____ *comparative* _____ form of an adjective or an adverb compares two

   things.

10. *We sang while we washed dishes* has a _____ *subordinating* _____ conjunction

    showing a relationship between two clauses that are not equal.

11. The first noun or pronoun following a preposition is its _____ *object* _____ .

12. The three moods of a verb are _____ *indicative* _____ , _____ *imperative* _____ ,

    and _____ *subjunctive* _____ .

> **Underline** each pronoun in the following sentences.

1. Mother went to <u>her</u> meeting, but <u>it</u> had been canceled.

2. No, <u>that</u> is not <u>our</u> Border collie; however, <u>you</u> can leave <u>it</u> with <u>us</u> until <u>you</u> find <u>its</u> owners.

3. <u>I</u> like zucchinis and tomatoes, but <u>you</u> prefer turnips and rutabagas.

4. <u>They</u> are not popular vegetables.

5. Does <u>anybody</u> here like kohlrabies or parsnips?

6. Occasionally <u>I</u> permit <u>myself</u> a special treat of green beans and almonds.

7. <u>Your</u> tastes are different from <u>my</u> tastes.

8. Although Manny was talented, <u>she</u> <u>herself</u> didn't like <u>his</u> kind of music.

9. Will <u>you</u> take <u>me</u> to the library?

10. <u>That</u> reckless driver should be arrested before <u>he</u> kills someone!

> **List** the personal pronouns in sentences 1-10 in the proper column below.

	Nominative	Possessive	Objective
1.	it	her	
2.	you, you	our, its	it, us
3.	I, you		
4.	They		
5.			
6.	I		myself
7.		Your, my	
8.	she, herself	his	
9.	you		me
10.	he		

Posttest: Subjects & Predicates

> **Draw** a line between the complete subject and the complete predicate. Identify each subject as simple subject (**SS**) or compound subject (**CS**). Identify each predicate as simple predicate (**SP**) or compound predicate (**CP**).

          SS   *SP*

1. The Amish | are a small group of the Pennsylvania Deutsch (German) settlers.

          SS   *CP*

2. The Amish | arrived in Lancaster, Pennsylvania, and settled there during the

1720s.

          SS   *SP*

3. The Amish | teach separation from the modern world.

      SS   *SP*

4. They | work hard at keeping their lives simple and their families together.

      SS *SP*

5. They | meet in each other's homes every two weeks for worship.

          SS   *CP*

6. The Amish | speak English at school and use a German dialect at home.

          SS   *SP*

7. Some Amish | drive horses and buggies.

      SS   *SP*   *SS* *SP*

8. They | do not have electricity in their homes, and they | send their children to

private, often one-room schoolhouses.

                    CS   *CP*

9. Progressive Amish and many Mennonites | do attend public high school and even

go on to college.

             CS   *SP*

10. Most Amish women and girls | wear modest dresses with long sleeves and full

skirts.

          CS   *SP*

11. Men and boys | wear broad-brimmed straw hats and dark-colored suits without

lapels.

            SS   *SP*   *SS* *SP*

12. Their clothing | is not a costume; it | is an expression of their beliefs.

      SS   *CP*

13. They | believe in simplicity and demonstrate its advantages.

          SS   *SP*

14. Amish communities | are now found in 23 states and in Ontario, Canada.

Posttest: Phrases

> Write sentences using the following phrases. Use each phrase as designated in parentheses.

1. to cut the tall grass (*infinitive phrase used as a subject*) *To cut the tall grass was very difficult.*

2. hiding in the tall grass (*participial phrase*) *Hiding in the tall grass, the rabbit eyed the lawn mower warily.*

3. a tiny, furry baby rabbit (*appositive phrase*) *The creature, a tiny, furry baby rabbit, trembled with fear.*

4. ears quivering (*absolute phrase*) *Ears quivering, the baby rabbit flattened itself in the grass.*

5. mowing the grass (*gerund phrase used as a direct object*) *I actually enjoy mowing the grass.*

6. to mow the grass (*infinitive phrase used as a direct object*) *I hate to mow the grass when it gets too long.*

7. in the tulip garden (*prepositional phrase*) *The rabbit now lives in the tulip garden.*

Posttest: Clauses

> **Underline** the dependent clauses. Label each adverb clause (**ADV**), each adjective clause (**ADJ**), and each noun clause (**N**).

1. The Arizona Poison and Drug Information Center, <u>which is located in Tucson,</u> *ADJ* handles about 15,000 cases per year.

2. Rattlesnakes, scorpions, and spiders—these are the species <u>that are among</u> *ADJ* North America's "most toxic."

3. Many people know <u>that these poisonous species live in Arizona and near Tucson.</u> *N*

4. <u>As Tucson's population continues to grow,</u> expanding neighborhoods and new *ADV* subdivisions invade these creatures' natural habitats.

5. <u>Whatever is constructed</u> becomes "home away from home" for snakes, <u>which</u> *N* <u>don't know what else to do or where else to go.</u> *ADJ*

6. Ninety percent of adult males are bitten on the hand, arm, or face <u>when they</u> *ADV* <u>encounter a rattler.</u>

7. The Poison Center considers most of these bites "illegitimate" <u>because snakes</u> *ADV* <u>can't jump.</u>

8. The Center staff know <u>that the person probably saw the snake, knew it was</u> *N* <u>dangerous, but picked it up anyway.</u>

9. Did you know <u>that a number of species of scorpions are crawling around in the</u> *N* <u>state of Arizona?</u> Among these species is one <u>that's a hairy, five-inch-long desert</u> *ADJ* <u>giant.</u>

10. <u>If you are stung by a scorpion,</u> don't panic. *ADV*

11. The dangerous exception is the inch-and-a-half-long *bark* scorpion <u>that may be</u> *ADJ* <u>deadly to children or to adults with heart problems.</u>

12. <u>What you need to remember</u> is wash the wound, ice it, and take some aspirin. *N*

Posttest: Kinds & Types of Sentences

Identify each sentence by the kind of statement it makes: declarative *(D)*, interrogative *(IT)*, imperative *(IM)*, or exclamatory *(E)*. Next, identify the sentence's structure: simple *(S)*, compound *(CD)*, complex *(CX)*, or compound-complex *(CD-CX)*.

D   *CX*   **1.** Scientists place metal bands around the legs of birds so that they can study the birds' flight patterns.

D   *CX*   **2.** Banding research began in 1899 when a Danish schoolteacher crafted his own metal bands and placed them on starlings.

D   *S*   **3.** Today almost 6,000 "banders" work together to solve the mysteries of bird biology and migration.

IT   *S*   **4.** Did you know that bird scientists are called *ornithologists*?

D   *S*   **5.** The numbered leg bands are important to ornithologists.

D   *CD*   **6.** America wants to conserve its wildlife for future generations, and accurate banding helps supply critical information.

IT   *S*   **7.** What kinds of research data are collected?

D   *CD-CX*   **8.** Research has revealed that the red knot shorebird flies 3,000 miles nonstop from Argentina before it reaches Delaware Bay; once there it must double its weight so that it can fly another 2,500 miles nonstop to the Arctic.

E
(or) IM   *CX*   **9.** Be careful when you band birds!

D   *CX*   **10.** Many species have beaks and talons that are extremely sharp and can cause injury.

Choose three to four facts from the sentences above. Arrange them into a sentence.

Ornithologists band birds so that they can study the flight

patterns of birds and thereby solve mysteries about bird migration.

Posttest: Subject-Verb Agreement

> **Underline** the subject and circle the correct verb choice in the following sentences.

1. Speech *(is, are)* a required course in most schools.

2. The first days of speech class *(is, are)* often a little frightening.

3. Each of the students *(is, are)* required to give six speeches each semester.

4. Of the six speeches, the first *(is, are)* the easiest to write and the most difficult to present.

5. Five different topics *(is, are)* suggested for the first speech.

6. All of the speakers *(is, are)* to be prepared on the same day.

7. Neither Bert nor Arthur *(is, are)* anxious to give his first speech.

8. The instructor *(understand, understands)* the nervousness of students giving their first speeches.

9. Either Janna or Joy *(is, are)* to give her first speech today.

10. Both Janna and Joy *(is, are)* well prepared.

11. "Economics for Small Businesses" *(is, are)* the title of Janna's speech.

12. Someone in the class *(is, are)* snickering as Janna is giving her speech.

13. Janna does a good job in spite of the distraction and *(hope, hopes)* to receive a superior grade.

14. Each member of the class *(write, writes)* a critique of each presentation.

15. The teaching staff *(establishes, establish)* the criteria for its evaluation.

16. Preparation and research *(is, are)* two of the components of a good speech.

17. Most of the students *(pick, picks)* subjects that are interesting to them.

18. Alex or Katia, I forgot which one, *(is, are)* researching a speech called "Biofeedback and the Rhesus Monkey."

Posttest: Pronoun-Antecedent Agreement

> **Correct** the pronouns in the following sentences so that each agrees in number, person, and gender with its antecedent. Underline the errors and write the correct words above.

1. One of the computers is missing <u>their</u> mouse. *its*

2. Judy chained <u>his</u> bicycle to the parking meter in front of the library. *her*

3. People who vote in the election should be the only <u>one</u> allowed to complain to *ones*
   their representatives.

4. Neither Dr. Jekyll nor Mr. Hyde could rid <u>their</u> nature of evil. *his*

5. Either Kevin or Maria left <u>their</u> jacket in the auditorium. *his or her*

6. Neither my mother nor my sisters golfed <u>her</u> best. *their*

7. Someone in the art class ruined the press, but <u>they</u> won't confess. *he or she*

8. The air force wants to beef up <u>their</u> image with faster planes. *its*

9. Both Greg and Bill are going to get <u>his</u> education at a state university. *their*

10. Each of the teams had <u>their</u> own strategy for winning the potato-sack race. *its*

11. "Those pieces of pie?" he asked. "I ate <u>it</u>." *them*

12. One of my brothers forgot <u>their</u> watch. *his*

13. Did everyone remember <u>their</u> handbook? *his or her*

14. The assembly voted to raise <u>its</u> annual salaries. *their*

15. Both of the girls gave <u>her</u> presentations today. *their*

16. The book club has changed <u>their</u> meeting place. *its*

17. Each person must clean up <u>their</u> mess. *his or her*

18. Both the salad makers and the pastry chefs keep <u>his or her</u> best recipes to *their*
    themselves.

19. Either the instrumentalists or the soprano vocalist missed <u>their</u> cue. *her*

20. Nobody can find <u>their</u> coat. *his or her*

Posttest: Combining Sentences

Combine the following sentences using the methods stated. You may use the same ideas in several sentences, and add or delete words as necessary.

Answers may vary.

Ancient Egyptian obelisks were single pieces of solid granite.
Ancient Egyptian obelisks weighed up to 440 tons.
Large teams of laborers spent years carving the obelisks.
Laborers placed the obelisks on timber sleds.
The Egyptian obelisks were lashed to the sleds with ropes.
Humans hauled the Egyptian obelisks up earthen ramps.
Ancient Egyptian obelisks were erected using levers.
Laborers tugged the obelisks upright to 90 degrees with brute force.

1. series _Ancient Egyptian obelisks were placed on timber sleds, lashed with ropes, and hauled up earthen ramps._

2. relative pronoun _Ancient Egyptian obelisks, which were single pieces of solid granite, weighed up to 440 tons._

3. introductory phrase or clause _Since the obelisks were single pieces of solid granite, it took large teams of laborers years to carve them._

4. a gerund phrase or a clause _Tugging ancient Egyptian obelisks upright to 90 degrees required brute force._

5. semicolon _Ancient Egyptian obelisks were single pieces of solid granite; they weighed up to 440 tons._

6. key word or words _Ancient Egyptian obelisks were carved with human labor, hauled with human labor, and tugged upright with human labor._

7. correlative conjunctions _Not only did the Egyptians devise timber sleds to move the obelisks, but they also created levers to erect them._

8. appositive _Ancient Egyptian obelisks, single pieces of solid granite weighing up to 440 tons, were carved by large teams of laborers._

Posttest: Sentence Problems 1

Edit the following sentences to eliminate fragments, comma splices, and run-ons. Also correct any rambling sentences. Use editing and proofreading marks when possible. Rewrite sentences that need extensive editing on the blank lines below.

Answers will vary.

1. Scientists ~~handling~~ *handled* the chemicals safely.

2. I hunted through the Yellow Pages to find a new pizzeria, *because* the deliveries from the old place kept taking longer and longer.

3. After she worked all day.

4. I tried to tie my sister's hair with a ribbon, *but* both got tangled around my fingers.

5. The movie theater was very comfortable. *I*t had reclining seats and cup holders.

6. The dolphins loved performing and they loved the treats they received and they kissed their trainer and the audience applauded enthusiastically.

7. The cat stretched his legs and his claws extended and his back arched and he yawned and then he curled up on top of my newspaper.

   3. After she worked all day, she still found time to jog or do yoga.

   6. The dolphins loved performing and eating the treats they received, so they kissed their trainer. The audience applauded enthusiastically.

   7. The cat stretched his legs, extended his claws, arched his back, and yawned. Then he curled up on top of my newspaper.

Posttest: Sentence Problems 2

Edit the following sentences to eliminate wordiness, unparallel constructions, and misplaced or dangling modifiers. Use editing and proofreading marks when possible. Rewrite sentences that need extensive changes on the blank lines below.

Answers will vary.

1. Washing dishes is okay, but ~~to dry~~ *drying* them is boring.

2. Your interview went badly and you did not answer the interviewer's questions at all well so it was not what you'd call a good interview; otherwise you might have gotten the job.

3. Wait for me ~~until I arrive~~ so we can go together ~~with each other~~ to the movies.

4. When only ten years old, my father taught me how to drive the tractor.

5. Hurrying up the stadium steps, the baseball flew past us.

6. The clowns rode past the tigers on unicycles.

7. ~~When I talk,~~ You don't seem to hear what I am saying ~~because you don't listen to me when I speak to you~~.

8. Jake likes playing the fiddle and ~~he likes to play~~ the harmonica, too.

    2. Your interview went badly; otherwise you might have gotten the

    job.

    4. When I was only ten years old, my father taught me how to

    drive the tractor.

    5. The baseball flew past us as we hurried up the stadium steps.

    6. The clowns on unicycles rode past the tigers.

Final Sentence Posttest

> **Draw** a line between the complete subject and the complete predicate in the following sentences. Label a simple subject **(S)** and a compound subject **(CS)**. Label a simple predicate **(P)** and a compound predicate **(CP)**.

1. Border collies and other working dogs | herd sheep. *(CS P)*

2. The sheepdogs | fetch, drive, and pen the sheep. *(S CP)*

3. Their handlers | twitter, whistle, and shout commands. *(S CP)*

4. The dogs | look like wolves to the sheep. *(S P)*

5. Sheepdogs | cannot move too quickly or get too close to the sheep herd. *(S CP)*

6. Then the sheep | may run wildly. *(S P)*

7. Dogs | have worked sheep for centuries, but the first sheepdog trial | didn't take place until 1873. *(S P S P)*

8. Border collies | now dominate other canine competitions, too—such as World Frisbee and Flyball. *(S P)*

> **Underline** the phrases in the sentences below and identify them as gerund, infinitive, participial, prepositional, or appositive.

gerund	**1.**	Grilling the steak made it tasty.
participial	**2.**	The person grilling the steak is our pastor.
prepositional	**3.**	Put the steak on the grill.
appositive	**4.**	The chef, Monsieur Crasie, grilled the steak.
infinitive	**5.**	We started to grill the steak.
participial	**6.**	The carefully aged and grilled steak tasted delicious.

> **Identify** each sentence as declarative (**D**), interrogative (**I**), imperative (**IM**), or exclamatory (**E**). Add end punctuation. Then underline each dependent clause and identify its type: noun (**N**), adjective (**ADJ**), or adverb (**ADV**).

<u>D</u> <u>ADJ</u> **1.** The distance between the rails on American train tracks is precisely 4 feet 8.5 inches, <u>which is a peculiar measurement.</u>

<u>I</u> <u>N</u> **2.** Wouldn't you think <u>that the engineers would have designed the rails to be an even 4 feet or 5 feet apart</u>?

<u>D</u> <u>ADV</u> **3.** Tracks have an unusual width <u>because American railroads were originally designed and built by British engineers and workers.</u>

<u>D</u> <u>ADJ</u> **4.** To design our tracks, they used the same patterns <u>that were used to build horse-drawn trolley lines in Britain.</u>

<u>D</u> <u>ADJ</u> **5.** In turn, those trolley patterns matched the measurements <u>that wagon makers had used.</u>

<u>I</u> <u>N</u> **6.** Are you wondering why old wagon wheels had <u>that particular spacing</u>?

<u>D</u> <u>N</u> **7.** It's <u>because British roads already had deep ruts that far apart.</u>

<u>D</u> <u>ADJ</u> **8.** The first ruts were made by Roman war chariots, <u>which were built to match the width of two horses side-by-side.</u>

> **Underline** each verb or pronoun that does not agree with the subject or with its antecedent. Write the correction above.

1. Some of the city's homes <u>was</u> ^*were*^ destroyed in the flood.

2. Each of the new cars <u>have</u> ^*has*^ a price sticker on <u>their</u> ^*its*^ side window.

3. The news <u>are</u> ^*is*^ grim no matter how you <u>looks</u> ^*look*^ at it.

4. The quartet carried <u>its</u> ^*their*^ instruments onto the stage.

5. Jack sold <u>her</u> ^*his*^ mother's cow to buy magic beans.

6. Negative four plus positive seven *equals* ~~equal~~ positive three.

7. I hear O'Reilly's *is* ~~are~~ selling its usual Irish imports.

8. Neither detergent nor bleach *is* ~~are~~ going to clean that stain.

9. Everyone *is* ~~are~~ invited to attend the bonfire after the game.

> **Rewrite** each sentence to eliminate fragments, run-on and rambling sentences, unparallel structure, wordiness, and misplaced or dangling modifiers.

1. I read that in 1871 a great fire destroyed Chicago in my new history book.

   I read in my new history book that a great fire destroyed Chicago in 1871.

2. This summer I plan to visit my grandparents, plant a vegetable garden, and I will be working full-time.

   This summer I plan to visit my grandparents, plant a vegetable garden, and work full-time.

3. The mouse ran past the tiger frantically squeaking.

   Frantically squeaking, the mouse ran past the tiger.

4. I am totally, like, bummed out and upset and stuff, because my mom told me to like, clean up the family room and, like, all my friends and I did was watch some videos and spill a little popcorn, and she really freaked when she found some gummy bears like, stuck, to the sofa. Can you, like, even believe it?

   I am upset because my mom told me to clean up the family room after my friends and I spilled some popcorn and left gummy bears stuck to the sofa. Can you believe it?

5. Don't touch that chair it has just been painted.

   Don't touch that chair. It has just been painted.

Final SkillsBook Posttest

Part 1: Identifying Common Errors

> **Test** your knowledge of usage, grammar, spelling, and other common errors by answering the standardized test questions below. Each sentence below is either correct—or one of its underlined sections contains an error. (No sentence contains two errors.)
>
> **Circle** the letter corresponding to the incorrect section. If the sentence has no error, circle the **E.**

>   *he*
> The other delegates and ~~him~~ immediately accepted the resolution
>   A   (B)   C
> drafted by the neutral states. No error
>   D   E

Note: The answer is B. This pronoun is part of the subject; it should be the nominative case *he,* not the objective case *him.*

1.   *it's*
   "I'm not sure whether ~~its~~ serious if
      A   (B)
   Leah misses her target on her first
                    C   D
   attempt," replied Chris. No error
                              E

2.   *badly*
   In spite of how ~~bad~~ he had begun the
      A   (B)
   race, Isaiah caught up with the other
                    C
   runners and finished third. No error
                   D   E

3. I knew that Elvis was planning
      A   B
   to appear, so I brought my camera.
       C   D
   No orror
    (E)

4.   *There*
   ~~They're~~ wasn't a trace of blood
    (A)   B
   anywhere, so how did the evidence
              C
   technician reach his or her conclusion?
                         D

   No error
    E

5. Cleopatra wanted to ask Caesar for

   his support,but she knew the palace
          (A)'
   guards would deny her entry; so she
                          B
   rolled herself up in a carpet that

   her servant Apollodorus boldly
            C
   carried past the guards and
                     D
   presented to Caesar. No error
                          E

6. Rayne emigrated from his home,
             A
   a village in war-torn Bosnia,
                B
   because he wanted to leave some very
          C
   painful memories behind. No error
                    D   (E)

7. The exact opposite of Julio and me,
          A   B
                she
   Scott and ~~her~~ are always very well-
            (C)   D
   groomed. No error
              E

8. A dependable pair of boots ~~have~~ *has* been
    A   B
crucial to a cowboy's well-being for
              C
more than a century.   No error
        D   E

9. After choosing the ~~most~~ *more* expensive of
        A   B
the two options, Lisa found herself
            C   D
once again in the thick of controversy.

No error
  E

10. In fact, every writer I know
                A
would be flattered to have ~~their~~ *his or her* short
        B   C
story accepted by a major literary

magazine as prestigious as the *New*
              D
Yorker.   No error
            E

11. Being quite athletic, Bruno my
        A   B
best friend excels at swimming,
        C
soccer, and tennis.   No error
    D   E

12. Despite his poor performance today,
        A
the pitcher who lost the game is not
            B
nearly as incompetent as he
  C
appeared to be.   No error
    D   E

13. Momentarily forgetting who she
                A   B
was, the usually sophisticated actress
                            C
began talking ~~loud~~ *loudly* with a mouth full
                        D
of food.   No error
            E

14. In the movie *A Room with a View,*
                A
one of the Americans ~~are~~ *is* portrayed as
            B   C
a well-meaning man who is less

civilized than his British counterparts.
            D
No error
  E

15. After Kadeem planned the

parent-teacher banquet, he called the
                    A
treasurer of the student council to
                            B
find out the course of action
                C
suggested by the principal.   No error.
                    D   E

16. "Just what are you implying by
                        A
telling me that it's your grandmother
                    B
who wore army boots"? asked the
                        C
company's director of personnel.
                            D
No error
  E

17. When Mom cooks rattlesnake, I
                    A
always wish she would make more of

the delectable, sweet meat that many
        B   C
people compare with the

white, delicate meat of chicken.
            D
No error
  E

18. Alicia's great-uncle $\underset{B}{\underline{\text{leads}}}$ a more
$\underset{(A)}{}$ *than*
active life $\underset{C}{\underline{\text{then}}}$ many people $\underset{D}{\underline{\text{who}}}$
are considerably younger than he is.

$\underset{E}{\underline{\text{No error}}}$

nor
19. Neither Dorothy $\underset{(A)}{\cancel{\text{or}}}$ her dog Toto

$\underset{B}{\underline{\text{expected}}}$ to experience $\underset{C}{\underline{\text{such a strange}}}$
variety of characters and adventures

$\underset{D}{\underline{\text{in Oz.}}}$ $\underset{E}{\underline{\text{No error}}}$

20. Why do you $\underset{A}{\underline{\text{think that}}}$ such a large
number
$\cancel{\text{amount}}$ of $\underset{C}{\underline{\text{professional basketball}}}$
$\underset{(B)}{}$
players come from the $\underset{D}{\underline{\text{Midwest}}}$?

$\underset{E}{\underline{\text{No error}}}$

21. I have a friend $\underset{A}{\underline{\text{whose}}}$ parents

$\underset{B}{\underline{\text{insist on giving}}}$ him a subscription to
the $\underset{C}{\underline{\textit{Weekly Reader}}}$ even though he
gets all the news he wants from the

$\underset{D}{\underline{\textit{New York Times}}}$. $\underset{(E)}{\underline{\text{No error}}}$

Part 2: Improving Sentences

> **Read** the following sentences, paying careful attention to the underlined sections. Beneath each sentence you will find five ways of phrasing the underlined part. Choice **A** repeats the original; the other four are each different.
>
> **Circle** the answer that best expresses the meaning of the original sentence. If you think the original is best, circle **A**. Your selection should produce the most effective sentence—clear and precise, without awkwardness, ambiguity, or errors.

> Laura Ingalls Wilder published her first book <u>and she was 65 years old then.</u>
>
>   (A) and she was 65 years old then.
>   (B) when she was 65 years old.
>   (C) at age 65 years old.
>   (D) upon reaching 65 years of age.
>   (E) at the time when she was 65.

Note: The correct answer is *B*. The original, and *A*, are awkward, as is *E*. Both *C* and *D* are wordy.

1. The ticket agent could not determine <u>the destination to which the woman intended to travel.</u>

  (A) the destination to which the woman intended to travel.
  (B) where the woman wanted to travel to.
  (C) the woman's intended destination.
  (D) where did the woman want to travel?
  (E) to where did the woman wanted to travel.

2. <u>If Carmen had correctly estimated the amount of problems she could do per hour,</u> she would not have had to finish them on Sunday.

  (A) If Carmen had correctly estimated the amount of problems she could do per hour,
  (B) If Carmen had correctly estimated the amount of problems she could have done per hour,
  (C) If Carmen had correctly estimated the number of problems she could do per hour,
  (D) If Carmen would have correctly estimated the number of problems she could do per hour,
  (E) If Carmen would of correctly estimated the number of problems she could do per hour,

3. To successfully complete his mission, Eric the Red knew he needed <u>accurate maps, a good crew, and to have adequate provisions.</u>

(A) accurate maps, a good crew, and to have adequate provisions.

(B) accurate maps, to have a good crew, and to have adequate provisions.

(C) accurate maps and a good crew, as well as adequate provisions.

(D) accurate maps, have a good crew, and have adequate provisions.

(E) accurate maps, a good crew, and adequate provisions.

4. Herbie and I think that Kim is <u>neither the best or the worst person for this assignment.</u>

(A) neither the best or the worst person for this assignment.

(B) neither the best nor the worst person for this assignment.

(C) not either the best or the worst person for this assignment.

(D) for this assignment neither the best nor the worst person.

(E) not the best but not the worst person for this assignment.

5. <u>Who do you think wanted the pale purple convertible—my mother or my father?</u>

(A) Who do you think wanted the pale purple convertible—my mother or my father?

(B) Whom do you think wanted the pale purple convertible—my Mother or my Father?

(C) Who do you think wanted the pale purple convertible? My mother or my father?

(D) Whom do you think wanted the pale purple convertible—my mother or my father?

(E) Who do you think wanted the pale purple convertible: my Mother or Father?

6. Mathias usually <u>chose candidates on the basis of his or her</u> position on environmental issues.

(A) chose candidates on the basis of his or her

(B) selected candidates on the basis of his or her

(C) chose candidates on the basis of their

(D) chose a candidate on the basis of their

(E) has chosen candidates on the basis of their

7. Sara willingly brought the oily rags out to the trash <u>barrel, then she made</u> the mistake of trying to burn them.

(A) barrel, then she made

(B) barrel; then she made

(C) barrel, she then made

(D) barrel, afterwards she made

(E) barrel; then she went on to make

8. <u>Akira was upset and the other members of the team were perplexed.</u>

(A) Akira was upset and the other members of the team were perplexed.

(B) Akira was upset and the other members of the team also was perplexed.

(C) Akira and the other members of the team were respectively upset and perplexed.

(D) Akira was upset; at the same time, the other members of the team were perplexed.

(E) Akira was upset, and the other members of the team were perplexed.

9. Annie Oakley entered the crowded <u>circus arena on a magnificent stallion</u> <u>firing both of her six-guns.</u>

(A) Annie Oakley entered the crowded circus arena on a magnificent stallion firing both of her six-guns.

(B) Annie Oakley entered, firing both of her six-guns, the crowded circus arena on a magnificent stallion.

(C) On a magnificent stallion, Annie Oakley, firing both of her six-guns, entered the crowded circus arena.

(D) Firing both of her six-guns, Annie Oakley rode a magnificent stallion into the crowded circus arena.

(E) Entering the crowded circus arena on a magnificent stallion, Annie Oakley, fired both of her six-guns.

10. Leah enjoyed physical education <u>almost as much as to have her</u> <u>wisdom teeth pulled or fixing a flat</u> <u>tire</u> on a cold, rainy night.

(A) almost as much as to have her wisdom teeth pulled or fixing a flat tire

(B) almost as much as having her wisdom teeth pulled or a flat tire

(C) almost as much as having her wisdom teeth pulled or fixing a flat tire

(D) nearly as much as having her wisdom teeth pulled or a flat tire

(E) almost as much as wisdom teeth being pulled or fixing a flat tire

11. The homecoming football game, <u>which started at 2:00 p.m., had</u> to be <u>called off; because, not only did it</u> <u>begin to rain and soak the huge</u> <u>crowd, but also lightning began to</u> <u>terrify everyone and make it</u> <u>dangerous to be outside.</u>

(A) The homecoming football game, which started at 2:00 p.m., had to be called off; because, not only did it begin to rain and soak the huge crowd, but also lightning began to terrify everyone and make it dangerous to be outside.

(B) Starting at 2:00 p.m., the homecoming football game had to be called off since it began to rain and soak the huge crowd, while lightning terrified everyone.

(C) The homecoming football game, which started at 2:00 p.m., had to be called off because rain had soaked the huge crowd and lightning had terrified everyone.

(D) Calling off the homecoming football game, which had started at 2:00 p.m., was necessary because not only did it rain and soak the huge crowd, but lightning was terrifying everyone.

(E) When lightning terrified everyone and rain had been soaking the huge crowd at the homecoming football game, which started at 2:00 p.m., it had to be called off.

12. Despite her immense talent, <u>Natalie desiring for glory led to a tragic turn of events.</u>

   (A) Natalie desiring for glory led to a tragic turn of events.

   (B) Natalie's desire for glory led to a tragic turn of events.

   (C) because Natalie desired glory, it led to a tragic turn of events.

   (D) Natalie's desiring glory led to a tragic turn of events.

   (E) Natalie desired glory; this led to a tragic turn of events.

13. The summer choir, <u>made up chiefly of altos and basses, have been making</u> a valiant attempt to compensate for their missing members.

   (A) The summer choir, made up chiefly of altos and basses, have been making

   (B) Made up of chiefly altos and basses, the summer choir have been making

   (C) The summer choir, which usually has altoes and basses, has been making

   (D) Made up of chiefly altos and basses, the summer choir has been making

   (E) The summer choir, chiefly made up of altos and basses, have been making

14. <u>Has she or will she ever find</u> true happiness in digging for night crawlers?

   (A) Has she or will she ever find

   (B) Has her ever, or will her ever find

   (C) Has she yet, or will she ever find

   (D) Has she found or will she ever find

   (E) Has she or will she find

15. If anyone finds the missing lapis lazuli necklace, <u>they will have solved</u> a 30-year-old family mystery.

   (A) they will have solved

   (B) he or she will have solved

   (C) they would have solved

   (D) they have solved

   (E) he or she has solved

16. <u>Brenda Sue and Glenda Lou, who are twins, are my cousins and they are also my best friends.</u>

   (A) Brenda Sue and Glenda Lou, who are twins, are my cousins and they are also my best friends.

   (B) Brenda Sue and Glenda Lou who are twins, are my cousins and they are also my best friends.

   (C) My cousins Brenda Sue and Glenda Lou, who are twins are also my best friends.

   (D) Brenda Sue and Glenda Lou are twins, are my cousins, and are my best friends.

   (E) My twin cousins, Brenda Sue and Glenda Lou, are my best friends.

17. Foreign languages generally mystified <u>Brendan, but</u> his fluency in Latin was <u>remarkable.</u>

   (A) Brendan, but

   (B) Brendan: however

   (C) Brendan—but

   (D) Brendan; yet

   (E) Brendan; but

18. One of the very few laws that Uma and Cherise obeyed <u>were the laws of gravity.</u>

   (A) were the laws of gravity.

   (B) was the law of gravity.

   (C) were that of gravity.

   (D) was the ones about gravity.

   (E) were those of gravity.

Part 3: Improving Paragraphs

> **Read** the following essay—a first draft in need of editing. Do not correct the text directly. Instead, answer the questions listed after the essay to identify and fix mistakes. Circle the letter next to the answer you think is best.

(1) A mysterious ancient monument known as Stonehenge is located in southwestern England. (2) You approach it by a broad avenue. (3) It consists of a series of huge, standing stones surrounded by an earthwork. (4) A circular trench about 320 feet in diameter, with a bank on the inner side, encloses the monument. (5) Inside the bank is a circle of 56 holes with a diameter of 288 feet.

(6) The mammoth stones are set in four series: two large outer circles, a horseshoe, and an oval. (7) The outermost circle of rocks, almost 100 feet in diameter, consists of sandstone rocks nearly 15 feet high and averaging 25 tons. (8) A continuous circle of smaller blocks stood on top of them. (9) The next circle consists of about 60 smaller stones. (10) An oval setting is inside that, with an altar stone in the center.

(11) The purpose of Stonehenge is a mystery. (12) Most archaeologists believe that it was used for religious ceremonies. (13) The exact nature of the religious ceremonies is not known. (14) Modern astronomers' discoveries have led them to believe that the stones and layout of Stonehenge were used as a calendar of the seasons and signal eclipses of the sun and moon.

(15) Over the centuries, some of the stones fell and others were moved a short distance or even removed and used to build dams and bridges. (16) Restoration of Stonehenge began in 1922, and it is now carefully maintained by the government.

1. Which sentence in the first paragraph shifts to a second-person pronoun and interferes with the unity of the paragraph?
   (A) Sentence 1
   (B) Sentence 2
   (C) Sentence 3
   (D) Sentence 4
   (E) Sentence 5

2. Which of the following is the best way to revise the underlined portion of sentence 8 in order to keep the verbs consistent throughout the paragraph?
   (A) circle of smaller blocks stood
   (B) circle of smaller blocks is standing
   (C) circle of smaller blocks stands
   (D) circle of smaller blocks has stood
   (E) circle of smaller blocks had stood

3. Reread the entire second paragraph carefully. Which of the following sentences should be added between sentence 9 and 10 to maintain the organization of the paragraph?

(A) Even though these are smaller, they are still quite large.

(B) The horseshoe shape is next, and that has really large stones.

(C) These are called bluestones, because of their color.

(D) Why the next shape is a horseshoe, no one really knows.

(E) Inside that is a horseshoe-shaped configuration of enormous stones—up to 22 feet tall and weighing 30 to 40 tons.

4. What is the best way to combine sentences 12 and 13?

(A) Most archaeologists believe that it was used for religious ceremonies, the exact nature of the religious ceremonies is not known.

(B) Most archaeologists believe that it was used for religious ceremonies, yet the exact nature of the religious ceremonies is not known.

(C) Most archaeologists believe that it was used for religious ceremonies, and the exact nature of the religious ceremonies is not known.

(D) Although most archaeologists believe that it was used for religious ceremonies, the exact nature of those ceremonies is not know.

(E) Believing that it was used for religious ceremonies, archaeologists don't know the exact nature of the religious ceremonies.

5. Which is the best way to correct the unparallel construction in sentence 14?

(A) Modern astronomers' discoveries have led them to believe that the stones and layout of Stonehenge were used as a calendar to predict the seasons and signaling eclipses of the sun and moon.

(B) Modern astronomers' discoveries have led them to believe that the stones and layout of Stonehenge were used as a calendar to predict the seasons and to signal eclipses of the sun and moon.

(C) Discoveries have led modern astronomers into believing that the stones and layout of Stonehenge were used as a calendar predicting the seasons and signaling eclipses of the sun and moon at Stonehenge.

(D) Stonehenge was used to predict the seasons and for signaling eclipses of the sun and moon according to beliefs held by modern astronomers.

(E) Stonehenge was predicting the seasons and signaling eclipses of the sun and moon according to the beliefs held by modern astronomers.

6. To conclude the final paragraph in the best way, which of the following sentences should be added after sentence 16?

(A) It is just one of many interesting places to visit in England.

(B) The admission fee is very reasonable.

(C) However, not all the stones were found.

(D) Today this mysterious monument is one of England's most popular tourist destinations, attracting more than one million visitors a year.

(E) What a fascinating place!